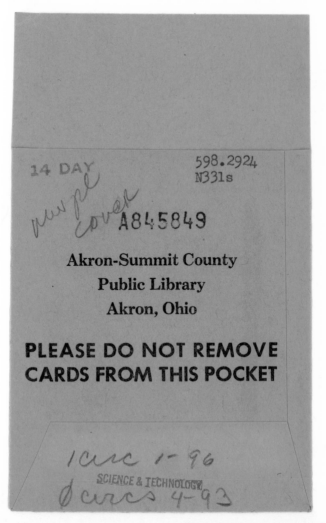

Seabirds

their biology and ecology

Bryan Nelson

Seabirds
their biology and ecology

A&W Publishers Inc.
New York

Foreword

Until recent years, many of us might have derided the very idea that divorce in a seabird affected its subsequent breeding success for two or more years after re-mating, or that birds from the centre of a group were more productive and themselves survived better in winter, than those from the fringes, or that the attentions of the male could influence the laying date of the female and hence the pair's breeding success. These are just three small examples of the increase in understanding that seabird researchers have brought about. In themselves, perhaps, they appear to be trivial, but they show that the long and tedious studies of life histories and breeding biology are giving us an increasingly refined knowledge. We are now, at last, *beginning* to understand some of the complexities of seabird reproductive and population biology. The years of watching, measuring, weighing, marking and experimenting have brought rich rewards, from all over the world.

The aim of this book is to offer the general birdwatcher some of the fruits of seabird work. It is not a compendium of scientific research, although there is much meat in it. Rather, it is an attempt to structure an approach to seabirds so that no major aspect of their lives is ignored. Naturally, 90 000 words go only so far in dealing with such a vast subject. But, by mixing generalizations with detailed examples, I hope that the reader will see both the wood and the trees, if the simile is not too inapt. It will be particularly pleasing if this book proved of interest to the knowledgeable bird student and biologist, but I will be more than satisfied if the average birdwatcher enjoys it and finds it useful. The questions I have asked are those that I hope have often occurred to him, but about which the evidence is not easily found outside scientific publications.

J.B.N.

* * *

Drawings by John Busby
Maps and Graphs by Raymond Turvey
Front jacket: part of the Gannet colony in Grassholm, Wales
Back jacket: Fulmars coming into land
Title spread: Sabine's Gull

First published in the United States of America in 1979 by
A & W Publishers, Inc.
95 Madison Avenue
New York, New York 10016
By arrangement with The Hamlyn Publishing Group Limited

Library of Congress Catalog Card Number: 78-65881
ISBN: 0-89479-042-0

Printed in the United States of America

Contents

Seabirds of the world   6

The oceans   24

Food and feeding methods   31

Breeding behaviour   64

Breeding biology   118
habitats, colonies and strategies

Breeding biology   154
eggs, clutches and mortality

Movements and distribution   170

Seabird populations   182

Seabirds and man   197

Appendices   214

Acknowledgements   220

Bibliography   220

Index   221

Seabirds of the world

This book is not meant to be a guide to the world's seabirds, and the purpose of the present chapter is merely to indicate the diversity of seabird species and of their biology.

Under the most favourable conditions, the sea can grow about as much food as the most fertile land. In the best ocean areas, production can be as high as 20 grams of carbon per square metre per day. And, although much of it is impoverished, the ocean covers around 70 per cent of the Earth's surface. The amount of green matter (phytoplankton) produced in the seas equals all the vegetation on the dry land of the world. So it is hardly surprising that seabirds are numerous. On the other hand, birds are mainly adapted to life in the air and on land, and only about 3 per cent of the world's total of some 8600 bird species are seabirds. The precise number depends partly on what one considers to be a species rather than a race, and upon one's definition of a seabird, but estimates usually fall between 260 and 285. The figure usually excludes the marine ducks, although without compelling reason.

It seems that almost all seabird orders and families originated in the Indo-Pacific Oceans, and radiated from there. The seabird fauna of the Atlantic is younger and less varied and is usually derivable from southern sources. Now, however, seabirds occur virtually from pole to pole, and although there are vast tracts of ocean that appear to be bereft of their cheering presence, it is equally true that there is a chance of seeing them wherever there is open sea, though they occur mainly in favourable areas, such as convergences, upwellings, and cold-water currents. It is common knowledge that each ocean-type, as defined by its climate and oceanography, has its typical marine avifauna. Frequently, one seabird group replaces another in equivalent, but geographically separate sea-areas, and although unrelated, evolves similar adaptive features. Thus the diving petrels and penguins of the southern hemisphere occupy much the same niche as some of the northern hemisphere auks. So the sixteen or so seabird families share out the world's seas in characteristic mosaics, and one can usually place each species in its zone, from antarctic to high arctic, although many wander between two or more zones at certain stages in their life histories or breeding cycles. A few span the globe from north to south on their annual migrations, and the great albatrosses girdle the Earth in the 'roaring forties' of the southern seas.

Seabirds diverged from ancestral terrestrial forms long ago in geological time. There is a fossil frigate 50 million years old, already recognizably a frigate (although with a somewhat greater resemblance to a sulid than modern frigates show), a fossil tropicbird of 60 million years of age and fossil cormorants 60–65 million years old. The ancestral pelecaniform must therefore have diverged much earlier still. Comparably, there are fossil albatrosses c. 50 million years old and the albatrosses were widespread by the Tertiary period, inhabiting northern seas from which they are now absent. Penguins date from the Lower Eocene (60 million years ago) and no fossils have been found outside the southern hemisphere. Penguins abandoned flight many million of years ago when cool, temperate conditions extended south to the polar continent, and have become (in some species) progressively adapted to the extreme antarctic conditions of today. Penguins presumably became flightless when no larger than the smallest living penguins of today, since wing-swimming and flying in air are incompatible with weights much above 1 kilogram. Gulls, terns and auks all existed in the Lower Eocene, some 60 million years ago. And so the four major seabird groups were all well differentiated by about this time. Indeed, some families contained many genera. There are, for instance, at least thirty-one fossil cormorant species.

During these long stretches of evolutionary time, seabirds have diverged even further to fill practically every available niche in the seas and on the land upon which they are compelled to (at least) lay their eggs. This adaptive radiation has, of course, occurred at all taxonomic levels: the major seabird groups carve out for themselves their major niches, and then each group itself diverges in innumerable subtle ways (bill structure, wing proportions, body size, etc.). This continues even at the population level, and different populations of the same species show different characteristics, both of body-form and ecology, which fit them to their particular locality.

seabirds could be more marine than the Emperor Penguin and the Arctic Tern, yet these two differ excessively. The penguin hunts, for months, in the stygian darkness of the Antarctic, often below thick ice, and the tern follows perpetual daylight from pole to pole; a creature of the air and sun. Flightlessness for birds is not intrinsically more dangerous than for marine mammals, which on land are even more helpless than penguins. It is a way of life opened up by the safety of the sea as a habitat, and so long as breeding could be carried out in remote fastnesses, it worked extremely well. Only the advent of man threatened to upset the applecart, both for fur seals and penguins, and turned it upside down for the Great Auk.

However, although the phenomenon of adaptive radiation is plain to see, it poses problems. Seabirds probably cover almost as wide an adaptive range as landbirds. There is nearly as

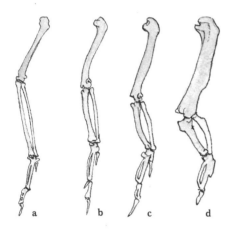

a	gull
b	Razorbill
c	Great Auk
d	Lucas Auk
e	penguin

The evolution of the wing bones in seabirds (not to scale). After R. W. Storer (1958).

The degree of divergence which has occurred in seabirds is enormous, and is well illustrated by the evolution of extreme dependence on flight (the frigatebirds) and complete flightlessness (the Flightless Cormorant) even within the same order. Both modes lead to considerable loss of the ability to walk, which so many seabirds have suffered as the price for their specializations, and which has had important consequences for the types of nesting habitat which they thus require. Within the wide range of adaptations to the marine habitat there is room for innumerable combinations of morphological and other characteristics. Perhaps, the most marine group is the albatross family and the least marine the darters, skimmers, and some of the pelicans, cormorants, gulls and terns. Few

much difference between the heaviest and lightest seabird as between the heaviest and lightest landbird, and the specializations in wing structure, form of bill, nature and position of legs and so on, is probably as great. Others have commented in opposing vein, to the effect that the adaptive radiation among seabirds has been into many very similar types, a phenomenon which they have ascribed to the relative uniformity of the marine environment. The point is, however, that, despite the uniformity of the seas, there is probably as much difference between feeding on small plankton and catching large, muscular fish as between feeding on nectar and catching hares, if it is even meaningful to make such comparisons. *Between* the extremes, however, there probably is a middle band, broader and more uniform in the seabirds; for example, there are perhaps more tropical seabirds, as a proportion of the total number of tropical species, that feed at least partly on squid, than there are tropical landbirds that feed on a single, comparably uniform food source. Nevertheless, different seabird groups have diversified to different extents. Gulls and terns, shearwaters, petrels, albatrosses, cormorants, frigatebirds, boobies, etc. have each split up into a number of fairly similar species. This may be because certain ways of feeding impose demands which can be met only within fairly narrow physical restraints. Thus, frigatebirds and to a lesser extent, gannets and boobies, could not function over a very wide range of shapes and sizes, whereas penguins can. So both processes – extreme adaptive radiation between widely separated groups and restricted radiation within groups are explicable.

Then there is the matter of the *distribution* of similar types. Broadly speaking, the same general types, in terms of size, shape, mode of feeding, etc. are represented in each of the major ocean zones, though the representative(s) of the type may be from very different groups. The phenomenon of adaptive radiation within groups has produced a range of physical structures which equip the group to take advantage of a wider band of the prey spectrum. The *total* range of feeding abilities shown by the composite seabird fauna of any major region enables it to exploit most, if not all, of the food in the sea. That this reduces competition between species need not imply that density-dependent competition operates in seabirds (see population chapter).

Because of their generally greater powers of flight and more uniform habitat, seabirds wander more than landbirds and transequatorial crossings have occasionally led to the establishment of closely similar forms in the two hemispheres, as in the Arctic and Antarctic Terns, the Lesser Black-backed and Kelp Gulls, the Great Skua of the two hemispheres, the Southern Fulmar and the North Atlantic Fulmar and some shearwaters, for instance. Ronald Lockley discusses ocean wandering and speciation in his book *Ocean Wanderers*, and I have insufficient space to follow suit. The only point I would pick up, concerns the proposition that wandering, pioneering, colonizing or whatever is a genetic mutation. It seems far more likely to be an expression of the normal range of variability inevitably thrown up by sexual reproduction, with its re-shuffling of genes. Segregation and recombination of genes is not the same thing as mutation.

One could explore many more general aspects of seabird phylogeny and distribution, but it is time to look at the characteristics of the four main groups, the penguins, the tubenoses, the pelicans and their allies and the auks and gull-tern-skua group.

Penguins

The penguins (Order Sphenisciformes, family Spheniscidae) comprise six genera and about eighteen species: *Aptenodytes*, King and Emperor Penguins; *Megadyptes*, Yellow-eyed Penguin; *Pygocelis*, Gentoo (several races), Chinstrap (no races) and Adelie Penguin; *Eudyptes*, Macaroni, Erect-crested, Rockhopper, Fiordland, Snares Island and Royal Penguin; *Spheniscus*, Magellanic, Humboldt, Galapagos and the Black-footed, Cape or Jackass Penguin of South Africa; *Eudyptula*, Little Blue and, though not recognized by some, the White-flippered Penguin. Odd though it seems, penguins are thought to be most closely related to petrels.

Penguins are highly specialized. Not only are they flightless (the flipper is derived from a wing and is not the modified forelimb of a walking ancestor, except insofar as all bird wings are) but their blubber, thick pile of modified feathers, moult process and their physiology associated with diving, are also special. Moult, for instance, is concentrated into a three or four week period during which time the birds cannot maintain their body temperature in water and lose almost half their pre-moult body-weight as a result of the energy used and the inability to feed. No other seabirds moult in this way, though some auks become flightless. The largest penguin, the Emperor, stands over a metre high and weighs up to 46 kilograms (usually about 30 kilograms) whilst the smallest, the Little Blue, stands 40 centimetres high and weighs, at most 2.1 kilograms (usually 1.1 kilograms), a weight ratio of 27:1, which is equalled by no other family and exceeded only in the much larger order, Procellariiformes, where it is considerably greater than 300:1.

Almost every antarctic and sub-antarctic island has two or more resident penguin species (some islands of the Scotia arc may have populations of several millions) and there are large

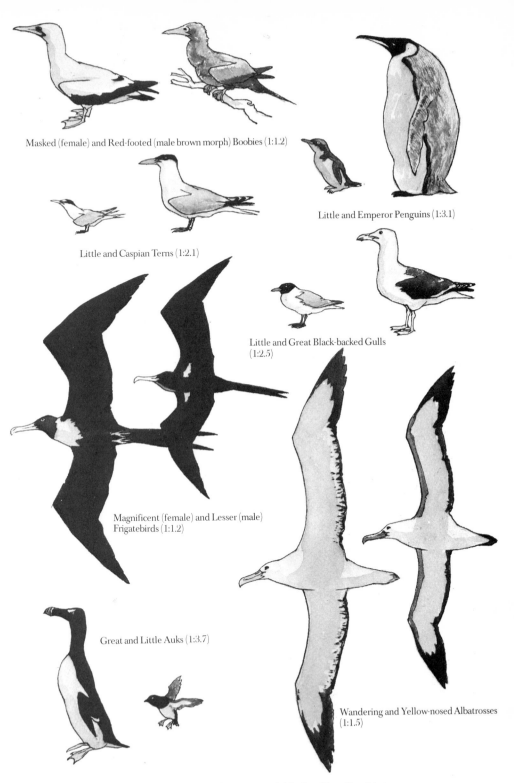

Masked (female) and Red-footed (male brown morph) Boobies (1:1.2)

Little and Emperor Penguins (1:3.1)

Little and Caspian Terns (1:2.1)

Little and Great Black-backed Gulls
(1:2.5)

Magnificent (female) and Lesser (male)
Frigatebirds (1:1.2)

Great and Little Auks (1:3.7)

Wandering and Yellow-nosed Albatrosses
(1:1.5)

Some examples of size-range within families of seabirds
(ratios of overall lengths are given in brackets).

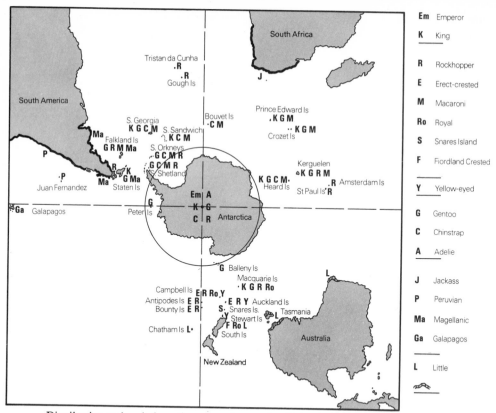

Distribution and main breeding areas of penguins (Spheniscidae).

Em	Emperor
K	King
R	Rockhopper
E	Erect-crested
M	Macaroni
Ro	Royal
S	Snares Island
F	Fiordland Crested
Y	Yellow-eyed
G	Gentoo
C	Chinstrap
A	Adelie
J	Jackass
P	Peruvian
Ma	Magellanic
Ga	Galapagos
L	Little

colonies, also, at places along the coast of the antarctic peninsula and continent. The spheniscids' excursions into warm or even tropical areas have been *via* cold water currents (Humboldt, Benguela). Emperors are confined to the high antarctic and together with Adelies, penetrate furthest south and are the most cold-adapted. Kings range through the sub-antarctic and on islands south of the antarctic convergence; they do not enter the pack-ice zone. Pygocelids, generally, are polar or sub-polar.

Most eudyptid penguins breed on temperate sub-antarctic islands. The Royal is confined to Macquarie Island and the Snare Island Penguin to the Snares, whereas the Rockhopper is widely distributed, including islands near Tierra del Fuego, the Tristan group, Falkland Islands, Marion Island and many islands south of New Zealand. Other eudyptids are intermediate in distributional range. There are some apparent anomalies in distribution. For example, the Rockhopper is absent from South Georgia which appears to be well suited to it, and is about as far from the antarctic convergence as is

Heard Island, where the Rockhopper is common. Several penguins are increasing at present, partly due to climatic changes which have uncovered more land for them to breed on, and partly to an increased food supply and reduced persecution. It has been estimated that the slaughter of whales has released enough krill to support an additional 300 million penguins per year.

Penguins utilize all the breeding habitats open to them, from sea-ice (Emperors), to cliff-faces (some Rockhoppers) and burrows (Little Blue), with, in between, boulder-strewn slopes (Chinstraps, often adjacent to Adelies or Gentoos), scree-slopes (Rockhoppers), tussock grass (Gentoos), raised beaches (Adelies), flats or slopes (Macaroni), bare rocks (Erect-crested), natural cavities or beneath vegetation (Magellanic, Galapagos, Snares Island). Colony size ranges from huge to small, often within the same species. Emperors with some two dozen colonies, range from less than 200 to more than 50 000 pairs, and colonies of Adelies may number more than a million pairs. Yellow-eyed

Penguins, by contrast, breed in small, scattered communities. Even the closely related Gentoos and Chinstraps differ in colony size, the former in small groups and the latter in tens or hundreds of thousands. Although penguins are basically annual breeders, the King Penguin breeds twice in three years, whilst the Galapagos Penguin breeds more than once a year. Both these departures from the typical periodicity are special adaptations to the environment: in the King's case, enabling the young to become independent at a time when there is abundant food after 'sitting out' the winter and in the Galapagos', allowing penguins to respond to temporary, non-seasonal (unpredictable) periods of relative abundance.

Generally, penguins produce only one chick, although all species except the Emperor and King, lay two or even three eggs, the eudyptids being peculiar in that the second egg is larger than the first, which is usually 'lost'. They show highly developed (ritualized) social behaviour and some species are unusual, though by no means unique, in 'crèching'; these aggregations of young are adaptive, anti-predator and energy-conserving devices and the chicks in them are fed only by their own parents. The burrow-nesting Little Blue Penguin is nocturnal, but others are mostly active during daylight hours.

Tubenoses

The order Procellariiformes—petrels, albatrosses, shearwaters probably contains more individuals than any other, although there are more species in the Lariformes. There are four families, the albatrosses (Diomeidiidae, two genera, thirteen species), petrels and shearwaters (Procellariidae, twelve genera, sixty-one species), storm-petrels (Hydrobatidae, eight genera, eighteen to twenty-one species) and diving-petrels (Pelecanoididae, one genus, four species).

The distinctive tube-nose of these birds may be partly for gauging the strength of air-flow and partly for detecting odours, at which some petrels are apparently extremely good. In addition to the tube-nose, and the hooked and plated bill, all members of this large order are distinguished by the structure of their stomach, the glandular part of which is greatly extended and produces the famous oil. A whole breeding strategy is based on this stomach oil.

The order spans the range between the most abundant (possibly Wilson's Storm-petrel) and the rarest seabird (the Cahow, or perhaps the Magenta Petrel) in the world, and between the largest (the Wandering Albatross) and the smallest (one of the storm-petrels). It also contains the most taxonomically complex groups, in the gadfly-petrels and the shearwaters. The order is distributed throughout the world's oceans, and over a dozen species can be seen at sea in one sweep of the binoculars—a phenomenon unequalled by any other order.

Only the Wandering Albatross has evolved a juvenile plumage followed by a series of immature ones. And the female is 'capped' whereas in other albatrosses the sexes are alike. However, several species occur in two colour-forms or morphs. The Wanderer is said sometimes to take thirty years or more to reach adult plumage, but since it may breed at seven, and has an average life expectancy of less than thirty, this seems unlikely to be true. Larger albatrosses moult only once in two years, whilst I believe all other seabirds moult at least once each year although some may retain their primaries for more than a year.

The albatrosses (Wanderer's wingspread up to 370 centimetres) are superb gliders with a long arm (up to forty secondary flight-feathers). They inhabit the windiest zones of the southern oceans, most of them between 30°S and 60°S. In winter and spring, the vast expanse from the 120th meridian of west longitude, to the Horn, is practically deserted by the great albatrosses but in summer it is the favoured region. As many as fifty have been seen together off Tristan da Cunha but usually they occur in threes or fours. Of the thirteen species, ten breed in the southern hemisphere, mostly in sub-antarctica, one (the Waved) in the tropics (Galapagos) and three (the Black-footed, Laysan and Short-tailed) in the sub-tropical Pacific of the northern hemisphere. The Wanderer (world population 50–60 000) is circumpolar in breeding range but the Royal (about 20 000 breeding birds) is confined to Chatham, Campbell, the Auckland Islands and the Dunedin area of New Zealand. Fossil albatrosses have been found in Britain and North America and the Black-browed occasionally strays into British waters, but, in general, the barrier of the windless Doldrums is presumably effective in confining them to the South Atlantic.

Except for the Sooty Albatross, which nests solitarily or in small groups, all albatrosses are colonial, breeding on open, windswept hillsides or terraces, often amidst tussock grass, or on flat ground. Some species, for example, the Shy Albatross, nests both on flat ground and cliffs. Buller's Albatross, of temperate waters, may breed beneath trees, as also may the Waved Albatross of the Galapagos. Whilst albatross colonies never attain the numbers reached by some penguins, pelecaniforms, terns or shearwaters, some reach a size of several thousands of pairs. Like all members of their order, albatrosses lay just one egg. All of them are seasonal breeders. Even the three North Pacific albatrosses lay in the southern summer, though for them it is the northern winter. Almost all of them breed annually, but the Wanderer, Royal and Grey-headed (at least) only once in two years. There is considerable overlap between albatrosses in the food (chiefly squid) which they take, but many authors believe that effective partitioning of the food has been achieved by differences in size, distribution, breeding season and so on.

The petrels and shearwaters, family Procellaridae, contains eleven genera and sixty-one species, made up as follows: group one, the fulmar-petrels, embraces two species of *Macronectes* or giant petrels; two species of *Fulmarus*, the fulmars proper; *Daption*, the Cape Pigeon; and *Thalassoica*, the Antarctic Petrel. Group two contains the prions *Pochyptila*, with six species. Group three contains the shearwaters, *Puffinus* with thirteen species, (some authors give seventeen); *Calonectris* with two species; and *Procellaria* with four species. Group four contains the gadfly-petrels, *Pterodroma*, with twenty-five species and *Bulweria*, with three species.

Even among specialists, some of these groups engender much disagreement, which I certainly cannot judge, nor even begin to present here. The giant petrels (southern and northern), the largest procellariids, are as big as small albatrosses, but less aerial. They nest right around the South Pole, in colonies. Like the other fulmars they have much less-highly ritualized social behaviour than the albatrosses. They are notable scavengers on land—the vultures of the antarctic—and in some areas voracious predators, taking shearwaters, prions, penguins, gulls, etc. in considerable numbers. In other localities, though, they are extremely timid and, in addition to marine food, take only carrion. The Antarctic Fulmar occurs widely on the antarctic coast. It gave rise to a northern

species, which has split into three forms, the fulmar of the Pacific polar basin and two forms of the Atlantic Fulmar, one of them dark and short-billed from the high arctic (it ranges to within five degrees of the pole) and the other lighter and larger billed and found south of the arctic, as around Britain. But there are intermediates. All fulmars like icy waters, rich in planktonic crustacea. They nest in colonies, which are sometimes huge, on cliffs or slopes. They live a long time, breeding annually and seasonally and have a low recruitment rate.

The prions specialize in straining out plankton through comb-like plates on each side of the mouth, each species having its own bill shape and size. They are small and fly fast and erratically. They are all found only in the southern hemisphere though the Broad-billed Prion nests further north than the others, close to the subtropical convergence. They are nocturnal, colonial burrow-or-hole nesters, mainly on islands, and are distributed widely in the reaches of the Atlantic and Indian Oceans south of Capricorn, and particularly around New Zealand, where all except the Thin-billed and Medium-billed Prion, breed. The former nest as far south as the pack-ice.

Of the shearwaters, the large group of medium-sized petrels within the genus *Puffinus* are among the world's most numerous seabirds, nesting from the sub-antarctic (Sooty Shearwater), through the sub-tropics and tropics, to the boreal Westmann Islands (Manx Shearwater). The fragmented, circum-global distribution of some shearwaters suggests an earlier distribution continuous throughout the so-called 'Middle Seas' that used to exist in a belt around the world, taking in the Caribbean and Mediterranean. Some species are widespread as breeders, whilst others, though numerous, are confined to a single island group. In the Bass Straits, mass flights of Short-tailed Shearwaters have been described of such dimensions and duration that many millions must have been involved. Several species migrate between hemispheres. Probably because they are largely nocturnal, they are modest in plumage, dressed in soft grey, brown, white and black and without colour adornment, or, in adults, brightly coloured soft-parts. Nor do any of them occur in two or more very different colour-forms, though the Sooty and Short-tailed Shearwaters show a dark and light form, and the Manx occurs in three races (Atlantic, west and east

wind direction

Dynamic soaring in an albatross.

Mediterranean) distinguishable in the field. Perhaps because of the fairly uniform feeding methods, their adaptive radiation is not spectacular and the ratio of lightest (the Little Shearwater) to heaviest (the Shoemaker, Cape Hen or White-chinned Petrel) is only about 1:5. Few seabirds are more mysterious than shearwaters, with their vast colonies, nocturnal habits, weird cries, sometimes bizarre nesting places, for example, on mountain tops, and even among forest trees (as in the Pink-footed Shearwater), extraordinary migrations, huge feeding concentrations, rafting habits and so on.

Most *Puffinus* shearwaters breed annually, but Audubon's breeds at approximately nine-monthly intervals in the Galapagos. As with so many Galapagos species, this is an adaptive response to the non-seasonal and fluctuating food. The *Procellaria* shearwaters – Pediunker (or Grey Petrel), Shoemaker (or White-chinned Petrel), Westland Black Petrel and Black Petrel – are the largest of all, and at a distance can even be mistaken for small albatrosses. The Shoemaker, Murphy says, is so called because 'he sits in his shop and sings'. Like the others, they are colonial burrow nesters, the two first named breeding together on several antarctic and sub-antarctic islands, always near to the convergence between the surface waters of these two zones. The Pediunker, very much a pelagic species, is a particularly good plunge-diver. The

Westland and Black Petrels are extremely alike, and breed in mountainous country in New Zealand and the latter also on offshore New Zealand islands. The Westland Black Petrel has an estimated population of 3–6000.

The group of gadfly-petrels (*Pterodroma* and *Bulweria*) is large and complex in plumage and taxonomy. The *Pterodroma* group is widely distributed in the tropics and sub-tropics, particularly in the Pacific, some of them south to about 50°S and east to the south-eastern Pacific islands of San Felix, San Ambrosia, Ducie, Henderson, etc. Some, such as the Trinidad Petrel, are circumpolar, nesting in all three major oceans. Although colonial, some gadfly-petrels, as, for instance, the Great-winged Petrel, may nest solitarily or in vast dense colonies. They are similarly flexible in choice of nest sites, which may be in burrows, in the open or on cliffs. Although many species are abundant and familiar, the gadfly-petrels accommodate several of the world's rarest and least-known seabirds (the Diablotin or Black-capped Petrel and the Cahow or Bermuda Petrel, both of the Caribbean, and the Magenta Petrel of the Chatham islands), which have been reduced by exploitation and pests. Many islands hold two, three or four species of breeding gadfly-petrels, as well as shearwaters and storm-petrels, and although each gadfly-petrel is seasonal, sometimes strictly so, different species, on the same island, may breed at opposite seasons of the year, as, for example, the Great-winged and White-headed Petrels on Kerguelen. These dashing petrels, sometimes nesting in wild and inaccessible mountain country, as do some of the shearwaters, are an altogether fascinating and attractive group. The Blue Petrel (*Halobaena*) is often grouped with the prions, but Murphy considered it closer to the small gadfly-petrels. It has a circumpolar distribution and breeds in the customary large, dense colonies.

The storm-petrels, family Hydrobatidae, are the smallest and perhaps the most primitive procellariforms. They are considered to have diverged into two main groups, one in each of the two hemispheres—the southern genera (*Oceanites*, *Garrodia*, *Pelagodroma*, *Fregatta* and *Nesofregatta*) with long legs and short, rounded wings and the northern group (*Hydrobates*, *Halocyptena* and *Oceanodroma*) with short legs and more pointed wings. The short wings, (only ten to eleven secondaries) and, often, square tail facilitate the characteristically buoyant and fluttering flight. Some are extraordinarily abundant and widely distributed, others restricted to a limited ocean area. Wilson's Storm-petrel migrates from its antarctic breeding grounds, which include the entire ice-free coastline of the Antarctic continent, to the sub-arctic. The British Storm Petrel is also a transequatorial migrant, whilst the Galapagos Storm-petrel, and other tropical and warm temperate species, have a limited range and no true migration.

They are all blackish, black and white or grey and white petrels, often with white rumps, wing bars, facial markings or underparts. They are highly vulnerable to predators, and nest in burrows or crevices which they visit at dark, although the Galapagos Storm-petrel visits its colonies in thousands during the day. Here, however, the only predator is the Short-eared Owl, which is not numerous enough to take a significant toll. As with all the procellariforms, only one egg is laid. Although so small, they are extremely long-lived, (twenty years or more can be attained) and probably usually form long-term pair-bonds and return to the same burrow. A notable feature of their colonies is the high proportion (perhaps 80 per cent) of 'unemployed' birds that take part in the mass, nocturnal flightings. Most of these may be young birds, some from other colonies. They do not breed until about four or five years old,

which for such small birds is unusually late. The petrels are exciting little seabirds.

Finally, among the Procellariiformes belong the four diving-petrels or Pelecanoididae, an odd, tightly-knit little group of supposedly primitive petrels broadly distributed in the south temperate and sub-antarctic zones of the southern hemisphere. They are birds of rough seas, grey clouds and high precipitation, requiring cold water throughout the year. The Potoyunco, or Peruvian Diving-petrel, has penetrated furthest north *via* the cold Humboldt current. Their short, stiff-feathered wings buzz them along in a most un-petrel like manner and they commonly fly through waves crests, as well as beneath the surface. More than half a century ago, Murphy pointed out the astonishingly close resemblance between the Magellanic Diving-petrel and the Little Auk of the northern hemisphere. Due to convergent evolution, not only size and proportions, but colour and texture coincide remarkably. The plumage is oily and compact and diving-petrels are unique in their order as, like some auks, they become flightless during moult. They are great burrowers, the Georgian Diving-petrel coping successfully with ground that is frozen hard. Like others of the order, colonies, which are visited nocturnally, contain many unemployed birds although one would expect fewer than in other groups, for diving-petrels breed in their second year, which is unusually early for a petrel. As in other procellariforms, there is a pre-laying exodus of breeding birds, presumably fattening up for the task of laying and incubating.

Pelicans and their allies

Within the order Pelecaniformes are placed six families—the pelicans (Pelecanidae; one genus, seven species), the gannets and boobies (Sulidae; one genus, seven species), the cormorants (Phalacrocoracidae; one genus, twenty-nine species), the darters (Anhingidae; one genus, two species), the frigatebirds (Fregatidae; one genus, five species) and the tropicbirds (Phaethontidae; one genus, three species). The pelicans are the heavyweights of the order, at about 11 kilograms some twenty times heavier than the lightest (the White-tailed Tropicbirds). The largest frigates, with a wingspan of 2·4 metres or more, make a respectable approach to the great albatrosses. But the order shows nothing comparable to the tiny petrels. Pelecaniformes have webs between all four toes. The

Galapagos Flightless Cormorants one of the world's rare seabirds. It is the only modern flightless seabird outside the penguin and auk families.

upper mandible is hooked in pelicans, cormorants and frigates but not in the other families, although some sulids closely approach the condition. Whereas the tubenoses have huge external nostrils, the pelecaniforms have none. In reflecting feeding behaviour, the tail has achieved a wide range of shapes and sizes in the order – short and rounded (pelicans); long and tapered (sulids); very long and graduated (darters); long and rounded (cormorants); long and deeply forked (frigates); centrally elongated (tropicbirds). Although there is not yet complete agreement about the relationships within the order, the pelecaniforms are thought to be from procellariform stock with the branch giving rise to the pelicans, gannets and boobies, cormorants and darters (sub-order Pelecanidae), these diverging earlier than that giving rise to the frigates and tropicbirds (each given, by some, sub-ordinal status). Apart from the penguins and the auks, the cormorants are the only seabird family which has modern, flightless members.

The order contains many colourful species – the pelicans and also some cormorants and the darters, with their conspicuous head adornments; the boobies with brightly coloured faces and feet; the beautiful tropicbirds and the nuptially adorned male frigatebird with his scarlet gular pouch. The pelecaniforms are globally distributed but are largely tropical and warm temperate birds. Several genera are circum-tropical (some boobies, frigates and tropicbirds) whilst there are tropical representatives of the others. Sulids nest from within the Arctic Circle (Atlantic Gannets) to the sub-antarctic (Australasian Gannet), and the cormorants beat this by nesting in the arctic and the antarctic; the Common Cormorant, alone, breeds from Iceland and Norway to New Zealand. From present numbers and distribution the order appears to have had its centre of origin in the southern hemisphere. The pelecaniforms are less marine than the procellariforms, for although a few members can be seen in mid-ocean, most are birds of inshore seas and many (some pelicans and cormorants and the darters) of inland waters. The tropicbirds, Red-footed and Masked Boobies are undoubtedly the most pelagic members, though frigatebirds also range far from land.

Pelecaniforms use practically every available nesting habitat except burrows – there is not one true hole-digger among them, although the tropicbirds nest in natural holes. But if the procellariforms outshine them in digging, the pelecaniforms make up for it by using trees and bushes extensively (pelicans, frigates, some boobies, some cormorants and darters). In fact they are the most arboreal order of seabirds.

They are all colonial nesters, although to varying degrees. Their biggest colonies, the Guanay Cormorants and Peruvian Boobies, number millions of birds, but this applies only to the special circumstances of the Humboldt; a few hundreds, or thousands, rarely amounting to 100 000 pairs, is much more typical of the order.

The pelicans are almost cosmopolitan. They contain two species (the Eastern White and the Dalmatian) which breed in Eurasia and northern Africa; the Pink-backed which breeds in Africa south of the Sahara; the Brown and the American White Pelican in the Americas; the Spotted-billed Pelican in Asia and the Australian Pelican. Pelicans are essentially birds of warm latitudes and of estuarine, coastal or inland waters, not (except sometimes the Brown) of oceanic islands. They are the fourth heaviest seabirds, behind the two largest penguins and the great albatrosses, and show little range in size. Because they are so large, and often nest in considerable colonies, the waters in which they fish must be capable of supporting a huge biomass and pelicans will travel great distances from the breeding colony, to feed. Their social behaviour seems less diverse and highly ritualized than that of the boobies and cormorants. The nestling pelican's habit of joining a 'creche' of youngsters is unique within the order. After breeding, pelicans disperse or migrate, even crossing deserts–the only seabirds except for some gulls and terns that habitually do so. But, as remarked, most pelicans are not true seabirds. Because of their dependence on inland waters, which tend to be drained or to become polluted, they have declined markedly in Eurasia, and probably Africa, within recent decades.

No pelican has departed from an annual cycle, although opportunistic breeding means that it is often not markedly seasonal. As befits birds feeding inshore or on locally abundant sources, clutch size may be large (up to six, which is about as many as any seabird ever lays). For the same reasons, pelicans rear their young in a relatively short time, and breed at an earlier age, by far, than procellariforms a fraction of their size.

The gannets and boobies are quite pelican-like in appearance, especially when they distend their gular skin. They are very much a marine family, all of them plunge divers, and they show a greater range in size and weight than the pelicans. There is more difference in weight between the sexes, too. The heaviest (Atlantic Gannet) at 3000 grams is some four times heavier than the lightest (the male Red-footed Booby). The sulids fall into three or four groups: the three Gannets (Atlantic, African or Cape, and Australasian) are all extremely similar and perhaps best regarded as one superspecies. They are often placed in a separate genus, *Morus*, although many authors use *Sula* both for gannets and boobies. All three, but especially the Cape and Australasian are of fairly restricted distribution and are clearly birds of cool, rich waters. Two of the three pan-tropical boobies (Brown and Masked Boobies) are sufficiently closely related to hybridize, even though they differ greatly in appearance. Behaviourally at least, they seem fairly close to the Blue-footed Booby, which has a markedly discontinuous distribution on the fringes of cool-water areas, the three main loci being a stretch of the west coast of South America, the Galapagos, and the Gulf of California. The Blue-footed, in turn, is extremely closely related to the Peruvian Booby, which is restricted to the cool waters off Peru and Chile. These four perhaps form the 'core' of the boobies, leaving the Red-footed and Abbott's Booby, both of which are tree nesters, to accommodate. Abbott's is definitely aberrant and is now restricted to one island (Christmas Island in the Indian Ocean). It seems more primitive than other sulids and if the Gannets deserve generic status, then Abbott's does, too. The Red-footed is pan-tropical and not so clearly aberrant. How close it is to the 'core four' it is difficult to say.

All sulids except Abbott's Booby are highly colonial nesters with a rich display repertoire. Clutch size and breeding strategies vary considerably within the genus–more so, perhaps, than in any other seabird genus, for we see clutches ranging from one to four, breeding frequency from once in nine months to once in two years, breeding success from less than 10 per cent to more than 80 per cent, and so on. This is due, possibly, to the great range of environmental conditions embraced by the sulids. Maturity is not deferred for as long as in the

The buzzard (a) shape (positive dihedral) is stable whereas the frigatebird (b) shape (negative dihedral) is unstable and ideal for trick flying.

procellariforms.

The cormorants and shags are the most diverse of the pelecaniforms. They are mainly tropical and temperate on marine coasts and inland waters but extend to the Arctic and Antarctic. They are all inshore underwater-pursuit swimmers, using their feet. Their wings eventually become soaked and incapable of protracted flight, although their body feathers are completely waterproof. Otherwise, no bird could survive prolonged immersion in icy water. Some authorities, nevertheless, claim that the body plumage of all cormorants *is* pervious to water. All cormorants are social birds typically nesting in small- to medium-sized colonies on the ground or bare rocks, slopes or rocky outcrops, cliffs, trees and bushes. Their displays are complex and highly ritualized, yet in many species nest sites and pair-bonds are relatively impermanent. Clutches are typically larger than in any other seabird family, growth rapid, and maturity less long-deferred. Many are said to make good eating, although in Scotland it is generally thought necessary to precede consumption by a period of decent burial (of the bird, not the consumer).

The frigatebirds are among the most spectacular of seabirds. The wings of the great albatrosses may be sail planes but the frigates, because of their negatively-dihedral shape and low wing-loading, are consummate trick-fliers, all the more breath-taking because of their great size. Related to their aerialness is the reduction in legs and feet. Frigates neither swim nor walk, but simply perch. The family is compact in size and shape, the ratio of lightest to heaviest being 1:2 and of wingspread, only about 1:1.2. The basic features of plumage are that adult males tend to be almost entirely black, (with a sheen on the back) with, at most, a white patch on the abdomen (Andrew's

A pair of Ascension Island Frigatebirds. The male is showing his inflated pouch. Note the ground nest site which is unique among frigatebirds.

Frigate) or tiny white slots in the armpit region (Lesser Frigate), whereas females (except the Ascension Frigate) have large white areas on the breast, extending, in Andrew's, onto the underwing and as a collar onto the sides of the neck (Andrew's, Lesser and Magnificent Frigates). Juveniles (except Magnificent and Ascension Frigates) have rufous on the underparts and the distribution of black and white differs from that in females. Although the eye-rings and feet may be brightly coloured (pink, blue) there is little to diminish the overall effect of black soberness, except the astonishing scarlet throat pouch, found on males of all species in the courtship season.

The frigates, like the boobies, contain widespread (pan-tropical) species in the Great and Lesser Frigates, as well as species confined to one island (Andrew's on Christmas Island in the Indian Ocean and the Ascension Frigate on Ascension in the Atlantic) and a species (the Magnificent Frigatebird) with a restricted (mainly Caribbean) distribution. The family is unique in that, so far as is known, all species breed less often than once a year, probably once every two years, a trait enforced by the excessively long period required to produce an independent youngster. Frigates are characterized by single-egg clutches, extremely low breeding success, and presumably by longevity and long-deferred maturity, though concrete figures for these are still lacking. Because of their biennial breeding, permanent sites and pair-bonds are impracticable. Their colonies are usually only medium large, and none as large as 10 000 breeding pairs.

Finally, the tropicbirds, the smallest pelecaniform family (if the darters are placed with the cormorants) consists of only three species, the Red-tailed, Red-billed and White-tailed (or Yellow-billed) Tropicbirds, although the Red-tailed is divided into five sub-species. The generic name is well chosen, for, to me at any rate, nothing evokes the sensation of the hot tropical sun and seabird islands more than the sight and sound of these graceful birds. The Red-tailed and Red-billed are closely related, the former being distributed in the west and central Pacific and in the Indian Ocean and the latter in the east Pacific and the Atlantic. The White-tailed occurs in the Atlantic, Indian and Pacific Oceans, but not in the eastern part of the latter. Tropicbirds are highly pelagic, and, at home, form scattered colonies, breeding in

holes and natural cavities. Breeding strategies are varied, from annual seasonal to non-annual, semi-continuous. There is relatively little complex display associated with breeding.

The pelecaniforms, unlike the procellariiforms, have failed to take advantage of the plankton-feeding niche and have no groups comparable to the vast assemblages of petrels, auks or penguins. They are pre-eminently fish-eaters and the main area of adaptive radiation, within families, has been predictably perhaps, restricted, within the inshore-feeding cormorants. All the rest are small families. But between families, there has been adaptive radiation every bit as extreme as in any other order.

Gulls and their allies

The fourth major group of seabirds, the gulls and their allies, and the auks, is the largest of all. It is variously defined as the order Lariformes or the Laro-limicolae within the great order Charadriiformes (we will use the former). There are eight genera (forty-two to forty-five species) of gulls, nine genera (thirty-nine to forty-two species) of terns, one genus (three species) of skimmers and thirteen genera (twenty-one to twenty-two species) of auks.

Most gulls are grey and white, often with black wing tips and black breeding adornments on the head. Legs, feet, bills and eye-rings are often brightly coloured, and some of these features are used in display and in parent-young interactions. Their breeding habitat ranges from arctic willow-bog and tundra to antarctic islands, taking in sea-cliffs, lava desert, marshes, buildings and much else, en route. The legendary Ross' Gull, when, for the first time, found nesting in 1905, was in marsh alder 160 kilometres south of the tree line, although its non-breeding habitat includes the bleak reaches of the east Siberian pack-ice.

The gull family contains more species than any other. They are predominantly northern hemisphere birds that have colonized the south. The Herring Gull superspecies extends around the world, over vast tracts of the northern hemisphere, and has, in response to the different conditions thereby encountered, sub-speciated into at least seventeen different forms. The Lesser Black-backed Gull (itself closely related to the Herring Gull with which it will hybridize) has a southern form, the Dominican or Kelp Gull, which has colonized Australia, New Zealand and the sub-antarctic. It appears to be spreading into the range formerly occupied by the Pacific Gull, itself a southern version of the (northern) Great Black-backed Gull. The Black-headed Gull breeds from the Atlantic seaboard, across Eurasia to the Sea of Okhotsk, and between Siberia in the north to the Caspian Sea in the south, whilst outside the breeding season dispersing further south still. It has given rise to the closely related Silver Gull, now abundant in Australia and the New Zealand area and breeding also in New Caledonia and South Africa. Comparably, the Common Gull extends widely, from Iceland across northern Eurasia and in northwest America, where it overlaps with, and, in eastern Canada, is replaced by, the Ring-billed Gull. Vastly adaptable, wandering birds, the gulls have spread and speciated widely throughout the world. Specialized forms have arisen which now occupy difficult niches. Such is the Dusky (Lava) Gull of the Galapagos lava-flows (a dark, small, Herring Gull type); Audouin's Gull; the Grey Gull of the burning Peruvian desert; and Ross's, Sabine's and the Ivory Gull of the Arctic (the latter overwintering in this bleak habitat). There are few truly oceanic gulls, but the plankton feeding and extremely abundant Kittiwake ranges over the North Atlantic, and is a pan-arctic breeder; it has a race in the North Pacific. However, several other gulls occur at times in mid-ocean. It is perhaps surprising that rather few have exploited the plankton niche, though, besides the Kittiwake, the Black-tailed Gull feeds extensively on the swarming euphasids off the coast of Japan.

Some idea of the success achieved by gulls may be gauged from the estimate that, in the western Palearctic alone, there are more than two million 'large' gulls and four million 'small' ones. However, gulls do not form excessively large colonies, nor do they (except Kittiwakes) nest extremely densely. They are strongly territorial; the *Larus* gulls are often highly predatory and cannibalistic. Clutch size does not exceed three, and the Swallow-tailed Gull is unusual in being restricted to a single-egg clutch. Breeding cycles are almost always annual, but in response to the lack of seasonality and high failure rate of the tropics, the Swallow-tailed Gull has evolved a cycle of approximately six-months.

The skuas which consist of two genera, and six species, are the gulls' closest relatives. The Great Skua, like the Fulmar, has a bi-polar distribution, but unlike the Fulmar, the skua probably originated in the north and colonized the south, and is, by some authors, treated as one species. The present northern population (c. 10000 pairs about half in Iceland and half in Shetland) is regarded as a recent recolonization by the southern form. Though migrating mainly to Biscay and north Africa, some northern Great Skuas wander well into the southern hemisphere, and Antarctic Skuas reach into the northern, the two thus intermingling. The Antarctic Skua is divisible into clearly different ecological forms, one feeding at sea, mainly on fish, and the other a scavenger and predator. Their entire breeding systems differ on account of this and the case is an interesting demonstration of the differences between populations of the same species. The northern Great Skua or Bonxie is highly predatory and cannibalistic, though it feeds much by honest fishing.

The smaller skuas (Arctic, Long-tailed and Pomarine) are all birds of the far north, the Arctic Skua breeding from the high arctic to Scotland, and the forest zones of north Europe, Asia and America. The Pomarine is restricted to the arctic tundra. The Long-tailed is probably the least numerous of the three small skuas. Interestingly, only it and the tropicbirds have evolved highly-elongated central tail-feathers, though the Blue-footed Booby approaches them, and the mobile tail of the frigate can effectively act as a long narrow tail. This feature enables its possessors to execute rapid shifts in direction, associated with their hunting techniques. The Arctic Skua occurs in two very different colour morphs, with associated ecological differences. Skuas are colonial, becoming densely so when (as on Foula in the Shetlands) increasing population puts pressure on space.

The terns almost equal the gulls in number of species and diversity of habits. There are nine genera according to some, and as few as three (black-capped terns or *Sterna* spp., noddies, *Anous* spp. and the Inca Tern, *Larosterna*) according to others. However, they are basically more marine than the gulls and are mainly a tropical group, with about thirty species (about 70 per cent) in the Pacific, mostly in the tropics and sub-tropics, twenty-five species in the Atlantic and Mediterranean, and nineteen in the Indian Ocean. No fewer than seventeen terns breed on the shores of the North Atlantic. The Arctic Tern nests as far

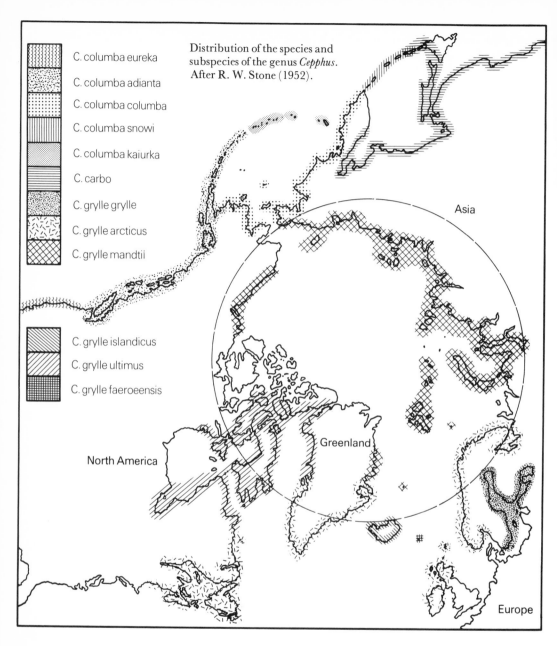

Distribution of the species and subspecies of the genus *Cepphus*. After R. W. Stone (1952).

C. columba eureka

C. columba adianta

C. columba columba

C. columba snowi

C. columba kaiurka

C. carbo

C. grylle grylle

C. grylle arcticus

C. grylle mandtii

C. grylle islandicus

C. grylle ultimus

C. grylle faeroeensis

Asia

Greenland

North America

Europe

north as land goes, and, in the form of the Antarctic Tern, almost as far south too. It thus beats even the Great Skua. It seems that its origin was the Antarctic, as otherwise it is difficult to understand why it undergoes such a fantastic migration when it could find suitable winter-quarters much, much nearer to the Arctic. There are areas in the northern sub-tropics which provide massive quantities of small fry at the appropriate time of year.

Terns are exceptionally aerial birds, more slender than gulls. They are great wanderers, apparently capable of virtually living on the wing for long periods. The largest tern (the Caspian) is almost as large as a small booby. The ratio of its weight to that of the smallest tern (the Little Tern) is 12.5:1, compared with 5.5:1 for gulls (Great Black-backed and Little Gull).

Like the gulls, they are predominantly black, grey and white birds often with colourful bills and feet, some species have black on the head, though as a cap rather than a hood. The Inca Tern is the only member of the gull-tern-skua group that has evolved colourful facial adornments. As in gulls and skuas, the young are downy and usually cryptic, but the first juvenile plumage is often more adult-like than in the gulls. Also like the gulls, they are immensely social birds and have developed highly ritualized displays. They utilize an even greater variety of nesting habitats than gulls, including the bare branches of trees, without even a nest (Fairy Tern), and floating vegetation (marsh terns). In size, the colonies of the Sooty Tern far exceed those of any other lariform, or perhaps any other seabird. Terns have evolved an enormous variety of breeding strategies. Sooty Terns vary their cycle length according to area; some tern chicks crèche; some nest densely

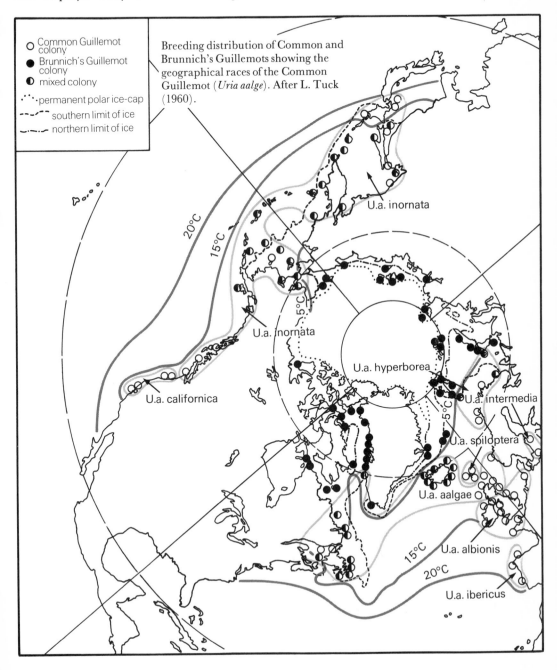

Breeding distribution of Common and Brunnich's Guillemots showing the geographical races of the Common Guillemot (*Uria aalge*). After L. Tuck (1960).

○ Common Guillemot colony

● Brunnich's Guillemot colony

◐ mixed colony

⋯⋯ permanent polar ice-cap

--⁀- southern limit of ice

-⸱-⸱- northern limit of ice

U.a. inornata

U.a. inornata

U.a. hyperborea

U.a. californica

U.a. intermedia

U.a. spiloptera

U.a. aalgae

U.a. albionis

U.a. ibericus

20°C
15°C
5°C
5°C
15°C
20°C

without prior territorial behaviour; some species nest opportunistically rather than returning to fixed areas whilst others are more conventionally territorial; some prolong post-fledging care throughout a lengthy migration and whilst in winter quarters, and so on. Like the gulls, they have taken advantage of inland waters, including lakes, rivers and marshes, and even of dry-land habitats and terrestrial prey. More terns, than gulls, are restricted to single-egg clutches, and this is doubtless related to their more pelagic habits and thus less frequent returns with food.

Finally, we come to the Alcidae or auks. These comprise thirteen genera, with about twenty-one species. It seems certain that auks, which are cold-water birds, differentiated in the North Pacific basin, from which there are fossils dating from the Lower Eocene (about 60 million years ago) and some of the advanced and specialized forms there became extinct before the Pleistocene. The North Pacific is still the main area for auks. In the Atlantic there are now only six although the Great Auk counts as 'modern'. Probably the auks entered the Atlantic through the Bering Straits and North American arctic. There are twelve species breeding along the arctic shore between the two oceans. The Puffin is probably a late immigrant to the Atlantic and is closely related to the Horned Puffin of the North Pacific, and these two (*Fratercula* spp.) to the Tufted Puffin. The Little Auk, one of the most successful of all seabirds, is a high-arctic plankton feeder, filling the niche of the Pacific auklets.

Horned and Tufted Puffins breed together throughout about half of their breeding range but the Horned outnumbers the Tufted in the northern areas. One big separating factor is nesting habitat, the Horned usually requiring natural holes and crevices whereas the Tufted Puffin, like the Atlantic bird, digs its own burrows. Interestingly, at least six alcids may be found nesting on the same island; Pigeon Guillemot, Parakeet, Crested and Least Auklets, Horned and Tufted Puffins all nest on St. Lawrence Island, Alaska. A record equalled only in the much larger order of tubenoses.

Auks comprise seven natural groups: (1) the Razorbill (*Alca*); (2) the Common and Brunnich's Guillemot (*Uria*); (3) the Little Auk (*Plautus*); (4) the Common and Horned Puffin (*Fratercula*) and Tufted Puffin (*Lunda*); (5) the six auklets of the north Pacific—Crested, Least

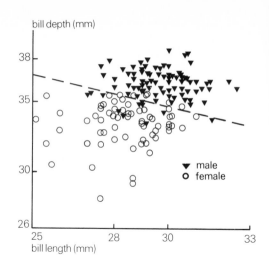

Measurements of 158 Puffin's bills. The male bills are larger than females (mainly because they are deeper) but there is much overlap. After P. Corkhill (1972).

and Whiskered Auklet (*Aethia*), Cassin's Auklet (*Ptychoramphus*) and the Parakeet Auklet (*Cerorhinca*); (6) the Marbled and Kittlitz's Murrelet (*Brachyramphus*); (7) Xantus's Murrelet (*Endomychura*) and Ancient and Japanese Murrelet (*Synlithiboramphus*).

Like some of the penguins, with which they invite obvious comparison, some auks have evolved ornate facial adornments. Also like penguins, their body plumage is mainly black above and white below, though some murrelets are brown. Their underwater-flying when feed-

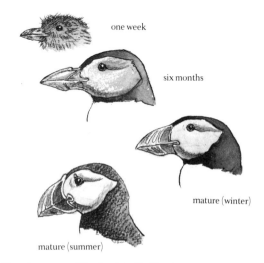

Development of the beak in Puffins (experts can distinguish between Puffins aged 3, 4, and perhaps 5 years using fine details of bill-bands).

ing has led to reduced wings. Adaptive radiation has led to the evolution of a range in sizes comparable to that in penguins, to a range of bill and palate structures adapted to different food preferences and, within several species, to considerable sub-speciation. Six species (Little Auk, Crested, Least, Parakeet, Whiskered and Cassin's Auklets) possess gular pouches, which are bag-like extensions of the buccal cavity. These are important structures, which develop only at the first breeding attempt and enable the auklet to carry up to 25 grams of zooplankton (15 per cent of adult weight). This means that the young can grow excellently on one trip per parent per day (compare up to seven by some puffins!). The pouch is also a useful way of separating birds that have bred or are breeding from those that have never bred.

The auks range widely in all aspects of ecology. Their colonies are huge as in Little Auks and guillemots to small as in tysties or even solitary pairs as in Marbled Murrelet. Nesting habitats include cliff ledges (guillemots), boulder and scree slopes (tysties), burrows (puffins and auklets), tree-holes several kilometres inland (Marbled Murrelet), cliffs up to 30 kilometres from the sea (Little Auk) and mountain scree many kilometres inland (Kittlitz's Murrelet), but never open congregations on flat ground. On St Lawrence Island, Least Auklets, Crested Auklets, and Parakeet Auklets nest on mountain slopes which, when the birds first return, are covered with snow. Breeding cycles are mostly annual and seasonal except that Cassin's Auklet produces eggs over a long seasonal period and is said to be double-brooded on the Farallon Islands, California.

Many auks, unlike the penguins, attend their partly-grown chicks at sea and in some species, certainly feed them. There are three distinct patterns of post-hatching development. Most alcids (fifteen species) are semi-precocial, that is the young are fed in the nest until nearly fully grown, (although the growth rates vary according to the species' feeding ecology), but four species are truly precocial (mobile and capable of finding their own food and keeping warm soon after hatching) and three are intermediate between these two categories. The precocial alcids are Xantus's, Craveri's, Ancient and Japanese Murrelets, which go to sea with their parents soon after hatching. The intermediates are the Razorbill, and the two Guillemots. In the arctic, late young may be deserted once the main crop has fledged, as the parents are unable to follow the food supplies and still fly back and forth from the colony. I fully agree with Spencer Sealy, that the main factor leading to early fledging among those alcids that do so, is not enhanced safety from predators but is the opening-up of access to food, which early dispersal from the colony makes possible. The young that can feed or part-feed themselves early, free themselves from a serious limitation and gain a big advantage. Their post-breeding dispersal patterns vary widely, some, for example the Guillemot, showing well defined movements and others, like the Puffin, apparently dispersing widely out to sea. But none undertake long, directed migrations. None are distant-foragers during their breeding season. Some, for instance the Marbled Murrelet, seldom feeds more than 500 metres from shore at this time. Nevertheless, most auks lay single-egg clutches, though several, for instance the tysties and the Ancient Murrelet, lay two. Many auks breed for the first time when two or three years old. Perhaps the main reason for their great success in the boreal and arctic regions is their almost exclusive occupation of a broad feeding niche consisting mostly of small fish, often at considerable depth, and zooplankton.

Reconstruction of the early Eocene frigatebird *Limnofregata azygosternon*. After Storrs Olson.

The oceans

The world ocean is vast, rich and complex. The Pacific basin alone occupies more than a third of the Earth's surface and the north equatorial current flows westward, unhindered from Panama to the Philippines, a distance of over 14 000 kilometres. Marine communities, like any other, depend on food, which in turn is affected by the nutrient content, temperature, salinity and exposure to sunlight, of the water. These are controlled by climate, wind and earth-spin, which are responsible for currents and other phenomena, such as turbulence and the degree to which waters with different properties become mixed. The microscopic phytoplankton which forms the base of the food pyramid at whose apex stands the Leopard Seal, Man, or the frigatebird, supports a mass of ocean life too stupendous for the mind to grasp. Take, for example, the single fact that the Sperm Whale consumes around 260 million tonnes of squids and octopuses each year. Thus, just one predator eats a weight of cephalopods equal to forty-five times the entire world catch of fish. And as an example of the oceans' complexity, the North Atlantic receives some 6 million cubic metres per second from the South Atlantic, via the equatorial current. The return payment is made partly, at very deep levels, in cold arctic water from downsinkings (2 million cubic metres per second) in the Labrador Sea and areas southeast of Greenland, and partly in warm, salty Mediterranean water. It is this scale of phenomenon that greatly affects the abundance and distribution of food and hence that of seabirds. Often, in my opinion, the seabirds themselves have no significant impact upon their food supply.

The present-day configuration of the world's oceans differs from that of the past. From at least 61–63 million years ago, until geologically recent times, the eastern Pacific and Caribbean were connected, and from there eastwards into the western Pacific stretched an unbroken belt (the middle seas). Most seabird groups date from at least 63 million years ago, and the present circum-tropical distribution of, for example, some petrels, terns, boobies, tropicbirds and frigatebirds date from these circumglobal middle seas.

The seas are still inter-connected even where they do not stretch unbroken around the world, as they do in the southern ocean between Antarctica and the land masses to the north – the global sweep of the great albatrosses. It is therefore more meaningful, in seabird terms, to zone the oceans according to natural features rather than by man's artificial boundaries and the map of the world's oceans (see inside covers) divides them up in this way. Even such climatic (latitudinal) zones are far from uniform and where food is rich as at convergences, seabirds and other predators congregate. Their distribution is patchy, though the gaps between patches are much larger in the tropics and sub-tropics than elsewhere. Locally rich waters, due to vertical mixing which makes nutrients available, can be caused by many things, such as the meeting of water masses (currents due to wind, etc.), the shape of the sea-bed, unequal heating due to atmospheric conditions, unequal salinity, convection currents around islands or ice and the nature of the coastline bounding the ocean. Even in mid-ocean, there are locally rich areas, and seabirds have to find them. Chance variations in the characteristics of the sea (surface temperature, salinity, evaporation) may influence food in the foraging areas of seabirds, and thus affect breeding biology. There is, for instance, some evidence that 1964/5 and 1968/9, in which particularly large proportions of Laysan Albatrosses withheld breeding, were poor food years due to definable climatic

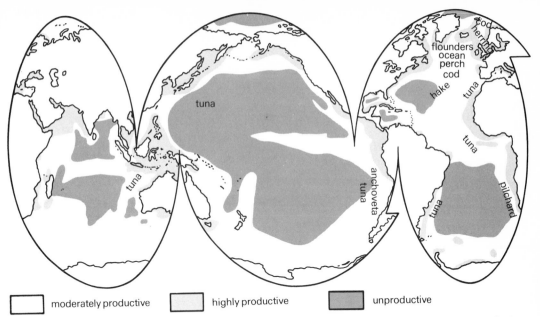

tuna

flounders
ocean
perch
cod

hake

tuna

tuna

tuna

anchoveta
tuna

tuna

pilchard

☐ moderately productive   ▨ highly productive   ▦ unproductive

Distribution of primary productivity in the surface waters of the Earth's oceans. The map also indicates certain fish stocks which are in grave danger of being overfished by man.

factors. But the difficulty of making precise correlations in these areas of study can be easily imagined.

The main ocean zones

The antarctic zone stretches from the edge of the antarctic continent to a water-boundary (the antarctic convergence) at which cold antarctic water begins to sink and to move east and north (circulation in the southern hemisphere, due to the Earth's spin, is anti-clockwise, and in addition, winds in these latitudes are strong, westerly). The antarctic convergence is quite sharp; it lies at about 60°S in the Pacific but almost 10° further north in the Indian and Atlantic Oceans.

The 30 million square kilometres of the Antarctic Ocean are richer in phytoplankton, mainly diatoms, than is any other comparable area. Under the intense and almost continuous sunlight of the short antarctic summer, productivity is enormous, as is the supply of nutrients adequate to sustain it. Even though 90 per cent of the energy 'fixed' from the sun, by the photosynthesis of the diatoms, is lost at each step up the food chain (it takes 1000 kilograms of diatoms to make 1 kilogram of penguin) multiplication is so rapid that the predators, prolific though they are, cannot check it. The small zooplankton filter-feeds on the phytoplankton,

which may be as small as 0.005 millimetres in diameter—invisible to the naked eye—and the larger, carnivorous zooplankton and the fish, squids, etc., feed on the primary zooplankton. The top predators gorge on the krill, fish and squids. Crustacea, such as the krill, the 'insects of the sea', are the most numerous marine herbivores (some 6000 species) and in places average 30 000 individuals per cubic metre of surface water. The famous *Euphasia superba* of the antarctic can live two years and measure 5 centimetres, which is about as large as an animal can become and still live on microscopic particles. Some 1 million million kilograms of krill may be produced annually and upon the size and prolificity of this shrimp rests most of the antarctic's teeming higher-life. Despite the climate, seabirds thrive, though in biomass rather than species—five penguins, six petrels, a skua and the sheathbill.

The more temperate zone though still cold, which lies north of the Antarctic (see map), is properly called the anti-boreal. Driven by the strong westerlies of the forties, the west wind drift takes vast quantities of cold, rich antarctic waters east and eventually north, to sweep up the western coasts of South America and Africa. There, in conjunction with the upwelling that occurs in these regions, it supports vast populations of seabirds.

Blue-eyed Shags feeding at sea in the Antarctic Ocean. The southern hemisphere is particularly rich in numbers and species of cormorants.

The rich antarctic convergence area in particular, but also the entire anti-boreal, supports large numbers of seabirds: penguins, albatrosses, a bewildering variety of petrels and shearwaters (at least thirty-four species are to be seen off southern South America), the Australasian Gannet, cormorants, skuas, gulls and terns. The Russian marine zoogeographer, Shuntov, lists seventy-four species characteristic of the anti-boreal zone, of which no less than half have a circum-polar distribution. At higher latitudes, the proportions of circumpolar species is even higher.

The sub-tropics are by and large, areas of high pressure and weak winds, with clear skies (and consequently much sun) and, near the surface, warm, salty water. In the southern hemisphere the sub-tropics extend from about 40°S to the Tropic of Capricorn, but the limits vary seasonally. The sea looks blue because it is clear, and the water molecules scatter the light, unlike the green, phytoplankton-loaded waters of the antarctic. Clear, warm and salty water may be ideal for the human bather, but it is barren for seabirds. Apart from those favoured pastures where, with audible hissing and visible turbulence, opposing water masses meet, and great feasting goes on, the sub-tropics are often impoverished. In the eastern Indian Ocean, north to 15°S, plankton, flying fish and seabirds are all scarce. Further north there are ten times as many. Presumably the seabirds which nevertheless forage even within the less productive areas quarter the seas in search of localized banquets, or of the ubiquitous squid, surely one of the world's most important foods (there are some 700 species, or more than twice as many as the world's seabirds, and their abundance is unbelievable).

The southern sub-tropics support a breeding seabird fauna less distinctive than that of the antarctic and anti-boreal zones. The colderwater areas within it (and these include the upwellings off western South America and Africa) support species found, also, in more southerly latitudes whilst the warmer areas share species with the tropics. The breeding list thus includes penguins, gulls, terns, cormorants, pelicans, boobies, gannets, frigatebirds, tropicbirds, petrels, shearwaters, diving petrels and albatrosses. Even those dominant tropical species, the bluewater boobies, tropicbirds and frigatebirds breed, in a few places, south of Capricorn and of the 23°C surface water isotherm (this temperature being perhaps the most meaningful criterion of tropical water, since the sub-tropics and tropics are not easily separable).

When the surface temperature drops, as for example in the Indian Ocean during the southeast trades, when the 20° isotherm moves north, several typically antarctic and anti-boreal seabirds move into geographically sub-tropical or even tropical waters, as for instance the Yellow-billed Albatross, Wandering Albatross, Cape Pigeon, Giant Petrel and some prions. But they are merely feeding, not breeding.

The tropics, on these terms, extend between seasonally-moving limits of the 23° isotherms, south and north of the equator. Tropical waters can rise to 29°C near the equator, and, like deserts, can show as great a temperature range in a day as in a year. The persistent trade winds, help to produce the great equatorial currents (east to west in both hemispheres) of the Pacific and Atlantic; and also cause moderate seas over much of the tropics, in contrast to the relative calm of many central sub-tropical areas. Towards the equator, however, the winds weaken, seas are calm, warm moist air rises, there is more rain and the surface water is less salty. The equatorial countercurrent here runs west-to-east, in the weak wind belt between the strong trades. There is enough vertical mixing of the water along the equator to bring nutrients to the surface and to encourage the growth of plankton, and equatorial regions can be highly productive. The Indian Ocean is strongly affected by the monsoons, which cause much greater seasonal changes than the analagous shifts in the wind systems of the Pacific and Atlantic. North of the equator, between October and March, the dry, light north-east monsoons blow, giving a westward drift over the northern Indian Ocean. From about May, the stronger south-west monsoon blows and causes upwellings off Arabia and Somalia, which attract many seabirds.

In the vast areas of the tropics, the basic seabird food is squid and flying fish. The dominant seabirds are boobies (Red-footed, Masked and Brown), terns (particularly Sooty), frigatebirds, tropicbirds and a few tropical procellariforms (shearwaters, gadfly-petrels, storm-petrels and the tropical albatrosses).

In the northern hemisphere, only the Pacific and Atlantic oceans have sub-tropical zones. In the Pacific, these extend close to 42°N, which is near to the 19°C surface isotherm. The main mass of water circling in the north Pacific derives from the North Equatorial Current, turning clockwise and mingling, off Japan, with cold water from the Arctic. Continuing eastwards across the Pacific and eventually turning south to rejoin the North Equatorial Current,

this cold water washes California as the California Current and supports the seabird concentrations there and in the off-lying Revillagigedos, Tres Marias and Marietas.

The mid-ocean area of the north Pacific sub-tropics is relatively calm, like its Atlantic counterpart, but there is plenty of variation, and its islands, for instance the volcanic chain of the Hawaiian Leewards, support large numbers of tropical and sub-tropical seabirds. On the one small island of Kure Atoll, the breeding seabirds comprise Black-footed and Laysan Albatrosses, Wedge-tailed and Christmas Shearwaters, Bonin Petrels, Red-tailed Tropicbirds, Masked, Brown and Red-footed Boobies, Greater Frigatebirds, Sooty, Grey-backed and Fairy Terns, and Brown Noddies. Nor, as their breeding success shows, do these birds have to combat the sort of food shortages that occur in some tropical areas. In the northern sub-tropics as a whole, roughly seventy species of seabirds breed.

The North Atlantic sub-tropics take in the seabirds of the eastern seaboard of North America from Florida to Cape Cod, and in the east, the Canaries, Azores, Bermuda, islands off north-west Africa and most of the Mediterranean. The Mediterranean supports rather few seabirds. It is very salty and its temperature varies greatly over the year. The plankton level is so low that, at least in winter, most of the seabirds (for example, the whole population of Cory's Shearwater) moves out into the Atlantic.

The boreal zone is, by some, inserted between the sub-tropics and the sub-arctic, whilst others use boreal and sub-arctic synonymously, leaving the arctic to be divided into low and high arctic. Following the latter course, the boreal zone extends northwards from the sub-tropics, at approximately 40°N, to the low arctic, taking in cold-water upwellings at latitudes as far south as the Iberian coast and islands off Japan. Much of the boreal area is shallow, which facilitates wind-generated mixing and many boreal species are inshore feeders. There is nothing quite comparable to the antarctic convergence, for in the North Atlantic the Gulf Stream flows into high latitudes and the circulation is complex. The water (3–14°C) is as cold as that of the corresponding anti-boreal region, wind-swept and rich, supporting large fisheries and great seabird populations. For example, south of 55°N off eastern Newfoundland, where the Labrador Current and Gulf Stream meet, there are large concentrations of seabirds. And the importance of *local* feeding areas should be emphasized. Around Prince Leopold Island, and in the general area of Barrow Strait and Lancaster Sound, strong currents produce considerable upwelling and the large concentrations of seabirds on Prince Leopold depend on this. Even the Black Guillemot, which doesn't forage far, number 4000 birds there. The boreal community comprises Fulmars, Manx Shearwaters, storm-petrels, Gannets, cormorants, several gulls, terns and skuas and many auks.

The extremely rich feeding areas of the Sea of Okhotsk and the Bering Sea lie within the boreal zone and, besides their breeding birds, support vast populations of moulting shearwaters and petrels from the southern hemisphere. As in the anti-boreal seabird community, direct feeding upon the larger zooplankton, here often *Calanus,* is important (Kittiwakes, Fulmars, shearwaters, petrels, some auks) though the larger seabirds are fish-eaters.

The low arctic, which can be defined as the region in which the water is a mixture of arctic and non-arctic, embraces the teeming seabird stations of Greenland, arctic Canada and arctic Russia. The Arctic Ocean is quite shallow, with large continental shelves, and during much of the year is covered with pack-ice, although open leads allow seabirds to feed. It has warmed up this century, with corresponding and important changes in the distribution of fish, several of which (Coalfish, Haddock, Cusk, Ling, Basking Shark, Horse Mackerel, Swordfish, etc.) have moved further into the arctic zone. But the most important fish for the seabirds of this region are Capelin, the clupeids and Sand-eels.

Most boreal seabirds are found, also, in the low arctic, the dominant low arctic species being, in the Atlanto-Arctic segment, auks (particularly Little Auk and Brunnich's Guillemot), Fulmars, Kittiwakes and skuas. In the north Pacific there are eighteen auk species—thirteen in the Bering Sea alone, this being the probable 'origin area' of the auks.

The high arctic is dominated by ice, even in summer. A permanent sheet as much as 4.5 metres thick covers the central basin. Seabirds live in the high arctic only in summer, with the exception of the Ivory Gull which remains even in winter. Sabine's, Ross's and Thayer's Gull are also high arctic species. The Fulmar penetrates the high arctic, as does the Puffin,

Black Guillemot and that swarming, pre-eminently arctic alcid, the Little Auk.

The physical basis for the patchiness of seabird food, and therefore of seabird distribution, deserves a brief mention. The energy for the movement of vast masses of seawater comes from the atmosphere—mainly from the planetary winds, generated by the Earth's spin and by the heating and cooling of air-masses. Winds generate currents which transport water around the globe, producing friction and mixing. The major current and wind systems combine to produce important areas in which surface water is replaced by that from deeper layers (the process of upwelling), containing the minerals necessary for the growth of phytoplankton. The deep water is *itself* replaced by slowly creeping currents which, for example, over thousands of years, may transport water from the Weddell Sea all around Antarctica and far into the northern hemisphere in all three major oceans. In fact it reaches the Grand Banks, off Newfoundland, where it mixes with deep water from the Arctic Ocean. Similarly, water from the North Atlantic crosses to Antarctica beneath the warmer surface layers of temperate and tropical latitudes.

The ocean currents
The Earth spins from west to east, so most of the ocean surface is dominated by wind driven currents, flowing from east to west, which, upon encountering the shores of the continents, deflect more or less north and south, in north and south hemispheres respectively, forming the 'boundary' currents. Thus the great North Equatorial Current of the Pacific (which, before the Isthmus of Panama was formed, must have been a continuation of the Atlantic North Equatorial Current) sweeps 14 400 kilometres west until deflected to the north as the Kuro Shio Current off Japan. Then it bears eastwards as the North Pacific Current before flowing past California and rejoining the North Equatorial Current. A similar clockwise-circulation, or gyre, occurs in the North Atlantic, where the westward setting North Equatorial Current deflects north as the Antilles Current and then carves its way back across the Atlantic as the Gulf Stream—a 'river' 152 kilometres wide and 1.6 kilometres deep, with a temperature gradient across its boundary so sharp that a vessel may have its bows in water 20° colder than that washing its stern. Where it meets the cold

Brown Pelicans diving for fish off the coast of Peru. The Humboldt Current, a marked upwelling off this coast, provides a tremendously rich supply of food, supporting large numbers of seabirds.

Labrador Current, dense fog banks ensue.

In the northern hemisphere, the major westward setting currents, produce, on their western boundaries, a much sharper delimitation between coastal and open-ocean circulation than occurs on the eastern sides of the ocean basins. The latter are characterized, as we have seen, by the displacement of water to the west, with resultant upwelling, rich feeding and great seabird concentrations.

In the south Pacific the South Equatorial Current crosses from east to west and sets south and east. It is joined by cold antarctic water driven by the westerlies and eventually washes the west coast of South America as the Peru, Humboldt or Antarctic Current. Similar processes give the Benguela Current off south-west Africa and the Western Australian Current.

The South Atlantic is virtually a mirror image of the north. The South Equatorial Current which, past St Paul's Rocks in mid-ocean, is a westward-setting mill-race, splits upon reaching Brazil. The northern half becomes the Gulf Stream, part of which crosses the Atlantic at high latitudes, where it produces complex systems with icy currents flowing south from both

sides of Greenland, (an area of huge seabird colonies). The other part completes its circulation by sweeping south as the Canaries Current, past Iberia, and north-west Africa. In both of these regions, the typical eastern-boundary current diffusion and upwelling produces rich feeding areas. After giving off the Gulf Stream to the north, the southern half of the South Equatorial Current circles south as the Brazil Current and then east as the South Atlantic or Antarctic Current. With cold water picked up in southerly latitudes it completes its anti-clockwise circulation by sweeping up the west coast of South Africa as the Benguela Current and rejoining the South Equatorial.

In the regions of the eastern boundary currents, riches accrue not only from the contribution of currents derived from colder areas but, more importantly, from the upwelling which follows wind-generated displacement of surface water. Despite constituting only 0.1 per cent of the ocean area, upwellings are vitally important to seabirds. One need only mention the rich fisheries and spectacular seabird populations associated with upwellings off Peru, California, Iberia, Algeria, Morocco, South-west Africa, Java, Western Australia, Arabia and Somalia to appreciate their importance. Upwellings have carbon production rates (a measure of green-plant growth) up to ten times greater

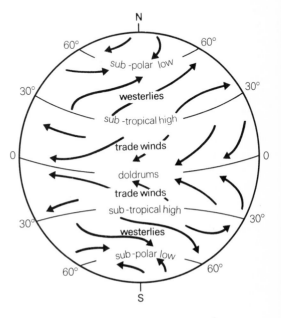

Prevailing wind zones and surface atmospheric pressure over an idealised Earth. After Lamb (1974).

than the open ocean and the importance of a continuous supply of new water in maintaining the production of phytoplankton can be judged from the fact that usually it can sustain maximum productivity for only a few days before exhausting the nutrients in the surface layer. Even 'rich' ocean water contains, for example, only about five parts of usable nitrogen per 10 million parts of seawater. Fertile soil contains 30000 times as much.

Where water masses of different properties 'front' or converge, even in mid ocean, there is sinking, turbulence and mixing. Birds and other predators flock to these rich feeding areas (convergences) and feed along them by the million. Often, there is visible and audible evidence of the mixing; the water there may be a different colour, with white tops to the breaking waves, hissing, and what has been described as the sound of distant surf breaking along a shore. Large marine communities may be uplifted bodily from deeper layers, for the predators to feast upon. Many accounts describe the scenes, as does the great seabird pioneer, Murphy, for the equatorial Pacific: 'It was as though all the life of the ocean had congregated there; yet, ten yards [ten metres] from the line, on either side, the water appeared empty of life. The most obvious creatures in sight were the seabirds, tropicbirds, boobies, frigates and phalaropes. On one side of the line, the sea was dark and rough, and on the other, lighter and smoother. White caps marked the shared edges of the two great currents whose meeting place was the convergence.'

The oceans' currents are infinitely more complex than my spare account suggests. There are, for instance, 'meanders' or 'eddies' in which bodies of water take off from the main current and move, intact, with their marine communities, to places where they do not normally occur. An eddy may persist for years and provide a rapid source of change in the ocean's budget, with far-reaching effects on local climates, fisheries and, nowadays, the removal of pollutants. Gulf Stream eddies, for example, moving offshore from the Georgia/Carolina coast, cause vertical mixing and take large quantities of nutrients to the shelf waters. It seems intrinsically more likely, to me, that the basic cause of dramatic changes in seabird numbers is change in natural food, related to such phenomena, rather than hand-outs of offal from fishing boats or even depletion of stocks by man.

Coastal waters (less than 180 metres deep) are extremely important feeding areas for seabirds; their shallowness encourages mixing and they receive minerals from the waters of inflowing rivers. As a consequence, they are at least twice as productive as the deep sea. In proportion to their extent, which is a mere 9.9 per cent of the ocean's surface, coastal waters support vastly more seabirds and most major fisheries are concentrated on continental shelves. Another factor which helps to make them more productive is the greater economy of their food chains. In the open sea, the food chains are long and complex. Only very small phytoplankton grows in the ocean, and only small herbivores can subsist on it. This increases the number of steps in the food chain, each with its attendant 90 per cent loss of energy. Rich areas, such as upwellings, contain a large proportion of diatoms that can aggregate into clumps or filaments which fish can eat direct. This is one reason why anchovies are so incredibly prolific in the Humboldt.

The small and shallow North Sea is one of the rich seabird areas of the Northern Hemisphere, supporting several million seabirds. And despite its smallness, it is far from a uniform mass. There are areas with their own physical features. For example, an area in the north and north west has high salinity, low temperature and low silicate concentration and corresponds with the limits of intrusive Atlantic water. Others are less salty and contain more silicate and suspended solids. These two types support different seabird concentrations, the first attracting more Fulmars, Gannets, auks, skuas and shearwaters than the second. This, it is suggested, may be because the second has a higher concentration of heterotrophic bacteria which recycle the phytoplankton before it can be eaten by the larger zooplankton and thus become available to seabirds.

The oceans, then, are food-contoured, if not as much as the land, then certainly enough to determine the pattern of seabird distribution and abundance. The sea's subtle ecological diversity is shown by the fact that more than 6000 species of crustacea, 700 kinds of squid and 10–11000 species of fish have evolved in them. The seabirds, depending as they do on the products of the sea, depend ultimately on the physical forces which produce water movements. If they keep pace with changes, they survive and speciate, or they become extinct.

Food and feeding methods

In one way it is meaningless to say that feeding is the most important thing a seabird (or any animal) does, for the same can be said about reproducing or even minor activities such as sleeping and preening, without which it couldn't survive. But feeding, nevertheless, is the primary activity to which all else is geared. It determines basic anatomy and morphology (not the other way round), and distribution and breeding strategy. Seabirds perform the most extraordinary behaviour to tap the riches of the oceans, and bend their breeding habits to fit their feeding habits in ways which place heavy demands on their evolutionary inventiveness.

Seabirds are adapted not only to the seizing and handling of their main prey, whether large fish, small fish, squid, plankton, etc., but to the position of the prey (surface, medium water, deep or bottom), its density and distribution (whether it is reliable and abundant or patchy and scarce) and its seasonal distribution. The latter is just as important as any other factor, for it is no good being well adapted to take advantage of food which is abundant for ten or eleven months of the year if you cannot cope with the other one or two months. Interrelatedness is such a universal phenomenon that not even physical adaptations can be assessed in isolation from each other, let alone from other systems. A plunge diver cannot have the neck and wings of a cormorant or a frigatebird and an auk or penguin adapted for flying underwater cannot have the wings for the sustained air travel of an albatross, although the diving-petrels come near to doing both. Usually, one, or a few related, modes of feeding stamp their necessary pattern on the species' anatomy and in some cases, plumage. Other things, such as breeding habitat and strategy, then 'slot in'.

Seabirds could not survive without the ability to handle the large amounts of salt taken in with seawater. They excrete this by means of salt or nasal glands, of various shapes and sizes, which lie in or around the orbit, above the eye, in shallow depressions in the skull. They have one or two ducts on each side, which lead into the nasal cavity. In many seabirds, ridges along the edge of the beak prevent the fluid flowing into the mouth and lead it, instead, to the tip of the beak, from which it drips or is shaken off.

The main types of feeding practised by seabirds are: (1) picking food from the surface, or just above or below it, whilst on the wing, sometimes with pursuit-plunging; (2) exploiting the surface layer mainly whilst swimming, with pursuit-diving; (3) deep plunge diving; (4) diving from the surface and collecting prey by extensive and deep swimming; (5) piracy; (6) scavenging and innovative feeding, although this is not so much a different method as a different source, which is tapped using the existing methods.

Surface feeding whilst flying

This is predominantly the method used by small and aerially agile seabirds, mainly tubenoses and terns, but one group of large seabirds, the frigatebirds, have specialized in it too.

Storm-petrels (Hydrobatidae) feed from the wing and for all their ability to swim (and in some species even to dive) they rarely do so. Wilson's Storm-petrel flits endlessly back and forth, lowering its feet, webs spread, every time it drops to the water and using them, mainly together, to patter over the surface. Upon touching the water it keeps its wings up and may 'stand' on one spot, scanning the surface with a downward pointing head. The Storm Petrel descends from its skimming flight to hover and trip over the surface, using its feet alternately and keeping its wings upraised. Other petrels have their own modes of flight—

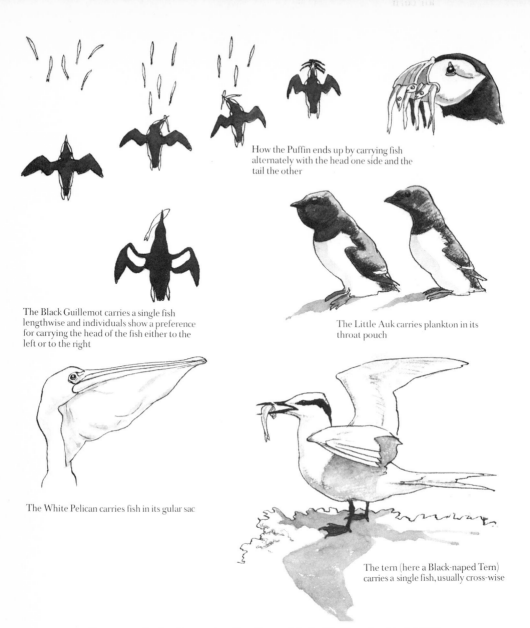

How the Puffin ends up by carrying fish alternately with the head one side and the tail the other

The Black Guillemot carries a single fish lengthwise and individuals show a preference for carrying the head of the fish either to the left or to the right

The Little Auk carries plankton in its throat pouch

The White Pelican carries fish in its gular sac

The tern (here a Black-naped Tern) carries a single fish, usually cross-wise

Some methods of carrying food in seabirds (Puffins after Nash 1975).

in fact flight is probably the best way to recognize them—but they use basically the same surface-picking method. Their food consists of minute floating animals or zooplankton (which may give them their orange stomach oil) copepods, and other crustacea. Off California both the Black Petrel and the Least Petrel feed largely on the larvae of the Spiny Lobster and the shrimp-like euphasids are an extremely important item for many petrels. Small fish such as Sardines and Anchovies, squids, any oil-containing offal and scraps are also taken. Perhaps

the main adaptation of the storm-petrels is for feeding on microscopic particles, which require almost incessant effort to collect. This is a very different system than the gorge-and-rest of many large seabirds and could not sustain a large body (the case of large whales that nevertheless subsist on small crustacea is different because they do not pick them up one at a time from the surface but swim through groups of them, gathering tonnes in a day). Some plankton feeding petrels (Leach's Storm-petrel, Storm Petrel and some prions) forage both by

Cape or Jackass Penguins
of southern Africa. This
species is highly threatened,
at present, due to
increased oil pollution.

An Emperor Penguin with
its chick. The male of this
species incubates the egg
through the antarctic
winter so that the chick
can take advantage of the
increased food supply
during the spring and
summer.

Right A Wandering Albatross, over Drakes Passage, south of Cape Horn. These magnificent seabirds inhabit some of the windiest zones of the southern ocean. Note the strength and direction of the wind indicated by the wave pattern.

Below right Part of the courtship display between a pair of Buller's Albatrosses on Little Sister Island, off New Zealand. This is probably the terminal stages of a bout of courtship display on the potential nest-site.

Below Grey-headed Albatrosses nesting amongst Black-browed Albatrosses on Campbell Island, off New Zealand. Most of the albatrosses are colonial, often breeding on open windswept hillsides.

Above left A mixed flock consisting mainly of Great
Shearwaters with some Sooty Shearwaters and
Fulmars.

Below left A Westland Black Petrel, from the
Scotchman's Creek colony, New Zealand. This is one
of the rare petrels with an estimated population of
3,000–6,000 birds.

Below The Giant Petrel is also known as the 'vulture'
of the Antarctic. Here a pair are scavenging the
remains of a King Penguin.

Right A colony of King Shags on Punta Tombo, Argentina. Further north on the Pacific coast by the Humboldt the related Guanay Cormorants nest two or three times more densely.

Below Eight White Pelicans group fishing.

Left A British colony of Cormorants – they often breed on rocky ledges and level sites near water. When the Cormorant and the British Shag nest in the same area they will use different island sites.

Part of a colony of Magellanic Penguins.

day and by night, sometimes in large flocks. They wander extensively and often gather in areas of high plankton density in cold upwellings, as at the polar convergences. Wilson's Storm-petrel breeds near high-density plankton areas in sub-antarctic zones and gathers in dense feeding flocks which must contain hundreds of thousands. Even in sub-tropical latitudes major feeding concentrations probably always are in the region of cool currents and convergences, though between breeding and wintering areas many species cross huge areas of impoverished ocean.

The prions are agile aerial feeders, though they often feed from the surface and dive extremely well. Some, such as the Antarctic Prion, are equipped with platal lamellae for filtering micro-organisms from the water, though they also take large items such as euphasids. Murphy long ago described the hydroplaning feeding method of the Antarctic Prion: '. . . the birds worked along with an odd creeping motion, resting their bodies lightly upon the surface but holding the wings just above it, the feet apparently furnishing all of the motive power. Then, as they scurried forward quite rapidly, their heads would be thrust underwater and the laminated bills would scoop for food'. Not all the six prions feed exactly alike. As in every other seabird genus, they have been under pressure to diversify. The Antarctic Prion, for instance, feeding by day, chiefly on krill, has a much more robust bill and a floppier, more laboured flight than the smaller, dainty and acrobatic Thin-billed Prion, which lacks functional palatal lamellae. The Thin-billed Prion feeds chiefly at night where it dashes helter skelter over the surface, feeding on surface plankton, particularly amphipods, pattering on the water with its feet and vibrating the wings through short arcs, so rapidly that it can hover over one spot. Sometimes it settles and picks like a Cape Pigeon.

Frigatebirds are extraordinarily light and agile, mostly weighing around 1.5 kilograms and with a wingspan of more than 2.5 metres. An albatross with a similar wingspan might weigh at least five or six times as much. Frigates range hundreds of kilometres from land in the tropics and sub-tropics but rarely settle on the water. They are opportunistic feeders. They fly with deep, steady wing beats, gliding frequently and descending acrobatically in pursuit of airborne flying fish, fish or squid near enough to

Wilson's Storm-petrels dabbling with two Cape Pigeons which usually feed from the surface.

the surface to be caught by dipping, for they seldom actually plunge into the water. They are adept at skimming the surface at full speed and with downbent head, plucking food from the surface layer, a method which is facilitated by their long neck and long, sharply hooked bill. Although famous for their audacious piracy, frigatebirds obtain most of their food by fishing. In impoverished seas their quest is often long and

Magnificent Frigatebirds competing for a fish.

Pomarine Skuas unearthing lemmings.

unrewarding and in the Galapagos a Greater Frigatebird sometimes stays away from the nest for a fortnight at a time, leaving its partner to incubate unaided. When feeding at sea they often hunt in pairs, as do tropicbirds, though nobody seems to know why. They may congregate in thousands at rich food sources and I have seen mixed flocks of frigates, terns and boobies fishing off Aldabra. Whilst they will readily take almost anything that offers itself – young turtles, eggs and young of other seabirds and, in some localities, of their own species, offal and carrion, jellyfish and larger plankton, etc. – their staple diet is undoubtedly flying fish and squid, though other fish species, such as Menhaden, are locally important.

The frigate's extraordinary dexterity is due to its low wing-loading, unstable wing shape (see page 17) and huge forked tail, which is highly mobile and can be used in many shapes. Whilst the males of all species are almost entirely black beneath, all the females except one (the Ascension Frigate) and all the juveniles have considerable areas of white below. Yet, even then the white is never on the head or forehead. On the assumption that in plunge diving birds the white is hunting camouflage which renders the bird more difficult to see from below, it might be expected that the frigate's forehead would be white. In fact, the white pattern of female frigates may be concerned more with enabling the courting male to recognize overflying females of his own species than with fishing.

Often, two species of frigates breed on the same island, Greater and Lesser being the commonest pair. In such a case, as on Aldabra Atoll, conventional wisdom would suggest a partition of the food resource. But Tony Diamond found that the differences were surprisingly slight. In the wet season the Lesser Frigatebird took more squid, relative to flying fish, than did the Greater, whilst in the dry season the two species took different proportions of the two main genera of flying fish (*Exocoetus* and *Cypselurus*), though the difference was not large. Nor did the smaller bird always take smaller average prey. In the dry season there was *no* size difference but in the wet, the Lesser Frigatebird's tendency to take more squid, which are on average smaller than flying fish, meant that, overall, its prey size was less than that of its congener. But the interesting point is the slightness of the differences.

The combination of what seems to me to be a particularly difficult feeding method (it appears much easier to sit, albatross-like, on the sea at night, picking up the phosphorescent cephalods which rise all around) with an often impoverished feeding area, have made it difficult for frigates to feed their young. Consequently, these grow so slowly that the breeding cycle takes well over a year and frigates can breed successfully only once in two years. This, in turn, has raised many problems for them in terms of site and mate retention.

Some terns, notably the noddies and particularly the Sooty Tern, are surface-dippers, hovering and picking up fish driven to the surface by predators. Of the truly marine terns (about thirty-four species) many are superficial plunge-divers, mainly in coastal and offshore waters, except when migrating. Sooties are the most pelagic, though several other species forage far from their breeding sites. Some terns (Common, Arctic, Sandwich and Little, for instance) dive from low or moderate heights (up to 10 metres), often hovering first and usually striking

a Brown Pelican plunge-diving (sequence of positions in one bird).
b A group of Blue-footed Boobies synchronising their dives after a signal (whistle) from one of them.
c The superficial plunge of a tern.
d Collaborative hunting by swimming in a group of White Pelicans.
e Sighting, pursuit, capture and holding of fish by a Guillemot. The feet are used as well as the wings.
f Albatrosses feeding on squid near the surface.
g Storm-Petrels pattering on the surface and picking up plankton.

Some methods of feeding in seabirds.

A Common Tern poised ready to catch a fish. Most truly pelagic terns are superficial plunge-divers.

the water at a fairly shallow angle – 'flop-snatching' – rather than penetrating cleanly. Noddies, Sooty Terns and Fairy Terns, typical tropical terns, usually do not strike the water in this way. They snatch fish and squid from the surface or from the air when these jump clear to avoid tuna or other predators. Noddies use their feet extensively to push off from the surface and are more prone to flop onto the water in a 'pursuit plunge'. They are less aerial than Sooties, which easily become soaked and therefore do not usually splash to the water and certainly do not sit on it, as noddies often do. In fact noddies sometimes swim about seizing surface prey such as small crabs and fish fry among weeds. These 'contact dipping' terns all have slender, more or less straight bills, narrow at the tip, which whip quickly through the water. The white forehead or cap of Sooties and noddies maybe camouflages them to make the downward pointing head less visible to fish against the light sky. The Sooty sometimes fishes at night, together with shearwaters, etc., but noddies seem to be fully day-time feeders.

The beautiful Fairy Tern feeds mainly by snatching small fish from the very surface or the air and is not a plunger or a 'patterer'. Evidently it is often a crepuscular feeder. Squid, and some fish which come to the surface mainly at night, seem to figure more importantly in its diet than in those of other sympatric terns. Its pure white plumage and extraordinarily translucent wings and tail may make it inconspicuous against the sky in dim light.

Surface feeding whilst swimming

Many seabirds, especially shearwaters and albatrosses, feed whilst sitting on the surface or by forcing themselves slightly below it. Whilst the storm-petrels feed from the wing on small surface prey, the shearwaters and albatrosses feed more on fish and larger squid, many of the shearwaters, in particular, combining plunge-diving with surface-swimming.

The Cape Pigeon, one of the commonest antarctic birds, feeds in vast flocks, usually from the surface. It paddles vigorously to bring plankton to the surface and pecks pigeon-like, from side to side. Although principally a crustacean feeder (euphasids are an important item) it dives well for fish and squids, both from the surface and from the air, as well as scavenging industriously. It is distinctly predatory and will take wounded birds. Despite this catholicity it is clearly adapted for filter-feeding, with serrations on the insides of the mandibles and a small gular pouch to retain the sievings. Like the fulmar-petrels to which it is related, the Cape Pigeon has a flexible hunting mode and a varied diet. Giant petrels feed mostly on the surface but dive well from it. Fulmars feed predominantly on crustacea whilst floating or swimming, and on other floating animal matter such as polychaetes, pelagic snails, etc. However, in pursuit of fish they can dive from the surface to a depth of several metres using their feet and wings. Off California, the Pacific Fulmar eats jellyfish – a watery diet one would think. Like the Cape Pigeon, Fulmars often congregate in thousands at rewarding food sources, whether these be the plankton-rich areas receiving the minerals from a glacial run-off, or the offal patches attending fishing and whaling. The Antarctic Petrel feeds in flocks on surface plankton, but neither by hovering and picking nor by swimming and pecking. It hovers and plunges, though shallowly and with outspread wings. Like the other fulmar-petrels, it scavenges enthusiastically. The gadfly-petrels, a varied group of medium-sized petrels, dive for cephalopods and crustacea, which they take, also, whilst swimming and floating on the surface.

The albatrosses catch their prey whilst floating or swimming. They feed mainly on large cephalopods such as the cuttlefish *Amplisepia*, though also importantly on fish, crustacea and offal. The great albatrosses have been seen to eat the formidable *Physalin*, or Portuguese Man-o'-war Jellyfish. Albatrosses often, perhaps mainly, feed at night. Sympatric species may differ significantly in diet. They feed by dipping head and bill into the surface layer and only occasionally, plunge dive, though several including the Royal and Wanderer have been seen to do so. The long, powerful bill is hooked with strengthened cutting edges. Most albatrosses have pale underparts for camouflage from beneath and they feed singly or in loose groups, with no suggestion of co-operation.

The Royal Albatross is the largest and heaviest seabird in the world with a wingspan of more than 3 metres and a weight of up to 10 kilograms (compare the 2 metre wingspan and less than 2 kilograms of Andrew's Frigate-bird!). These huge petrels have developed their long narrow wings, torpedo-shaped body and short, square tail, as adaptations for fast gliding. They girdle the Earth in the windswept latitudes of the '40's' and below. This vast nomadism enables them to take advantage of rich but widely separated patches of food. Linked to these high powers of flight are lengthy forag-

ing trips when breeding, and to these, the useful ability to store, if not to manufacture, oily stomach contents as they go, instead of merely gathering a cropful of fish. In turn, the ability to deliver huge feeds of nutritious oil underpins their breeding strategy, enabling the young to go for long periods without food.

Many of the shearwaters feed whilst swimming on the surface but all of them dive in pursuit, mainly from the surface and to no great depth, using half-opened wings and chasing surface swimming shoals of fish and squids. They will take, also, crustacea and offal. Several shearwaters plunge-dive from the air, the Great Shearwater, perhaps, best of all, power-diving steeply from 6 metres to 10 metres above the surface, but even it feeds mainly by pursuit plunging from much lower heights, or from the surface. Cory's Shearwater, which replaces the Great Shearwater fairly sharply in the warmer zones of the sub-tropical convergences, dives rather less and feeds more from the wing, skimming along over the surface, and dipping.

Shearwaters which dive freely from the surface include the Flesh-footed, Manx, (which also plunges), Little and Audubon's. The surface diving shearwaters, of which the Christmas Island Shearwater is a good example, show adaptations for fast swimming, such as strong but streamlined legs, large webs whose big toes enable them to fold neatly between strokes, and compact plumage which enables the bird to sink more easily. Many shearwaters feed in dim light or at night. Some, for example the Slender-billed and the Manx, often feed in dense flocks whilst others, for instance, the Little and Audubon's, are mainly solitary or occur in small groups at sea.

Plunge-divers

Some terns, gulls, skuas, shearwaters, etc. qualify as plunge divers, but whilst the boundary between surface plunging and deep plunge-diving is merely one of degree, we will reserve the term 'plunge-diving' for the select few that really dive, and consider the others to be superficial plungers, often but only partly immersing and, at most, remaining below the surface for a second or two. Heavy plunge-diving is virtually confined to the Pelecaniformes and even there, to the tropicbirds and, spectacularly, the Gannets and boobies, whilst most pelicans are not plunge-divers, but take fish mainly whilst swimming on the surface, though the Brown Pelican plunges shallowly. The dive looks a bit like the fall of a weighted eiderdown but is in fact expertly controlled. During it, the neck is bent to take the head over the shoulders rather than retracted into itself as in the Gannet. The result is that the diving pelican looks much less stream-lined than the bullet-like Gannet, but it uses the same technique of angling the wings, rotating the body but keeping the head stable, and shooting its legs and wings right back just after the bill hits the water. The pouch balloons out and surrounds the fish whilst the upper mandible closes rapidly to chase it in. The pouch can be expanded to hold about 10 litres of water, which effectively immobilizes it. The head is then raised vertically, the water flows out of the still submerged bill, taking up to a minute to drain away, and the pelican swallows the fish with a characteristic toss of the head. Australian Pelicans empty their pouches by tucking their bills against their breasts, contracting their pouches and ejecting water from the corners of the gape.

Brown Boobies diving for fish. These birds are one of the pale-headed forms from the Pacific Ocean.

Tropicbirds dive from 10 metres or more, and probably rely on the impetus of the dive to carry them to their prey. But the long, pendulant tail feathers seem ill-suited to powerful diving and it may be that they feed mainly from just above the surface, by dipping or aerial capture, when their tail would be a useful stabilizer and direction-changer. Furthermore, the White-tailed (Yellow-billed) Tropicbirds are too small and light to penetrate far, though the more powerful red-billed species could certainly dive more deeply.

All nine sulids are spectacular plunge-divers, although they differ in style. There is relatively little difference in size and weight between the smallest (the male Red-foot of the central Pacific) and the largest (the male Atlantic Gannet); they differ by a factor of only 4:1 in weight and 1.5:1 or less in size, presumably because a penetrating plunge-diver requires to be reasonably heavy (terns, by contrast, differ in weight by a factor of 17:1). Nevertheless, the physical differences between the various sulids are highly important adaptations to their respective feeding environments. The Red-foot lives in the tropics and sub-tropics, which are often impoverished. It feeds mainly on squids and flying-fish, in search of which it ranges up to at least 150 kilometres from the breeding station. Often, it takes flying fish in the air,

agilely changing tack as the fish break surface in all directions. It is also markedly nocturnal. Its far-ranging habit is itself a form of insurance against its scattered and often scarce food; in such circumstances the longer a bird stays away from base the less likely it is to come home empty handed, which, when you have travelled a long way, is a prime consideration. It does mean, though, that the Red-foot can manage to feed only one chick, and even that one grows slowly. Of its tropical congeners, the Masked and Brown Boobies, the former is larger and more powerful. It, too, forages far from base. It tends to dive steeply though rather inflexibly, and to penetrate deeply (dives from a height of 100 metres have been estimated). It can handle larger prey than can the Red-foot and takes less on the wing and at the surface. Unlike the Red-foot and, particularly, the Brown Booby, there is little difference between the sexes in size, perhaps suggesting that it takes prey in areas and at depths at which no useful purpose would be served by dimorphism. The Brown Booby tends to fish nearer the shore, often, indeed, in very shallow water, and the smallness of the male may fit him to do this more than the female. Brown Boobies, and probably the others too, pursue their prey by swimming beneath the surface, using feet and wings. The most specialized of all the inshore fishers is the male Blue-footed Booby, whose particularly long tail and small size gives him the ability to dive headlong into less than 0.5 metres of water, though the larger female often goes far out to sea and, out of the breeding season, so does the male. The Blue-foot has achieved the distinction of perfecting a truly collaborative form of fishing in which a group of hunting birds dive synchronously at a signal whistle from one of them (usually a male). Other sulids call excitedly when fishing, but not as a signal to others. This raises the whole question of the function of communal fishing and allied aspects (see below).

Atlantic Gannets are much the heaviest members of the family and this enables them to plunge with terrific force. Like others, they may commence by power-diving, with wing-beats, or simply incline into a gravity plunge, slanting or vertical. They hunt by beating upwind with a downward-pointing beak and binocular-gaze. Undoubtedly they spot and pursue an individual fish, adjusting their angle and position minutely on the way down. The wings are partially or fully angled, tips moving and body rotating if necessary. The tail is spread and worked and the feet act as flaps. Gannets may hustle down in one straight air-slide, corkscrew or even tip backwards of vertical before shooting their wings behind them and entering the water like an arrow (the old Cornish name for the Gannet—saithor—means arrow). Even so, it is unlikely that Gannets penetrate more than 10 metres, at the most. Usually, they remain submerged for less than 10 seconds, during which time they swallow their prey, which they probably seize when their speed has slackened, or on the ascent. It is ideally built for penetrating air and water, with a pointed, tapered bill, torpedo body and pointed tail. Well-developed air sacs cushion the impact of the dive and occluded nostrils prevent the ingress of water. Robust tarsi and large webs allow vigorous thrusting through water. There is a protection reflex movement of the nictitating membrane across the eye, upon contact with the water. The Gannet's weight and strength enables it to cope with powerful fish such as large Mackerel, one of its two principal prey species (the other is the Herring), of which it can swallow four or five in succession. Its weight depends partly on an extensive fat layer, which has the further functions of insulating the bird from the rigors of the arctic conditions in which it lives for much of the time and of providing fuel to tide it over the periods in which stormy weather prevents fishing. One could accurately say that the Gannet's survival is based on the ability to gorge and fast in hostile but food-rich seas. The Atlantic Gannet is, I believe, a modified version of the African Gannet, whose ancestor penetrated northwards and adapted to the opportunities and demands of a more exacting climate and richer seas by becoming stronger and heavier.

The dazzling white plumage is an extraordinarily effective social signal, attracting other Gannets to the fishing area. Communal (though *not* collaborative) fishing is extremely widespread among seabirds, usually involving several species, though not so much in the Gannet's case since, usually, no others can reach or handle the prey. Often, no doubt, several species gather merely because the prey is there, perhaps made vulnerable by underwater predators driving it to the surface, or perhaps concentrated at a convergence. The birds are probably hunting independently, neither helping nor hindering, except that, in extremely dense feeding flocks there is likely to be some competition. It may be that in other cases, however, and the Gannet is one such, the individuals in the feeding flock are actually helped by each other's activity, and therefore the plumage which helps them to see each other and to gather in one place is a positive advantage both to the 'summoner' and the 'summonsed'. That the aid is involuntary and non-collaborative makes no difference. It could work by confusing, disorienting and fatiguing the shoaling fish on which Gannets mainly feed. A hail of Gannets striking thickly into the water gives the fish no time to recover and evade and each Gannet may well end up with more captures than it would have gained singly. The apparent competition would thus not really be competition at all. However, this story has its loose ends, for the Masked Booby is even more dazzling than the Gannet and yet it feeds singly and rarely has the chance to benefit in the way described above. However, its white plumage may have a completely different function, namely that of heat-regulation. The safest generalization in biology is that it is unsafe to generalize.

Plunge diving as a profession is highly restricted; as a hobby it is quite widespread. Even shags and auks occasionally indulge. But to the few who have perfected it, substantial feeding niches have been opened and sulids, though a small family, are widespread and (until man intervened) were numerous. That the tropicbirds are less successful may be in part due to their specialized requirements for nesting sites.

Diving from surface and underwater pursuit

Many seabirds have become expert at underwater pursuit. But because of the difference in the density of air and water, it is difficult to use wings for flying in the air *and* for flying underwater. It requires immense force to swim rapidly through water and thus large birds are at an advantage because their power increases with volume whilst the resistance offered by their body surface increases only as the square of their length. However, flying underwater *and* in air, is practicable only in small birds. Hence, small auks can do it, but the Great Auk could not and even the Guillemot is approaching the limit. All penguins have opted solely for underwater flying and so have been able to evolve into the small Fairy (Little) Penguin and the massive Emperor. Large underwater swimmers that fly well in air, such as the shags, cormorants and divers, use their huge feet synchronously for propulsion under water, usually keeping their wings tightly folded against their bodies although underwater use of wings has

Feeding rafts of Spotted Shags off New Zealand. These birds sometimes form dense flocks when food is particularly abundant.

been seen in some species. Diving-petrels and shearwaters use both wings and feet, but they are not large birds, nor are they so specialized for this mode of feeding as the auks, phalacrocoracids and penguins. Clearly, underwater swimming opens up an important feeding niche. Even a cormorant can descend to depths unobtainable by simple plunge-diving and can quest along the sea-bed, flushing concealed prey such as flatfish, whilst an Emperor Penguin can descend to the almost unbelievable depth of 265 metres.

Common Cormorants usually forage singly or in loose groups, fairly well inshore and often in fresh water far inland. They seldom remain submerged for more than a minute and rarely dive deeper than about 10 metres although reportedly they have been netted at a depth of 37 metres. Shags can remain submerged for 3–4 minutes, though usually much less (around 40 seconds) and probably hunt more in midwater and less along the bottom. They, too, are usually solitary hunters but sometimes gather in dense flocks where prey is particularly abundant. They seem never to collaborate, though Double-crested Cormorants, Little Black Cormorants and others form lines and circles, herding and concentrating fish. Almost 2 000 Double-crested Cormorants have been seen feeding together. Smaller flocks feed in tenuous lines, larger ones in lines up to three or four deep, which move forwards together as the birds dive and resurface. Guanay Cormorants, pied cormorants and others, feed in enormous rafts, but independently; birds continually fly

over the backs of their feeding companions to the front edge of the moving group. Where several species live together, they tend to divide up the feeding habitat. Thus of four shags that feed in the New Zealand coastal waters two (White-breasted and Black) feed close inshore, seldom in water more than 3 metres deep, Pied Shags often feed in water of 3–10 metres up to 300 metres from the shore and Spotted Shags feed in deeper water up to 15 kilometres offshore.

Coarse fish figure largely in the diets of many phalacrocoracids. The Common Cormorant in Britain eats mainly flatfish, especially Flounders, but also lots of shore and estuarine fish such as blennies and sea-scorpions. One survey found only 10 per cent of marketable fish in Cormorant stomachs. The Shag's diet, as its foraging habits would suggest, differs markedly from that of the Cormorant. Other members of the family also have their own food spectra; the Little Pied Cormorant, for example, takes freshwater crustacea, insect larvae, waterbeetles, tadpoles and other small fry while the Red-faced Cormorant takes a lot of crabs.

The two darters (Anhingidae) are freshwater relatives of the cormorants and have perfected the novel method of capturing fish by stalking or pursuing them underwater and spearing them. Their beaks lack a terminal hook and are shot forward as the S-shaped neck is powerfully straightened, using a special hinge mechanism. The impaled prey is then brought to the surface, thrown up and swallowed. As Owre has detailed, darters are much less powerful swimmers than cormorants, and they have weaker pelvic girdles. Instead of pursuing their prey with speed and vigour, they approach stealthily, like the spear-gun fisher. They are less buoyant than cormorants, which helps them to remain submerged whilst swimming slowly. They seldom fly from the water, preferring, when soaked, to climb out onto vegetation, an accomplishment aided by their more generalized legs, freed from the heavy musculature of the power-swimming cormorant. Their light wing loading means that they have greater manoeuvrability when flying around forest-surrounded ponds.

The vast majority of the cormorants and their allies forage within 8 to 16 kilometres of base. This generally reduces the size of their colonies, although there are notable exceptions, principally the Guanay Cormorant, of which up to 6 million pairs have been estimated on Central Chincha, of the Peruvian guano islands. But this is the exception that proves the rule, for these birds nest on the doorstep of the Humboldt Current with its astronomical population of anchovies upon which the cormorants, along with pelicans, boobies, terns, burrowing petrels, penguins and sea-lions, feed with little more effort than it takes to open their mouths. In Britain, by contrast, the average size of a Cormorant or Shag colony is less than 200 pairs, though colonies of some southern hemisphere species, for instance, the Little Pied Cormorant, are much larger.

Of all diving birds, penguins are the most specialized. Emancipation from flight, (though at a price, as witness their restricted distribution) has removed the conflict, mentioned earlier, between flying and swimming. The result is that they have evolved the most extreme modifications for diving found among birds. Although certain penguins are capable of extraordinary diving feats, as a group they feed largely on fish, crustacea and squid which they catch fairly near the surface, not very far offshore. The shrimp-like krill is an abundant penguin food in offshore antarctic waters during the summer. Bernard Stonehouse paints a vivid picture of the amount of food, largely krill and larval fish, brought home by the 5 million Adelie Penguins of Lawrie Island at the height of the breeding season. He estimates that, at about 2 kilograms of food daily, they take up to 9000 tonnes of seafood each day, which is the catch of about seventy modern trawlers. Squids figure prominently in penguin diets; King and Emperor Penguins take them up to a metre in length. The penguins of South Africa and South America (the Black-foot, Magellanic and Peruvian) feed on the vast numbers of pilchards and anchovies in the Benguela and Humboldt Currents.

When covering long distances, King Penguins 'porpoise' through the water, travelling 3 or 4 metres through the air before re-entering and covering another 6–12 metres with the impetus so gained. They swim underwater with immensely powerful strokes of their flippers, which almost meet on the upstroke, and are held out from the sides when gliding, head tucked in and feet extended backwards, soles facing each other or uppermost. Kooyman suggests that penguin swimming speeds have been greatly over-estimated and that they are probably nowhere near as fast as porpoises and dolphins, precise measurements of which have shown a maximum swimming speed, for a very short period, of 39.4 kilometres per hour (Spotted Dolphin), the fastest reliable record for any marine mammal. The Pacific Bottle-nosed Dolphin managed a brief dash at 29.9 kilometres per hour but could long maintain a speed of only 11.1 kilometres per hour. Swimming between ice-holes, Emperor Penguins clocked a maximum speed of 9.6 kilometres per hour.

Emperor Penguins, the largest of all diving and the problems of heat loss or, during vigorous exercise, heat production. There are no grounds, at present, for claiming any special properties of the blood of diving birds which would help them to resist asphyxia. There is more myoglobin in the muscle than in land birds, but the oxygen bound to it is only about 15 per cent of the total store. Birds are one up on diving mammals because they possess an extensive system of air sacs which together with the lungs contribute about 50 per cent of the oxygen store; the remainder is carried by the blood. Unlike seals, which exhale almost half their breath before

King Penguins 'porpoising'; an economical mode of travel used over long distances (distance under water is 6 to 12 metres).

birds, are particularly fascinating because of their singular commitment to the shores of Antarctica and its fast sea-ice during the antarctic winter. This means that they not only dive and feed during winter darkness but, unlike other penguins, must at times do so in heavy pack-ice and, perhaps, even under fast ice. Kooyman's work shows that, when feeding, Emperors normally remain submerged for up to 9 minutes at a time. That this is well within their reserves was demonstrated by a bird that was seen swimming near the release hole 18 minutes after submergence and, in fact, never returned. By attaching depth recorders, it was estimated that birds dived to 265 metres at a maximum depth-change rate of 72 metres in one minute, even when encumbered with equipment weighing 700 grams! Such deep dives are probably in search of deep-dwelling squids.

Emperors often dive in tight, synchronized groups, surfacing in a breathing hole together and submerging as a group. The function of this behaviour is not known but could have to do with direction finding, since isolated penguins studied by Kooyman often seemed badly disoriented. They depend, it seems, on visual cues to return to open water from beneath the ice, for no acoustic signals could be detected.

Deep diving birds commonly have to overcome shortage of oxygen, the effects of pressure diving, penguins dive after breathing in. As the bird dives, its heart beat drops to a rate of about 1/5th of the resting rate and the supply of blood to the muscles is greatly reduced, though not nearly so much as in the seal. This enables the available oxygen to be used by those tissues which are absolutely dependent on it, leaving others to function without. The muscles, for instance, use their myoglobin and when that is finished, they function without oxygen and build up toxics (lactic acid) which the bird deals with when it surfaces.

The ability of diving birds to avoid decompression sickness remains a puzzle and, at present, it appears that the dives are simply too short to allow much nitrogen to be absorbed by the blood.

Penguins are marvellously well insulated against heat loss when swimming in icy water. Their feathers are extremely thick (11 or 12 to the square centimetre in the Emperor) and are short and narrow—more like fur than feathers. They are believed to account for 80 per cent of the insulation, the remainder depending on a thick layer of fat. Nevertheless, Emperor Penguins soon begin to shiver whilst resting in sea-water at −1.85°C and, after a time, even birds that are diving shiver during the breathing periods between dives. They comb their body plumage vigorously, presumably to refurbish it

Glaucous Gull with adult
Little Auk (Greenland)

Frigatebird chasing Red-
footed Booby to make it
regurgitate (tropical seas)

Great Skua hounding Sooty
Shearwater (northern
Atlantic)

Lesser Black-backed Gull
stealing a Guillemot's egg

White-tailed Tropicbird
evicting a Cahow chick
(Bermuda)

Tropicbirds have proved to
be a grave menace to this
tiny population of petrels
struggling to re-establish
themselves

Predation, kleptoparasitism and interspecific killing.

with air, which is squeezed out as the plumage compresses during dives. To keep warm in water, therefore, penguins have to expend a lot of energy–probably much more than seals.

Scavenging and piracy

Compared with the major ways of getting food, scavenging and stealing (piracy or klepto-parasitism) are considerably less important and the former is not even a 'method', as such, for it only employs techniques used in the aquisition of 'natural' food. Yet they are well worth notice. In partial, albeit inadvertent, compensation for his destructive forays against seabirds, man, by his other hunting activities, supplies some of them with a great deal of fish, whale offal and other refuse. In some areas, and for some species, this can have a marked effect on populations. In the small Irish Sea, for example, an estimated 25 and 34 million fish were dumped overboard in 1972 and 1973 respectively. For the scavengers, in this case mainly Herring Gulls (67 per cent) and Kittiwakes (25 per cent) but also other gulls, Fulmars and Gannets, such amounts may not be negligible, especially in helping young birds to survive their first year of life. In the North Sea, some tens of thousands of tonnes of fish waste are dumped every year. During the peak years of the whaling industry, colossal amounts of blubber and flesh were thrown away and nourished numerous members of the procellariforms.

The spectacle of excited crowds of seabirds attending fishing vessels is common the world over. Usually the scavenging flocks are composed of several species which compete strenuously. Gannets and Fulmars dominate gulls and even skuas in the North Sea and North Atlantic but there is no evidence that scavenging birds have any sort of a peck order within their own species, though they often fight. In southern latitudes, albatrosses, petrels, Cape Pigeons, etc. replace Fulmars, gulls and Gannets.

Many gulls scavenge at sewer outfalls, rubbish dumps, fish docks, farm feeding places, etc. and (if it is scavenging) behind the plough. Adult Herring Gulls are more successful than immature birds, at least on rubbish dumps, and in a feeding flock immatures are usually at the edges. It has been shown in Herring Gulls feeding at a fish dock that individuals become highly specialized in this one method. Not only do they attend regularly for years, possibly even exclusively, but they generally feed in only one

part of the dock and, moreover, feeding companions tend to nest together in the colony. The tendency for individuals to specialize on one type of food is well known from more casual observations and is likely to be a widespread phenomenon. There are specialist egg-robbers and specialist pirates among frigatebirds and skuas; specialist attenders at seal rookeries among giant petrels, and so on.

Piracy is confined mainly to two families, the skuas and frigatebirds, although some terns and gulls practise it also. Even here, only a small fraction of the total population practises piracy; the remainder feed 'honestly'. Piracy is not the same as supplanting, which is common to many seabirds. It is an active pursuit aimed at compelling the victim to drop or disgorge its catch. The skuas and frigates reinforce their pursuit with various forms of attack. When hounding Gannets, Great Skuas often seize a wing tip or tail and capsize the victim in mid-air, or, using their feet, push the Gannet down. Even so, only about 12 per cent of Gannet chases yield regurgitations for this skua. In the smaller and more agile Arctic Skua, 22 per cent of chases of Puffins yielded prizes at Hermaness and 50 per cent at an Icelandic colony. One strategem used by Puffins against skuas is to return to the colony among a crowd of non-breeding, or at least empty-handed, birds. The skua then sees it late, and birds which are fairly near home have been shown to retain food more stubbornly than ones for which the chase begins earlier. Indeed, it has been suggested that late breeding is selected against in Puffins because such birds have to return with food when their screen of non-breeders has largely dispersed.

Piracy is the principal feeding method of the Arctic Skua on Foula, in the Shetlands; Furness found that 90 per cent of its food (almost entirely sand-eels) is so gained, and, in fact, it rarely if ever fishes for itself in the breeding season. It relies on its great agility to out-fly its victim on level terms whereas Great Skuas, like frigates, circle above potential victims and then surprise them by stooping at great speed. Arctic Skuas tackle the agile terns and Kittiwakes more than do Great Skuas, and have a greater success with them. On the other hand, they are less successful with auks, which are presumably less afraid of them, and they don't even bother to try to rob Gannets. Furness found that skua success depended, in general, on the speed with which the victim reacted, its height (the higher the victim the better for the skua), visiblity (poor visibility favoured the skua) and the number of skuas participating (success rose with numbers). Similarly, Laughing Gulls, which parasitize terns, were more successful in larger than in smaller groups. They form groups not because there are too few terns around to do otherwise, but because a gull joining in after somebody else has started the chase gains more advantage than by chasing on its own.

Perhaps more surprising is that terns are pirates as well as victims. A few Roseate Terns, operating singly, patrol above incoming terns of several species and then carry out surprise fishing-dives in which they attempt to snatch the fish from the owner's bill. About 8 per cent of attacks on Common Terns were successful and contrary to what one might expect, short fish were obtained more successfully than longer ones. In Newfoundland, up to 61 per cent of landings by fish-carrying Puffins elicited attacks or robberies by gulls. In the north-east of Scotland, Black-headed Gulls stole food from the Sandwich Terns which nested among them, thus exacting a toll for their protection. After the tern chicks were a few days old, food stealing by gulls rose sharply, and almost a third of food-carrying terns were harried. Successful attacks rose to 6.5 per cent, and although the stealing did not affect the terns during incubation and early chick-life, it may have reduced the terns' fledging weight and thus, perhaps, their survival.

Frigatebirds intent on piracy are as exciting to watch as any predator. Homecoming boobies, particularly Red-footed with which the frigates so often nest, are pursued, often after a screaming descent by the frigate, but gulls, shearwaters, terns, tropicbirds and others are also chased. The percentage of successful piracies seems to vary; 12 per cent of chases by the Greater Frigatebird on Red-footed Boobies in the Galapagos were successful but 63 per cent on Christmas Island (Pacific). As with the Great Skua, piracy cannot be important for more than a small proportion of the frigate population, although for these few, it may confer significant advantage. Alternatively, perhaps a larger proportion use the method as a supplement.

It is but a short step from piracy to predation and Great Skuas are formidable predators. They take some adult seabirds, including not a few Arctic Skuas, and many Puffins, as well as young Kittiwakes, which they can often snatch from the nest. Frigatebirds, also, are significant predators at seabird colonies, taking young Sooty Terns and newly fledged shearwaters, prematurely unguarded boobies, etc. The Magnificent Frigatebird, in particular, takes eggs and young of its own species though in most cases this is probably because somebody has just disturbed them. The large gulls, too, are significant predators, especially on Puffins, Little Auks, various auklets, terns, shearwaters, petrels, and even other gulls. Herring Gulls entirely destroyed the large and ancient Black-headed Gull colony on Walney, and among the Lesser Black-back Gulls of Skokholm, Wales, the bulk of egg and chick losses were due to predation by adults on neighbouring nests. This, however, was probably due to the increasing density of the nesting gulls, due to the growth in the population.

Among terns, the Gull-billed Tern lives mainly on animals other than fish (frogs, small mammals, insects, etc.) and the Black Tern, which is one of the freshwater terns, feeds largely on insects. But these are aberrant terns; the mainline is distinctively marine and fish-eating.

Seabird diets

This brief survey of the feeding methods used by seabirds shows how effectively they garner the vast and varied resources of the sea. Can one make any useful, broad generalizations? Nobody has done more painstaking work than Philip Ashmole on the difficult subject of the food of marine seabirds and most of my generalizations on the way in which the world's seabirds divide up their cake are based on his analyses.

First, and hardly unexpectedly, the most important item in a seabird's diet is fish. About 138 out of some 270 seabirds species eat mainly fish and a further sixty-two eat at least a moderately important amount. Among the mainly fish-eaters are the pelicans, some skuas, many gulls and terns, the skimmers, all the sulids, several penguins, some shearwaters, virtually all the shags and cormorants and many auks.

Perhaps less obviously, at least forty species eat mainly crustacea and other invertebrates (excluding cephalopods) and no fewer than 138 species, in total, eat, among other things, a considerable amount of these small shrimp-like animals and their relatives. In terms of food-economy this is a very 'sensible' thing to do,

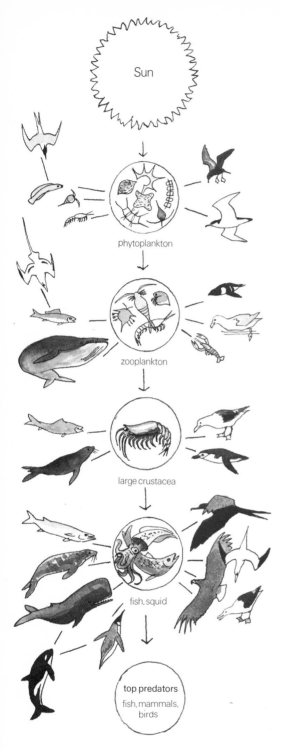

A simplified ocean food-chain. Notice how seabirds have adapted to take advantage of each level of this food-chain.

because birds that can live on crustacea and plankton are near the base of the food pyramid and therefore have much more available to them, since much is lost at each step to the apex. Among the groups subsisting mainly or substantially on crustacea, etc. are several penguins, many storm-petrels, the diving petrels, murrelets, the Little Auk, the Cape Pigeon, many shearwaters, the prions, fulmars, Snow Petrel and Blue Petrel whilst for Sabine's Gull, the Grey Ternlet and the Rhinoceros Auklet, they are about as important as fish. It is, however, useful to be able to switch to other foods, especially where crustacea are seasonal and most seabirds are opportunistic and will take what is available. Thus, the Fulmar, in a sample of 180 birds shot in the North West Territories held mainly fish (63 per cent), though in fact, on other evidence, they were searching for amphipods.

The third most important type of sea-food is the group containing squids—the cephalopods of which there are some 700 species. It is not commonly appreciated that cephalopods are not only amongst the most abundant sea-life but that they are extremely quick-growing and short-lived—eighteen months or two years is a good age for them—thus rapidly turning over the primary productivity of the sea and making it available for higher predators such as seabirds. Fifteen seabirds subsist mainly on squids and a further sixty-one eat considerable numbers of these animals. Those depending mainly on cephalopods include several gadfly-petrels, the three petrels belonging to *Fregatta* and *Nesofregatta* and nine albatrosses, whilst squid figure prominently in the diets of the other albatrosses and gadfly-petrels, many shearwaters, fulmars, storm-petrels, prions, the Antarctic Petrel, some penguins, the tropicbirds, frigates and boobies, some gulls and terns. Philip Ashmole has drawn attention to the key role played by squid in the economy of seabirds.

Flying fish, and squid, are a natural 'pair' in the menu of many tropical and sub-tropical seabirds because they occur together in the surface layer and in a wide range of sizes. Similarly, in colder southern latitudes, squid and crustacea figure together prominently in the diets of penguins, albatrosses, fulmars, the Antarctic Petrel, Cape Pigeon, Snow Petrel, some gadfly-petrels, etc.

Nor must the role of carrion, offal and the like be underestimated, for at least seventy-one

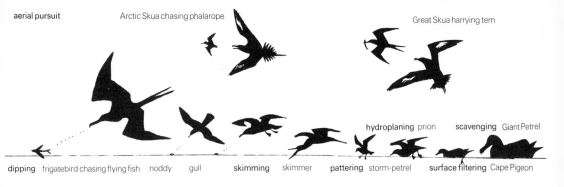

aerial pursuit   Arctic Skua chasing phalarope   Great Skua harrying tern

hydroplaning prion   scavenging Giant Petrel

dipping frigatebird chasing flying fish   noddy   gull   **skimming**   skimmer   **pattering** storm-petrel   **surface filtering** Cape Pigeon

surface plunging   tern   pelican   tropicbird   Gannet   booby

pursuit plunging   shearwater
surface seizing   phalarope   albatross

underwater   bottom feeding   scaup   eider   pursuit diving with feet   cormorant   pursuit diving with wings   diving-petrel   penguin   auk

Seabird feeding methods (after Ashmole, 1971).

species eat a considerable amount, although perhaps only the ugly and redoubtable 'Stinker' or Giant Petrel subsists mainly by scavenging and killing sickly birds.

Distribution of feeding methods

Just as there are particularly important items among seabirds' food, so, among the many ways of hunting, a few are of major importance. It is impossible to say, simply, which is the commonest mode of feeding, for many species use two, three or even more. But more species use diving from the surface and subsequently seeking or pursuing prey for prolonged periods of under- water swimming, as their main method, than use any other as the main one. This is due mainly to the twenty-nine shags and cormorants, the fifteen penguins and twenty-two auks and their allies, all of which are wedded to this habit, as are the four diving-petrels, the southern hemi- sphere equivalent of auks. Only one major group, the shearwaters, use it as an important subsidiary method whilst thirty-three other species, mostly from the Procellariiformes and including albatrosses and several prions, use it as a minor method.

Picking from the surface, or dipping, whilst on the wing, is the second commonest way of

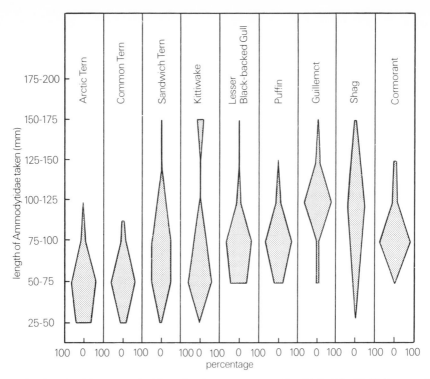

The length of the Ammodytidae taken by some species of seabird. After T. H. Pearson 1968.

gaining a living, if one includes 'pattering' by petrels, sieving plankton, and a modicum of pursuit plunging. No fewer than fifty species from twenty-two genera use dipping as their main feeding method.

Among the genera for which surface dipping and pattering is an important feeding method, may be mentioned nine storm-petrels of the genus *Oceanodroma,* and the British Storm Petrel (*Hydrobates*), three skuas (Pomarine, Long-tailed and Arctic), no fewer than thirty-five gulls, twenty-six terns and twenty large petrels of the genus *Pterodroma.* Thus 152 species use this combination of dipping, with or without pattering and pursuit plunging, as their major, or as a main, feeding method.

Picking or scooping whilst swimming or floating, with pursuit diving in some cases, is the major way of feeding for thirty-four species, which include all the albatrosses and the pelicans, and is important in a further eighty-eight.

Again the difficulty of pigeon-holing becomes apparent, for Brown Pelicans plunge rather than pursuit-dive, and prions, which may be classed as swim-feeders from the surface, feed a lot from the wing. Again, thirty-eight gulls often use swim-feeding, just as thirty-five use

surface-dipping from the wing. At least, how-ever, the five filter-feeding auks – four murrelets, and Cassin's Auklet – are committed pursuit divers.

The great majority of seabirds feed by one or other of the three methods just described, leaving only a handful of specialists to perfect real plunge diving and piracy. The main plunge divers are the nine sulids. Twenty-eight terns, including the large terns, such as the Crested, Royal, Sandwich and Caspian, and the smaller Common, Arctic, Roseate and others, comprise by far the largest group of plunge divers. To these forty 'main living' plunge divers must be added a further fifty-five part-timers such as all the skuas and gulls, the noddies and Grey Ternlet, and all seven pelicans. Among those seabirds which dive occasionally may be numbered the two great (and perhaps other) albatrosses, several shearwaters and eight more terns (the three 'black' terns, the Bridled, Spectacled, Sooty, Fairy and Gull-billed).

Piracy is even more limited. There are no *species* which live principally by this means, although some *individuals* may do so. In addition to the frigates and skuas, piracy is reckoned to be an important feeding method in no fewer than twenty gulls and a minor one in a further fourteen, and in twenty-one terns. Thus the Laridae show a marked tendency to supplement honest fishing in this way. By carrying fish in their beaks, as so many do, they tempt their neighbours to snatch, and, being colonial, it is but a step to the adoption of piracy as a useful feeding method. Their strong family trait of courtship feeding also equips the females with the tendency to take food from other adults, and may have contributed towards the adoption of kleptoparasitism.

Scavenging is thought to be important in sixty-nine species. Again the gulls score highly (thirty-five) and emerge as extremely varied and opportunistic feeders, which is one reason for their great success. The other major scavenging group is the petrel genus *Pterodroma*,

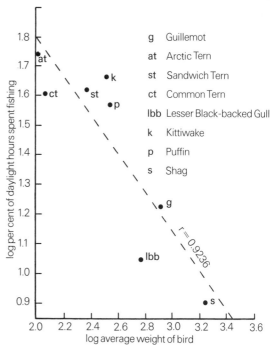

The relationship between the average weight of the bird and the percentage of the day spent in fishing activities. After T. H. Pearson 1968.

(twenty) and other scavenging tubenoses are: the Cape Pigeon, Snow Petrel, the fulmars, and eight albatrosses. In a further forty-two species, scavenging plays at least a minor part, again mainly in the tubenoses and the Laridae (particularly the large gulls).

Plumage and hunting

Having discussed the main feeding methods of seabirds, it remains to make some general points. It appears that seabirds are generally drabber than landbirds. There *are* ornate seabirds, such as the Horned Puffin, Whiskered Auklet, Inca Tern and Rockhopper Penguin, but decorative features and colours usually involve merely the head, facial skin and beak, and the feet. The body plumage is overwhelmingly black, white, brown, grey or combinations of these. Furthermore, sexual dimorphism is rare. Simmons has put together and interpreted our knowledge about seabird plumage in relation to feeding. He distinguishes three broad categories: mainly dark with restricted white areas and frontal aspect dark; dark above and white below, frontal aspect again partly or wholly dark; mainly white or light coloured, frontal

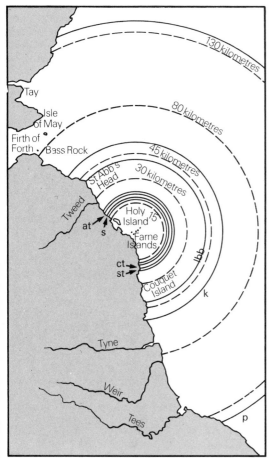

The average potential feeding ranges of seabird species breeding on the Farne Islands, off the British coast. After T. H. Pearson 1968.

aspect largely white. The primary seabird families fall into these categories as follows:

Family	Mainly dark	Dark above pale below	Mainly pale	Examples
Spheniscidae (penguins)	0	17	0	Adelie Penguin
Diomedeidae (albatrosses)	4	0	9	Sooty Albatross, Wandering Albatross
Procellariidae (petrels and shearwaters)	22	35	11	Wedge-tailed Shearwater, Manx Shearwater, Antarctic Prion
Hydrobatidae (storm-petrels)	13	7	1	Wilson's Storm-petrel Frigate Petrel Grey Storm-petrel
Pelecanoididae (diving petrels)	0	4	0	Common Diving-petrel
Sulidae[1] (gannets and boobies)	1	2	6	Brown Booby Blue-footed Booby; Gannet
Phalacrocoracidae (cormorants)	21	8	0	Common Cormorant Pied Cormorant
Fregatidae (frigatebirds)	5	2	0	Male Greater Frigatebird Female Andrew's Frigatebird
Stercorariidae (skuas)	4	3	0	Great Skua Light-morph Arctic Skua
Laridae: Larinae (gulls)	1	1	40	Lava Gull Hemprich's Gull Kittiwake
Laridae: Sterninae (terns)	7	0	38	Black Tern (Summer) Common Tern
Rynchopidae (skimmers)	0	3	0	Black Skimmer
Alcidae (auks)	9	15	2	Tufted Puffin Puffin Black Guillemot

[1] The Red-footed is polymorphic but I have taken the typical plumage to be that of the white morph.

There has been considerable discussion about the function of white plumage in seabirds, largely since Graham Phillips flew models over captive fish and demonstrated that birds with white underparts were not reacted-to as quickly as those with dark underparts. He proceeded to categorize seabirds as 'swimmers', in which the white is confined to the area below the water-line, and 'plungers', in which there is usually white on the head, breast and underwing as

well. A third plumage-type ('all white') doesn't correspond so neatly with a hunting mode. Whilst the light underparts seem clearly adaptive as camouflage against fish, the function of the dark, or for that matter white, upperparts seems less obvious. I have already commented on the function of the Gannet's dazzling upper plumage in fishing, as an attractant to other Gannets, thereby aiding both the summoner and the responder. It cannot, I think, be doubted that pure white is much more conspicuous against the sea than is brown or black. Dark upperparts, on the other hand, could aid social *inconspicuousness* whilst leaving the white underparts intact. All-black plumage is, so far, relegated to the dust-bin of 'special pleading'. It *could* be because of this or that, but there is no convincing interpretation. If social inconspicuousness is an advantage, the implication is that others would compete rather than help. There are cases, such as that of the Guanay Cormorants, where, notwithstanding dark upperparts, the birds always seem to fish in droves, but that may be just unavoidable where there are so many. Also, it might help to be less conspicuous to potential pirates, chiefly skuas and frigates. Then there is the important

a Fairy Tern: pure white plumage with a translucent quality. Feeds by aerial dipping.
b Sooty Tern: white beneath with white forehead, probably acting as camouflage, making the bird harder to see against the sky by the fish. Feeds by hovering and surface dipping.
c Common Noddy: mainly dark coloured but with white forehead. Feeds by surface dipping and occasionally by splash diving.
d Female Lesser Frigatebird: takes flying fish and squid by surface-snatching. But if its white under surface is hunting camouflage what of the male, which is all black?
e Brown Booby: mainly white ventral surface like all sulids (but see below). A plunge-diver.
f The all-brown morph of the Red-footed Booby is a plunge-diver but shows no white. Something of a puzzle.
g Guillemot: mainly white beneath. Pursues fish by underwater 'flying'. Presumably camouflaged against sky as it descends to fish.
h Shag: all dark. Pursues its prey by underwater swimming using feet, but often in turbid water and by flushing concealed prey.
i Great Shearwater: powerful plunge diver, also feeds by diving from the surface. Both modes may be helped by its white ventral surface.

Plumage and hunting in seabirds.

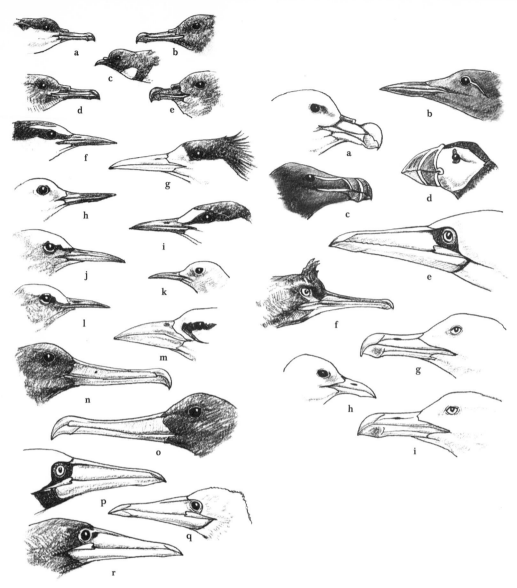

Christmas Island

a	Audubon's Shearwater	j	Common Noddy
b	Wedge-tailed Shearwater	k	Grey Noddy
c	White-throated Storm-Petrel	l	Lesser Noddy
d	Christmas Shearwater	m	Red-tailed Tropicbird
e	Phoenix Petrel	n	Lesser Frigatebird
f	Grey-backed Tern	o	Greater Frigatebird
g	Crested Tern	p	Masked Booby
h	Fairy Tern	q	Red-footed Booby
i	Sooty Tern	r	Brown Booby

Bass Rock

a	Fulmar
b	Common Guillemot
c	Razorbill
d	Puffin
e	Gannet
f	Shag
g	Herring Gull
h	Kittiwake
i	Lesser Black-backed Gull

A comparison between a tropical Pacific island (Christmas Island) and a cold temperate North Atlantic island (the Bass Rock, off the east coast of Scotland) in terms of the range of seabird bill shapes and sizes found on each of these islands. After Ashmole.

point, as in all adaptations, that plumage may be critically useful only under certain conditions or at certain times, but this may be enough to confer survival value on it.

Anatomically, seabirds show a vast range of modifications of the basic avian skeleton and musculature.

Basically, the range of size roughly parallels that of the raptors, which are the obvious, though not quite fair, land equivalents (unfair because seabirds comprise *all* seabirds but raptors only a fraction of all landbirds). The smallest seabird is the British Storm Petrel weighing about 25 grams and with a wing length of about 120 millimetres (carpal joint to tip of longest primary) and the largest representative, excluding Emperor and King Penguins on account of their flightlessness, is the Royal Albatross, weighing up to 12 kilograms and with a wing length of 680 millimetres (up to 710 millimetres) giving a total wingspan of up to 3.2 metres. The size, weight and mobility of the major groups are correlated with several aspects of their ecology and behaviour, but to attempt to describe these relationships would lead too far afield. The general concept, though, is an important one, and applies widely in the animal kingdom. Within groups, too, there is a range of size, which relates to the type and range of feeding.

Size is related to prey preference and results partly from the process of adaptive radiation by which animals diverge and come to occupy practically all available feeding niches. Straight variation in size and proportions within a family never occurs. The largest is never just a scaled-up version of the smallest. Always, the bill is proportionately either bigger, thicker, longer, differently shaped or whatever, the wing proportionately longer or broader; the tail longer or differently shaped; the legs thicker and webs bigger, and so on. Thus innumerable combinations of physical features are possible, even within a large family, whilst between families the possibilities are greater than the living avifauna ever demonstrates. There are, for example, extinct auks that went further than penguins in wing reduction, and fossil giant sulids with, among other things, much longer legs than any living member.

This process of physical differentiation presumably results from pressure to divide up the food resources. In every ocean, comparable overall feeding pressure has evolved, despite differences in the initial 'material' exerting the pressure. Thus there are the large and small penguins and the diving-petrels of the southern hemisphere and the large and small auks of the northern; the southern hemisphere petrels and the northern storm-petrels, the North Atlantic and Australasian Gannets, the plankton feeding auks of the North Pacific and the filter feeding prions of the southern oceans, the Great Skuas of the arctic and of the antarctic, and so on. In the case of the North Atlantic, (which probably was not the cradle for the evolution of any major seabird group, as the antarctic was for the penguins, the North Pacific for the auks, and the south-west Pacific and Australasian region for the Pelecaniformes) the two sides, east and west, contain remarkably equivalent spectra of seabirds. There are, of course, gaps. There are no northern hemisphere equivalents of the large albatrosses and no north Pacific sulids, but these are probably explicable in terms of physical barriers to dispersal, or nesting requirements.

The auk family is, as Bedard points out, an instructive example of adaptive radiation, insofar as it is the only northern hemisphere family which has utilized the various available feeding modes in the sub-surface waters. So its responses to these opportunities have been able to develop unmodified by competitors from other major groups.

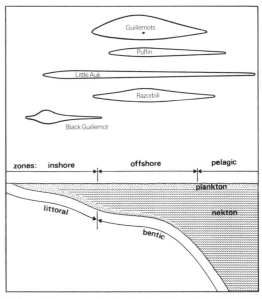

Winter biotypes and relative densities of the alcids in Newfoundland, Canada. After L. Tuck 1960.

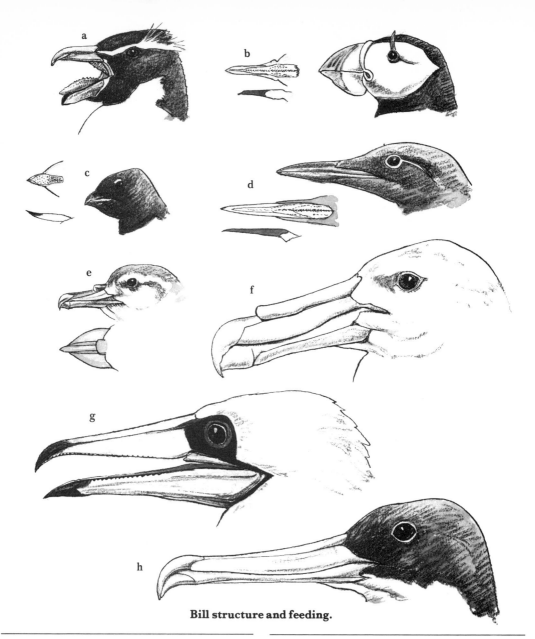

Bill structure and feeding.

a Snares Crested Penguin. The hooked upper mandible slots into a recess at the tip of the lower mandible. The tongue and palate are studded with horny papillae.

b The Horned Puffin with plan and side view of tongue. All three puffins eat both fish and plankton and have characteristics fitting them for both.

c The short wide bill of the Little Auk, its flattened palatal surface and fleshy tongue is adapted for feeding on plankton. The bird's small body size also goes with this method of feeding.

d The narrow, palatally grooved bill of the Guillemot is typical of the fish-eating auk. The tongue is less fleshy than that of the plankton-eater, and body-size can be larger.

e Broad-billed Prion with plan of bill showing the wide flanges or palatal lamellae which filter small organisms out of the seawater.

f The powerful, sharply hooked beak of the Giant Petrel can tear a young or sickly albatross to pieces.

g The long-strong and deeply serrated mandibles of Abbott's Booby are well adapted for holding struggling fish.

h The long deeply hooked bill of the frigatebird is ideal for whipping through surface water and snatching flying fish or squid.

Auklets specialize in plankton-feeding, importantly on copepods and euphasids. The Parakeet Auklet feeds largely on larger invertebrates such as arrow-worms, polychaetes, amphipods and cephalopods as well as upon fish larvae. Guillemots, Razorbills and tysties feed much upon shoaling fish. The puffins feed both on plankton and fish.

The bills of auks which feed on small soft-bodied organisms are wide at the base and have a flattened palatal surface, whereas fish-eaters have narrower, palatally-grooved bills, (comparably, the earthworm-eating kingfisher, *Clytoceyx rex*, also has a broad flattened bill). The plankton eaters have a greater amount of blade-edge, many more horny papillae on the palate, and a fleshier much thicker, tongue, than the fish eaters. Bedard suggests that the auks show a gradation from one 'feeding level' (plankton), through intermediates, to the fish-feeding level, which has been accompanied by a relative increase in body size with increase in prey size. A tiny bird could readily exploit the microplankton but would have an adverse surface to volume ratio, whilst a big plankton-eater would have an unfavourable energetic balance. So the plankton-eating auks are the small members of the family and the fish eaters are the large ones. Fish-eating auks, moreover, have acquired a stronger skeleton than plankton-eaters, and smaller wings for more efficient swimming. The largest fish-eaters (guillemots) are already close to being as heavy as they can be, compatible with flight *and* the use of wings for efficient underwater propulsion. The Great Auk, of course, exceeded this limit, and was flightless.

Where several auks have become plankton eaters, they all approximate to the ideal combination of body size and feeding adaptations, but differ in details. In the North Pacific and Bering Sea there are five plankton feeders whose ranges overlap to some extent, or did so. In the North Atlantic, the Dovekie or Little Auk alone fills the plankton niche, as does Cassin's Auklet in the eastern North Pacific, and both these species are of intermediate body size for plankton feeders. By contrast, the fish-eaters show a considerable and somewhat puzzling range of body sizes, coupled with a surprising degree of overlap between closely related species. Thus, whilst Xantu's Murrelet and the Ancient Murrelet both lack at least some of the adaptations of true plankton feeders (notably, they have no pouch to carry food back to the nest), they are nevertheless so tiny, both in body and bill, that it is doubtful if they could feed much on fish, or carry fish to the nestling. Instead, they have shortened the nestling stage to one or two days—shorter than in any other true seabird—after which the chicks go to sea with their parents. Yet, judged by the morphology of their feeding apparatus, they are true fish-eaters. At the top end of the size-scale, the two guillemots (Common and Brunnich's or Thick-billed) are but poorly differentiated and overlap greatly in range and habits. In between, the auklets of the genus *Aethia* are different in size and plumage but similar in ecology, whilst the two murrelets that replace each other around the coasts of the North Pacific (the Marbled Murrelet and Kittlitz's Murrelet) have nevertheless evolved significantly different feeding apparatuses whilst remaining similar in habits and plumage!

So the auks warn against a simplistic interpretation of feeding differences between closely related species. It is fallacious to think that the feeding habitat is neatly divided up between species so that there is little overlap in habits and associated biology. Whilst this is broadly true, as virtually any seabird taxon shows, and is true, also, between taxa, the picture is complicated, because *many* factors are involved in producing any one character, and it is virtually impossible to unravel the interactions.

This leads onto my final point in relation to feeding, which is the way in which it determines breeding strategy. The timing of breeding, brood size and the rate at which chicks grow, depend on the foraging and feeding characteristics of the adult. Two examples will serve. The Brown Booby of Ascension Island breeds about once every eight months; it lays two eggs but the brood is virtually always reduced to one as a consequence of the first-hatched killing its sibling, and often, even the remaining chick dies. It grows slowly and in extreme circumstances may be fed for a further thirty-seven weeks *after* it has become free-flying. Within the same family, the Peruvian Booby, of the famous guano islands, lays up to four eggs, all its young live amicably, and survive and grow well and, despite their numbers, *rapidly*. This is entirely due to the near proximity of the Humboldt Current, richly stocked with anchovies, upon which the birds feed with little more effort than it takes to gather them up.

Breeding behaviour

What is behaviour? An Adelie penguin is behaving when it throws itself into the 'ecstatic' posture. It is also behaving when it charges to attack a rival, walks normally, incubates its egg, 'stares' at a neighbour, preens or defaecates. But is it behaving when it draws breath, secretes from its salt gland or erects its crest feathers? Somewhat arbitrarily, one may exclude from behaviour involuntary acts such as secreting from glands or breathing. Voluntary movements, whether simple or strung together in complex sequences, are behavioural acts. This excludes crest-raising, although we have no proof that it cannot be done voluntarily and although it is an important element of display. We assume that a penguin can 'stare', that is, roll its eyes to expose the white sclerae, when it wants, but that it can't raise its crest at will, though in fact the reasoning behind this division is distinctly woolly. Basically, it leans on our knowledge that muscle contractions such as those moving limbs or eyes are under voluntary (central nervous system) control, whilst (for example) the secretion of glands, erection of feathers or movements of the gut are largely governed by the involuntary (sympathetic and parasympathetic) nervous system. But the voluntary and involuntary systems are by no means independent of each other. A rat, for example, can learn to control the rate at which its heart beats. Mostly, such esoteric uncertainties are quite irrelevant to the bird watcher, but they serve to remind us that behaviour occurs at several levels and, that on close examination, the boundaries between them become blurred.

Animals cope with life by behaving. Almost ceaselessly, a stream of messages impinge on them from the external environment, and from within, from glands, organs, and brain centres. They respond, often rapidly, precisely and predictably, using a particular and sometimes inherently improbable set of actions. A Gannet fouled by a neighbour will attempt to dispel the dirt by a special sequence of plumage-shaking acts. This behaviour does not depend on any particular internal state but merely on the external stimulus. On the other hand, a Gannet's greeting behaviour, which also has a special form, depends partly on hormones. Yet again, a Gannet returns to its colony in early spring and this, too, depends on its hormonal state although the behaviour it uses to do so has no special form; it is just 'flying'. So again, one can easily find difficulties in definition.

One of the major types of animal behaviour, notably including display, is communicatory in nature. This chapter describes display and other activities involved in breeding. Communication is more than merely the transfer of information. Communication means eliciting a response from somebody else. It is *only* the response that demonstrates that communication has been achieved. But a penguin's raised crest, or a woman's blush, can elicit a response though the emitters of these signals are not 'doing' anything. The events are just happening to them, willy-nilly. So one should think of non-verbal communication as both the behaviour and the *structural* features of 'A' that affect the behaviour of 'B' and vice-versa. Most ethologists assume that, man excepted, animals have no conscious understanding of the goal of their behaviour. Although this is certainly not true of the chimpanzee, we would be wise to accept that seabirds, complex and beautifully adaptive though their behaviour is, perform their many displays largely instinctively as a result of genetic programming, without understanding their goal. They know when they *reach* their goal, because the stimuli they then receive fit the expectations with which they have been innately provided, or which they have acquired. But it would be quite erroneous to say that they understand the goal in any way remotely akin to human understanding. This is staggering, to say the least, when one considers the number of tasks that a higher animal such as a colonial seabird must perform in its lifetime.

There are few seabirds that nest more or less solitarily, but the types of social organization that they exhibit are many and varied, and the cost/benefits of these are unlikely to be the same for any two species. No seabirds literally *ignore* their neighbours, but on the other hand, none *co-operate* in anything but the most rudimentary fashion, for example, in concerted mobbing of predators. Inbetween, hostility ranges from total to mild; display from bizarre and highly ritualized to extremely rudimentary. Perhaps typically, seabirds are highly gregarious but also territorial. Partial exceptions are burrow-nesters, perhaps principally the petrels and shearwaters, which show rather limited territoriality. Every species has its own *set* of selection pressures to contend with, and these affect the degree and nature of its sociality. The dense-nesting Royal Tern is notably unaggressive, territorially, but the dense-nesting Gannet is fiercely territorial, because, although both species nest densely, they experience vastly different selection pressures.

Territorial behaviour

Two of the most important and often difficult things a seabird does in its lifetime are to acquire a breeding place and a mate. Assuming that the male bird has returned to the locality of its birth (which most do) and is about to establish itself as a site-owner, it may first join an assembly of conspecifics, on the water around the breeding island. These 'rafts' are sometimes vast gatherings, and although largest in the pre-breeding period, they continue in nocturnal species throughout the season. Birds arrive in daylight and 'raft' whilst waiting to go ashore under cover of darkness. Rafts are, often, spectacular in shearwaters but are found in many other groups, for example gulls (particularly Kittiwakes), guillemots, puffins, Razorbills, Little Auks, petrels, penguins and albatrosses. Rafts have nothing to do with territory as such, though probably much to do with pair-formation and social stimulation, and they help seabirds to overcome their innate fear of the dangerous environment into which they must venture. They have their counterparts in, for example, the night-gatherings on land of Sooty Terns, which gather in dense groups, and perform mass flights, immediately after return to the breeding locality but before settling in the colony proper. Dreads or panics in which the mass of birds suddenly flies out from the colony are common in seabirds early in the season and are an expression of this fear. 'Clubs', common in seabirds, fall into a different category because, usually, they are composed largely of birds which will not breed that season.

The male who would carve out a territory has to be extremely fit. There is little known about this aspect, but enough circumstantial evidence to suggest that there may be a fairly inflexible threshold of condition below which no male will attempt to breed. Carrick has shown, for example, that the Royal Penguin male will not attempt to breed unless it reaches a certain weight, though it must be added that in Yellow-eyed Penguins the non-breeding ranks contain birds as old or older, and as heavy, as those of the breeders.

The first stages of site establishment are extremely variable. In general, the greater the subsequent fidelity to the site, the longer the period spent prospecting, establishing and guarding it before actually breeding. Gannets often spend a whole season faithfully attending their site without attempting to breed; Fulmars may visit an area and sporadically attend a particular site for two years or more before breeding; hole-nesting penguins and shear-waters are faithful to their sites and show lengthy pre-breeding attendance. Shags spend part or all of a season on a site, perhaps even building a nest, without laying. Sooty Terns may spend two or more years in the colony before breeding, and the same holds for the Waved Albatross. Here, however, the attendance is primarily to form a pair-bond and there is little or no attachment to a precise site. Indeed, the Waved Albatross commonly moves its egg many metres during incubation! Among species showing little pre-breeding attendance are Sandwich Terns which may lay two or three days after arriving, paired, at the locality in which they make their nest and even first-time breeders do not attend a site long before laying on it. Correspondingly, they desert breeding localities at the drop of a hat. This is an anti-predator device for they are so vulnerable that a disturbed colony might as well give up and go somewhere else, and by cutting down on time at the colony, they reduce the chances of such disturbance.

To recognize the initial stages in site establishment one needs marked individuals and a fairly continuous watch and even then what one did not see may nevertheless have happened. In species in which territorial defence is strict, new males ease themselves warily into the breeding ranks. A ground nester may take over an empty site or stake a claim on fresh ground at the perimeter. He does not abruptly, and without reconnaissance, plonk himself down in a suitable spot and stake a stubborn claim. On the contrary, he spends much time flying over and around the colony. Indeed, the young male Kittiwake or Herring Gull, and probably the Gannet, Fulmar, Manx Shearwater, Great Skua, Puffin, Shag, Royal Tern and others, may investigate *several* widely separated colonies within the space of a few days, exposing himself to their subtly different influences (size, spacing, composition, intensity of territorial and sexual behaviour). Tentatively, he prepares to settle in the colony of his choice. A new male Black-headed Gull is alert and shows more anxiety postures than an established one; a young male Fulmar may expect to be dislodged by a prior claimant, perhaps scores of times; a young Gannet flees precipitately if quickly challenged by a rightful owner. This eliminates the most damaging form of strife – that between two 'rightful' owners. Hole-nesters are in a more difficult position because visible display is impracticable. In tropicbirds the contesting of holes, which are often in limited supply, can be a cause of nesting failure and even death.

Fighting

During the first stages of site establishment fighting is, on the whole, rare. Disputes arise when a temporarily unattended site attracts a prospecting male. Rarely if ever will a prospector simply challenge an established bird, for fighting is potentially too damaging. Even when it does occur, it is in most species mere show. Herring Gulls grip beaks and push and pull, flailing their wings and jumping into the air; Kittiwakes grip beaks and twist to dislodge the opponent from the cliff ledge; ledge-nesting Black or Lesser Noddies peck and grapple, as do Fairy Terns; Sooty Terns grip beaks and shake their heads violently; Shags hardly fight at all, and attempt to disengage if gripped by an opponent; Adelie and Crested Penguins grip

Ritualized 'showing' of nest material is an exaggeration of the swing involved in picking-up and placing of a twig.

The post-hop recovery movement occurs in many cormorants as the basis of a display movement.

Symbolic nest-building has become a ritualized activity in some sulids (here the Brown Booby).

The origin of some ritualized behaviour (display).

'Saluting' by this incoming male Blue-footed Booby is a presentation of its vivid blue feet to his partner. It is an exaggerated 'braking'.

Auk 'butterfly' flight is due to altered depth and speed of wingbeat.

Waved Albatross 'sway-walk' is simply exaggerated counter-poise action.

Fighting, threat and aggressive display.

Overt fighting is seldom severe and damaging, but Atlantic Gannets are exceptional in the vigour of their fights

Fairly 'primitive' beak grappling in the Brown Pelican

At the boundary of its territory when at a point of balance between the tendency to attack and retreat from the rival a Herring Gull often re-directs its attack to the ground and pulls at the grass, treating it as it would a rival

Stylized display, as in this territorial 'bowing' of the Gannet, often supplements or replaces more direct aggression

In a flipper fight penguins beat each other resoundingly with the hard edges of their flippers

bill-to-axilla   sideways stare   alternate stare   point   gape

initial response to a model penguin

sideways stare

alternative stare

point

gape

peck

4.5   60   90   150

distance (cm)

charge

attack with chest contact

Aggressive behaviour in the Adelie Penguin. The series shows postures indicating increasing intensity of aggression

Attack gape in Waved Albatross. Birds run at each other in this posture

Pigeon Guillemots fighting on water

Cassin's Auklet using feet in ground fighting

69

with their beaks at the same time pushing with their chests, beating with their flippers and (Crested's) screaming loudly; King Penguins thump rivals with their flippers: 'the rookery resounded with the hollow thumps of flipper edges beating against resilient breast feathers' (Stonehouse); Guillemots usually peck and grip briefly although they sometimes fight fiercely, and fatalities may result. Brunnich's Guillemots fight for up to an hour and may tear a mandible off an opponent. In this species most of the intense fights appear to involve females, and sometimes non-breeding females. However, auks, in general, do not fight much in defence of territory. In them, most actual contests (as in so many groups) may be about partners rather than sites. Shearwaters lunge and snap; frigatebirds, despite their long, hooked bills, grapple and peck ineffectively; albatrosses run at each other with wide open beaks and bite vigorously at each other's head and neck but these encounters, anyway, are brief and usually concern disputed dancing partners, not sites. In none of these examples is fighting at all serious, but there are a few species in which it is. In the Atlantic Gannet territorial fights are savage, prolonged and exhausting, and sometimes seriously damaging, and of particular interest for this reason. Boobies, too, are in general aggressive birds but one, the forest-nesting Ab-

bott's Booby, is singularly inhibited from all contact behaviour since this carries the risk of falling beneath the canopy, which would be fatal. Natural selection would quickly eliminate fighters. Tropicbirds fight fiercely and sometimes fatally. Great Skuas sometimes crush the base of the opponent's beak with their powerful grip.

Probably, though there are notable exceptions, seabirds which nest on cliff-ledges and in holes or burrows, generally fight more than do open-ground nesters, for such sites are scarcer, safer and the subject of more competition. It may have been the competition for cliff-ledges and holes which forced some seabirds to adapt themselves to very curious alternatives. The lovely Golden Bosun, which is the Christmas Island race of the White-tailed Tropicbird, has taken to nesting in holes in jungle trees, sometimes kilometres from the sea, presumably to escape competition with the more powerful Red-tailed Tropicbird, and the Red-footed Booby may have adopted its tree-nesting habit

as a substitute for cliff-nesting. Most astonishing of all, the Fairy Tern's incredibly dangerous nest sites, such as bare branches, palm fronds, or frail forks of twigs, are perhaps ledge substitutes.

Species which remain largely faithful to their sites, once acquired, show greater overt aggression in their defence than do those which change a lot. Gannets, Fulmars, some albatrosses, Kittiwakes and Great Skuas, for example, stick to, and forcefully defend, their sites. On the other hand, frigatebirds, Sandwich Terns, Royal Terns, Sooty Terns and some penguins, all of which nest extremely densely, are either much less faithful, or completely unfaithful, and are less aggressive in defence. The adult Emperor Penguin is virtually non-belligerent and non-territorial because its survival whilst incubating during the antarctic winter depends on huddling together. Much depends on how difficult it is to gain a site in the first place. If a bird has to put a lot of effort into getting it, then it is better to defend it forcefully.

Usually, the male establishes the site but both sexes defend it. The striking resemblance between the sexes in most seabirds is often interpreted as an aid to shared defence, each sex thus presenting the same repelling stimuli to a potential intruder. It is also likely that, in many cases, the main value of plumage colour is in feeding, though the two functions are by no means mutually exclusive.

Display in site-defence

The function of the many striking and stylized postures and movements which birds perform when establishing and defending their sites is to signal the status and mood of the displaying bird, that is, to send a message and affect the behaviour of the individual who 'registers' the display. This effect can be perfectly well observed. Territorial displays are widespread in the animal kingdom and particularly well developed in birds. They are the expression of the bird's mood, be it aggressive in defence of territory, afraid (of attack or retaliation by a rival) or sexually aroused. Often, indeed, almost always, its 'mood' at any one time is made up of two or more conflicting tendencies. It may feel like attacking but also like fleeing, and this may result in incomplete (intention) movements towards or away, with all or part of the body. These intention movements, appropriately exaggerated to make them more conspicuous, can form one basis for display. Alternatively, the conflicting tendencies to attack and to flee can cancel each other out and leave the nervous system, and the muscles which it activates (including those which move the plumage) free to do something else. In other words, the animal can only do so much at a time and when it is momentarily unable to respond to the stimuli which urge it to attack or flee, it is free to attend and respond to, other stimuli. These may come from, say, nest material, or food, or tactile stimuli which are probably always coming in from the plumage. Over time, these 'other responses' can acquire the status of signals because they reveal something useful about the mood of the performer. By becoming stylized, exaggerated or repetitive, they turn into displays. Displacement activities, intention movements and re-directed behaviour are all important sources from which display derives. The gulls provide excellent examples of all this. Herring Gulls run the entire gamut from actual fighting, to re-directed fighting (grass-pulling—with, incidentally, 'displaced' nest-building occurring as a sideways flick at the end), to intention movements of pecking using a particular posture (the aggressive upright) which would facilitate this, to intention movements of fleeing, using a different posture facilitating withdrawal (intimidated upright), to actual fleeing. Unfortunately I have space for no more than a rapid overall survey of territorial behaviour in seabirds, but the broad comparative picture may be complemented by a closer look at diversification within one or two well-worked groups.

Gulls have a large repertoire of displays basic, more or less, to the entire family. The Herring Gull, which is typical of the large gulls, has at least four distinctive, stereotyped postures-cum-movements, shown on page 82, which it uses both in territorial and sexual encounters. The '*upright*' is common in boundary disputes and expresses the gull's readiness to peck downwards and to use the carpal joint of its wing to deal blows. The '*forward-posture*', has the carpal joints somewhat raised and rather like a bird partly in the 'long-call' position but about to start 'choking', (see below) is accompanied by the 'mew' call—an eerie moan. Perhaps its main context is in parading with the mate, both mewing, to a spot where choking can begin, but it is also used in boundary clashes. The '*forward-oblique*' is the best known of all gull postures and the loud, yodelling call, or territorial 'song' which accompanies it, one of the unforgettable sounds of a gull colony. '*Choking*' is mainly performed by mates on a potential nest-site, but single birds engaged in

hostilities may choke. In addition to all these postures and movements go three postures (forward, hunched and facing away) whose main function is to reduce the likelihood of aggression. These clearly signal that the performer is putting itself in a non-attacking position. Together with actual attack and the unmistakable, high-intensity threat indicated by grass-pulling, all these postures equip the Herring Gull with an effective vocabulary, capable of expressing fine nuances of mood. The way in which order is restored to a disturbed colony shows how it works. The disturbed birds float overhead, giving the anxious 'ha-ha-ha' and the alarmed 'kleow'. Some of them 'long-call' in flight and attack infringers of their aerial space. Then they drop down into their territories. After landing, they shuffle their wings restlessly, their flight threshold being still low. One after another they throw back their heads and 'long-call'. Violated boundaries are restored with quick skirmishing, grass-pulling and aggressive upright postures. Mates approach and stand parallel or face away. Then the females hunch and head-nod. Males mew and choke, often eliciting similar behaviour from their mates. The colony is a bedlam of alarm calls, moans, and yodelling. Then, gradually, postures relax and other activities, such as preening or returning to incubate, creep in and the colony resumes its ordered state.

---

a The female Gannet (*right*) averts her bill in a facing-away posture, when the male bites her.
b Mutual preening, as in these Gentoo Penguins, is usually a form of pair-bonding behaviour rather than plumage care.
c The hunched posture of the female and young Lesser Black-backed Gull is the opposite of the male's upright threat and is an appeasement posture.
d The slender walk of the Adelie Penguin is used by the bird when it has to pass through neighbours.
e Guillemots use three postures when passing alongside or through neighbours. (1) walking through dense groups; (2) walking alongside a dense group; (3) walking along empty ledge.
f Here, a pair of Brown Boobies interact, the left-hand bird in the 'bill-up-face-away' posture and the right-hand bird 'bill-tucking'. Both postures avert the beak.
g A pair of Abbott's Boobies 'cut-off' the sight of the other by closing the eye on the appropriate side only. This facilitates close proximity without engendering aggression.

Other gulls are both similar and yet different, and it comes as no surprise to find that those most closely related taxonomically are most alike in their behaviour. The Lesser Black-back is so near to the Herring Gull that the two will happily interbreed if they have been artificially cross-fostered. Even so, their 'long-calls' differ enough to give their respective females clearly different cues which may be at least partly responsible for maintaining reproductive isolation.

The hooded gulls look so strikingly different from the white gulls that one might expect marked differences in behaviour, but in fact the hood can be misleading. Some hooded gulls (Hemprich's is one) are simply Herring Gull types that have gained a hood, whilst others, such as the Black-headed, are truly hooded. Also, the hood is probably easily lost or gained, in evolutionary terms and is not a reliable indication of affinity. Thus the New Zealand Silver Gull lacks a hood but is nevertheless extremely closely related to the Black-headed, which it greatly resembles in display. It has probably only recently lost its hood. 'Hooded' is in any case a loose description. Some authors distinguish 'masked' gulls, which include the Black-headed, from 'primitive hooded gulls', which include the Laughing, Dusky and Franklin's Gulls.

The **skuas**, though strongly territorial, do not display nearly so much as the gulls. The Great Skua performs the ubiquitous territorial 'oblique-cum-long call', but with wings stretched up, displaying the large white patches. The upright postures are clearly marked, and the ones with forward stretch and bill straight are most likely to be associated with attack (nine combinations of bill and neck angles can be distinguished). Great Skuas lower their breast and head in a posture apparently equivalent to the Herring Gull's choking, and moreover utter a repetitive squeaking equivalent to the Herring Gull's muffled 'choking' noise. So the family repertoire remains basically intact.

Terns, which are highly specialized aerial larids, have penetrated everywhere and adapted themselves to an astonishing variety of nesting habitats, although, as with gulls and skuas, there are no hole-nesters except the Inca Tern. Breeding terns have conspicuously marked and ornamented heads: crested; capped black on white or white on black; white forehead on black cap; black nape; highly coloured ear

tufts and bright bills, are all found. These are much used in posturing but almost all of it in the context of courtship rather than territorial ground display.

Tern territorial behaviour is characterized by a greater emphasis on aerial fighting and display and less on ground fighting and ground display than in the gulls. Arctic and Common Terns show undoubtedly hostile, though non-ritualized, air-to-ground attacks and male-male, aerial pursuits (the 'upward flutter') which may continue until the birds are too high to be seen. In the Black Tern, too, most fighting is done in the air. The larger crested terns (Caspian and Royal) do not engage in prolonged aerial pursuits. On the ground, the aggressive upright postures so marked in gulls are either absent or indistinct in terns. The Sandwich Tern is hardly territorial at all, until after the egg has been laid, and even then, much less so than many other terns. This is because it protects its eggs and young differently from others, by crowding compactly into the centre of a colony of Black-headed Gulls, and lacks many of the aggressive, spacing-out mechanisms.

The terns' weaker territoriality may be connected with the much reduced size of their territories, in turn related to the fact that terns rarely kill each other's young as gulls do. Paradoxical as it may seem, and though there are notable exceptions, it is often true that, in seabirds, the densest nesters are less territorial than those species with larger territories.

Few seabird families have evolved such well-differentiated territorial behaviour as the gulls. The **albatrosses**, though remarkable for their elaborate courtship dances, are relatively ill-equipped with ritualized *territorial* behaviour. Whilst albatrosses will eject oil or stomach contents at man, they do not use this as a means of territorial defence against other albatrosses. Indeed, stomach oil does not appear in quantities until there are young to be fed. Frightened birds earlier in the breeding cycle eject greenish bile or digested food, with hardly any oil. All of them lunge and snap at intruders and perhaps it is these biting movements which have become speeded up to give the bill-clappering, universal in albatross courtship and used, also, against intruders, as for example in the Royal and Wandering Albatrosses. Established Laysan Albatrosses on-site react to potential intruders by performing a forward and downward 'bobbing' display which indicates the position of the

Arctic Skua gliding and long-calling.

Display in the Great Skua: (a) 'bend' posture (bird more aggressive than afraid); (b) bend posture with long-call; (c) oblique posture with long-call;

Wing-raising display of a pair of Pomarine Skuas against an intruder. The left-hand bird is in the first phase of the long-call.

Skua display (Great Skuas after M. Anderson).

nest-site (it is the same display that in the Waved Albatross, terminates a bout of 'dancing' between partners, after the male has led the female to the site). Sometimes a short sharp fight, which dislodges feathers and may draw blood, ensues. Laysan and Black-footed Albatrosses do not vigorously defend their territories, though they maintain a minimum distance. They often fol-

low the expulsion of intruders with a ritualized posture (the head-up and whine) though again, this is primarily a component of the dance which, like all courtship, is in part aggressively motivated. Waved Albatrosses often run at a rival, with vertically stretched neck, wide gape and loud whinny, and may bite and grapple, but this, in my experience, was usually a courtship fracas. However, an established male stationed in the area where it has previously bred and awaiting the return of its mate, will defend this territory, rushing at birds of either sex and forcing copulation upon them (a nice illustration of the close relationship between sex and aggression). The Wandering Albatross behaves similarly. A comparable link between aggression and enforced copulation is found in the White Pelican and the Australasian Gannet.

It seems that, for most albatrosses, nest-sites are generally plentiful and there are no compelling reasons, such as the need to avoid predation by achieving a central site, close to others, or to synchronize reproduction *via* social stimulation, which could cause them to compete for sites, and to evolve displays essentially for defence of territory.

In the **petrels and shearwaters** the situation is somewhat different. Giant Petrels, though powerful and pugnacious, do not fight over sites but they have a ritualized aggressive display, accompanied by a neighing call, in which they spread their wings and hold their fanned tail forwards, ruffle their neck feathers and sway their great heads in large arcs. This is directed against intruders but does not occur as a 'spontaneous' site-ownership display, so it still falls short of the most advanced territorial behaviour.

Head swaying with thickened neck, cackling and oil-spitting, is the typical territorial behaviour not only of the Fulmars but of open-ground nesting procellarids and of at least some burrow-nesting petrels and shearwaters. None of them fight in more than the most cursory fashion, though many have formidable bills. Unlike albatrosses, Fulmars eject stomach oil so forcefully and freely that the cliff behind a disputed ledge may be liberally smeared with their ammunition. Again, they have not developed a formal display signifying ownership. Instead they use the presumably more primitive procedure of simply repelling, in the manner described above, potential rivals who investigate by flying up to and past the site. Time and again the occupier launches into a frenzy of cackling and thick-necked head waving, perhaps 'spitting' and swallowing convulsively to get rid of oil brought up into the mouth. The thickened neck is doubtless associated with the effort of regurgitating. It is further in keeping with the primitive, undifferentiated nature of this behaviour, little changed from the original, that

it has not narrowed its context. Thus, in Fulmars, as in Cape Pigeons and other procellarids, it is also the main interaction between mates. Fulmar mates head-wave 'at' each other, making bill contact and nibbling movements. Oil seeps from the nostrils at this time, and the billing and nibbling may be all that is left of ancestral courtship feeding.

Most of the burrow nesting shearwaters are virtually unknown quantities when it comes to assessing territorial interactions. Little enough is known about their excited aerial manoeuvrings, but it is plain that they have to do mainly with courtship or social stimulation and not with territory. Two factors may contribute to the shearwaters' mild territoriality. First, it often seems easy for them to dig burrows – witness the vast size of so many shearwater colonies, notably the four million Great Shearwaters on Nightingale Island in the Tristan da Cunha. Second, their enforced nocturnal habits (anti-predator) largely preclude efficient territorial display, leaving only the functional grappling which is common among them.

Fighting, using the beak only and not (usually) spitting, occurs in contested burrow-chambers in the Manx Shearwater, the Slender-billed, Wedge-tailed and Little Shearwaters and no doubt others. The last named not only defends the burrow and its vicinity for up to four months before egg laying begins in the colony, but engages in apparently hostile rather than sexual, aerial chases. It may be that this apparently unusual degree of territoriality is associated with the Little Shearwater's nest-site requirements, for it is a tropical and subtropical species using crevices and holes rather than digging its own burrows. Also, it is partly diurnal. The cause of the noisy skirmishes, in the Manx Shearwater, and in many other procellarids, is the visiting of occupied burrows by unattached birds, including newcomers to the colony.

The petrels are much the same as the shearwaters in that at most, the nest-chamber may be defended by fighting (White-faced, Leach's and Madeiran Storm-petrel). Some, such as the Storm Petrel and Wilson's Storm-petrel, are described as non-territorial. As in shearwaters many birds may share a single entrance to a system of connected burrows. Many, if not most, of the petrels engaging in the mass flights over the breeding area (common to many species) are non-breeding birds visiting the colony. Ringed Leach's Storm-petrels have been recaptured flying around colonies on islands other than their own and 'visiting' Wilson's Storm-petrels were often found in company with, and apparently accepted by, one of the rightful occupants of a burrow. In breeding colonies of Pycraft's Petrel, New Zealand, about 80 per cent of the birds were believed to be unemployed, and an unknown, but large proportion of the Galapagos petrels, *Oceanodroma castro* and *O. tethys*, were similarly non-breeding visitors. So there is ample opportunity for intrusion and confusion.

The picture for the large and successful order Procellariiformes is thus quite different from that of the gulls and their relatives. Territorial behaviour is relatively inconspicuous and most display concerns pair relations or, perhaps, subserves ecological functions such as the timing of breeding.

Some pelecaniforms swing to the other extreme in territorial defence. **Gannets** not only fight with astonishing ferocity but have two displays derived from overtly aggressive movements. The threat display, though comparatively little ritualized, has changed enough, to give it a distinctive emphasis and style. The 'bow', on the other hand, looks nothing like an aggressive act, so polished and bizarre is it. Yet the bow itself is an incomplete ground-biting movement (redirected aggression akin to Herring Gull grass-pulling) and the headshake which follows is an exaggerated version of the movement by which moisture or dirt is shaken off the bill or head. The two have become coupled because ground-biting dirtied the bill. Now the display is so ritualized that the ground is not in fact bitten, but the shake remains. Gannets of both sexes bow throughout the long season and thereby signal, continuously and urgently, their ownership of the site. Unlike nocturnal burrow nesters, they are large and conspicuous birds in full view. All the other sulids have developed ritualized territorial display though less so than the Gannet. In most of them the basic movement is head-nodding, variously modified.

Pelicans are territorial. Males in particular, lunge and snap at intruders and neighbours, but hardly ever fight. 'Mood' is signalled mainly by the positioning and opening of the bill. The head movements are undoubtedly stylized, but simple. However, the Brown Pelican has a site-ownership display (bowing) which is comparable to the Gannet's, though more variable in form and used far less frequently. Again, there are doubtless good reasons why pelicans are less aggressive than Gannets. For instance, their extreme gregariousness permits the crèche system (q.v.). Strongly developed territorial behaviour always has to operate within the constraints imposed by the animal's other requirements.

Tropicbirds fight furiously in the vicinity of disputed holes but, as one might expect from a hole nester and, moreover, one so tied to the sea that it can scarcely hobble, ground displays are not used. Aerial displays are well developed, but again in the service of pair-formation and, perhaps, social stimulation, rather than territory. When contesting a hole rivals may crouch motionless for many minutes, looking at and then quickly away from each other, before abruptly grappling fiercely. Probably, the 'looking' period is not as inactive as it may seem. The birds' motivational thresholds are doubtless fluctuating furiously as slight cues are fed into the nervous system and affect the release centres in the brain. This is the period in which Herring Gulls would grass-pull and thus settle the issue by reducing each other's tendency to actually attack. But the tropicbird has no equivalent of grass-pulling and so it must wait until its internal state reaches precisely the point at which the external stimulus of the rival is enough to trigger attack. Hence the waiting periods.

The five **frigatebirds** are a curious group. They have a very long breeding cycle and manage to breed successfully only once in two years. I believe that this makes it impracticable for them to retain a permanent site. Possibly as a consequence they show little territorial behaviour. Prior to pair formation they have no fixed territory, because pair formation takes place on the male's display site and during this period he may move around. So there is no site ownership display at this time, nor even much individual space, for male frigates commonly display in actual body contact. After pair formation, when nest building begins, both sexes snap and lunge at intruders, calling and displaying, though the 'display' is basically uncoordinated wing-waving. Actual fighting is mild and short-lived. One of the most striking things in the Greater Frigates that I watched in the Galapagos was the way in which several males, successively or in concert, would attack a nest-owning male (occasionally even a female) and then fight among themselves. Possibly the nest itself is the stimulus for attack, since nest material is essential but hard to come by in most frigate colonies. These intraspecific squabbles cause great loss of eggs and chicks.

Shags and cormorants, have developed a rich repertoire of displays, though, yet again, mainly in courtship. They are all territorial. The Common Cormorant lunges and snaps at intruders and threatens with gaping bill, sometimes grappling briefly, but it has no stereotyped site-ownership display which is performed regularly and without any overt intrusion. It comes nearest to this after landing, when it assumes a distinctive head shape, points its bill forwards and down and calls loudly. The Common Shag has a somewhat more emphatic threat-gape, partly because it displays a vivid yellow gape and hisses loudly but also because it has ritualized the movement to a greater extent. It precedes the actual forward dart of the head by partly raising its wings, drawing its head far back and then snapping it forward with a violent sideways shake. However, like that of the Cormorant, this territorial behaviour is primarily or entirely a reaction to intrusion. Nor does it occur in any of the southern hemisphere shags, such as the pied cormorants of Australia, the king shags of Antarctica or the Guanay Cormorants of Peru. Indeed the latter, the densest nesting phalacrocoracid, shows less territorial behaviour than many of the others.

Neglecting phylogeny but in pursuit of behavioural convergence I propose to finish this survey of territorial behaviour in seabirds by looking at penguins and auks.

All **penguins** except the Kings and Emperors build a nest and therefore have a static territory, which in some species is retained for more than one breeding cycle. As part of its adaptive web for breeding in the most extreme parts of bird-inhabited Antarctica the Emperor, in particular, has abandoned territoriality. In general, penguins are noisy and aggressive and in most of the open-ground nesters threat behaviour is important. In the 'crested penguins' it has become mildly ritualized; the bird moves its head up and down from a forward stretched posture, whilst gaping and uttering deep growls. The pink gape is further emphasized by the exposure of the bill plate's fleshy edges. Although no penguin has developed a special display *solely* concerned with signalling site ownership, some

have evolved a highly ritualized display which (like the Herring Gull's 'long call') is performed *both* as a territorial display by lone birds *and* as a sexual display. Thus the crested penguin's vertical head swinging (raised head and foreneck swayed in an arc between raised flippers with bill gaping widely, after first bowing with loud throbbing sounds) is often seen from lone birds on-site, both well established and newcomers, but is common, also, as a pair interaction and possibly as a male advertising display. Nevertheless, its main function seems to be the demonstration of site ownership, and this is consistent with the retention of the site from year to year. Its equivalent in the Adelie Penguin may be the 'loud mutual display' which often occurs between fighting penguins, though with a particular (forward) orientation that marks it out from the 'loud mutual' used as a greeting ceremony. It is not at all unexpected to find the same or nearly the same display used in these two contexts. In the Gannet, for example, the three displays which subserve the three functions just mentioned (site ownership, sexual advertising and pair-greeting ceremony) are also closely related. All that has happened is that they have become more highly differentiated from each other in the Gannet than in the penguin. Nevertheless, the penguins have gone much further than the albatrosses, shearwaters or auks for that matter, in the evolution of complex, site-orientated display. The penguin's head-swaying, incidentally, nicely illustrates the way in which closely related species can develop their own distinctive versions of the same display, for by differences in amplitude and frequency of the head swaying, quite different effects are produced. The same thing was seen in the 'long call' of Herring and Lesser Black-back Gulls.

The Adelie Penguin's main threat display, the 'bill-to-axilla', is quite different from head-shaking but seems related. It begins with a forward movement at about 45° (the bow?) and then turns its head so that the bill points to the axilla. Indeed it often turns its head alternately from one side to the other. Again it is most frequently given by lone, on-site penguins. A similar movement is given in the ecstatic display.

Some other open-ground nesters, for instance Gentoos, perform simple bowing-with-calling, and vertical head raising with calling, at the nest. So, too, does the Little Penguin, which is partly a crevice or burrow nester. This is interesting because fully committed hole or burrow nesters of all families lack well ritualized territorial display.

The **auks** show little obvious behavioural convergence with the penguins, so far as display is concerned. Of course, no auk nests on flat open ground just as no penguin nests on true cliff ledges. In general, auk display is much simpler than penguin display. The Common Guillemot's great problem is how to operate whilst jam-packed with potentially aggressive neighbours for it is the densest-nester of all seabirds. Apart from jabbing and grappling, sometimes quite severely, it shows variants on upright and bowing postures but these are not particularly well-marked displays and are not easy to interpret. Immediately after landing, it stands bolt upright and gapes. This, however, is probably not a threat-gape but a 'fear' or 'appeasing' gape. Williams claims that it reduces aggressive and fish stealing acts by other birds. Birkhead lists six appeasement postures, three of them 'active', which he suggests mean 'please stop pecking me' and three 'passive', meaning 'please don't peck me', but his case for the former seems incomplete. Passive appeasement includes placing the bill out of reach. Low intensity aggression (and manifested aggression, perforce, can only *be* fairly low in the guillemot's situation) is expressed by 'footlooking' (a form of bowing) which occurs, also, in courtship (as 'mutual footlooking'). Bowing, or bobbing, a more vigorous movement involving more of the foreparts, is mainly a response to fear (alarm). The guillemot's close contact with many neighbours induces displays that reflect strongly conflicting, but largely inhibited, tendencies to attack and escape. The frequent upright posturing, bowing and displacement preening (mainly of the flanks) reveal this conflict. The 'footlooking', incidentally, seems appropriate as an aggressive, site-indicating display because the site is, in fact, somewhat mobile. There is no nest, and birds do tend to move their position on the ledge.

In many auks, and this applies to guillemots, Razorbills, puffins, tysties and Little Auks, one gains the strong impression that much of their display has more to do with social stimulation and courtship than with overt defence of territory and the prevalence and extended seasonal length of 'water dancing' and displaying bears this out. In the guillemot's case, dense and shifting crowds make sophisticated territorial display impracticable to say the least. This is confirmed by comparing Brunnich's Guillemot and the Common Guillemot. The two species tend to divide the cliff between them. The former inhabits small, static and relatively dangerous sites and it appears that the enhanced territorial competition which these imply is reflected in Brunnich's greater development of territorial aggression, and, interestingly, in the development of the post-landing posture into a site-ownership display.

This completes our brief survey of territorial behaviour in seabirds and leads us to courtship, which, due to its strong links with territory and aggression, has inevitably already obtruded.

Sexual behaviour

Gaining a mate is not as easy as it might appear. There are at least four ways of doing so. A male may first establish a territory and then perform a special display on it, indicating his readiness to receive a female, and the female prospects for just such a male. Typically, the most territorial seabirds, for example, Gannets and some penguins and gulls, do it this way. Or the pair may form outside the territory and then 'house hunt', as do Sandwich Terns and some albatrosses. Or the male may display for a female and *then,* but only if successful, make it his territory, as in the frigatebirds. Or a male may establish a site and then gain a female outside it, as petrels and shearwaters and tropicbirds probably do. Of course, in species with permanent pair bonds, the subsequent re-unions are easier than initial pair-formation, for there is a fixed meeting place. Thus, male shearwaters and tropicbirds return to their burrows and holes of last year and await the female there; albatrosses, fulmars, Gannets, and penguins wait for their mates on last year's nest site. Inevitably, we know more about pair-formation in those species where the male first establishes himself and then 'advertises'. How can one really follow what goes on in large gatherings on the water, or in aerial courtship, or in the mazy clouds of nocturnal petrels and shearwaters?

During the discussion of territorial behaviour it will have become apparent that many seabirds put more into courtship than into territory. After all, it is not necessarily mandatory to form a close relationship with one's territory, but all seabirds have to forge an efficient and usually complex relationship with their mate.

Puffins appose bills and 'push-bill' in a see-sawing motion

Mutual display in the Fulmar involves head-swaying and 'cackling'. Bills often appose and the nostrils seep oil.

The Masked Booby's greeting behaviour is a ritualized jabbing, hardly distinguishable from the real thing.

Shearwaters billing in their burrow. Much time is spent in this simple interaction.

Guillemots bill-touching.

Razorbill greeting posture

The Gannet's greeting ceremony is a protracted and visually arresting mutual display, in which bills are apposed and there is loud calling.

Abbott's Booby's well-developed greeting ceremony is conducted at a distance (anti-falling device).

'Head-up' display in the White Pelican is used during nest-relief. Here, both birds are performing simultaneously.

Some gull displays (based on Tinbergen).

That the overcoming of aggression between partners is one of the complexities of pair formation and maintenance is evident in the prominent role played in courtship by aggression/fear components. Many courtship behaviour patterns were originally more overtly aggressive or fearful acts and are *still* the expression of aggression/fear 'feelings', albeit now in the sexual context and therefore much modified in form and, of course, function.

Courtship and maintenance of pair-bond

The male Herring Gull's 'oblique-cum-long-call' attracts the prospecting female as effectively as it repels potential intruders. On approach, she may be attacked but she appeases the male by adopting the 'hunched' posture and by head-tossing, which is the food-begging behaviour of the chick and that by which the female solicits mating. Sharp turning away of the head (facing away) also occurs, although it is not so obvious as in the 'hooded gulls'. Once accepted, she is fed by the male and they can then mate. There is never, in any gull, any contact greeting ceremony comparable to those found in sulids, albatrosses, penguins and (in primitive form) auks. Perhaps instead, courtship feeding is important in gulls and terns and in some species, for example the Red-billed Gull, the male's abilities in this department materially affect the female's reproductive success.

The male Herring Gull then leads the female to a nest site within his territory, using the mew call and posture. When he gets there he performs a rhythmical head-bobbing from a forward-tilted position. This 'choking' becomes mutual and communicates their agreement about where to place the nest. *All* of these

---

1 Black-headed Gulls standing parallel in the forward posture (in which it long-calls), and 'head-flagging' (turning bill sharply away from each other and presenting edge of hood).
2 Herring Gull (a) long-calling (territorial);
(b) mewing in the forward posture with mate;
(c) 'choking' at nest-site. In (d) the bird is in a threat posture (aggressive upright) and in (e) the female is food-begging in the hunched submissive posture.
3 Kittiwake, with its brightly coloured gape and tongue, initiating pair-information by (a) 'choking' and displaying the tongue. The long-call (b) is delivered from the nest and in (c) one of the partners performs the rhythmic upward 'choking'.

---

displays are performed as warning signals as well as sexual ones, and once the pair has formed they 'long-call' in unison against their neighbours. It is interesting that the male continues to 'long-call' singly. If this results in the approach of another female his hostile response drives her away. Before copulation the female head-tosses from a hunched position and the male may remain mounted for several minutes, with greatly ruffled ventral feathers and extended wings, periodically shuffling and applying his cloaca whilst calling 'kwo kwo kwo'.

Pair formation in the Black-headed Gull is basically similar. 'Long-calling' attracts the female and when the two are close together, they adopt a distinctive 'forward' (horizontal) posture in which, often, they stand or move parallel to each other. They then 'headflag' sharply turning their heads away from and towards each other, which prominently displays the contrast between chocolate hood and white neck. 'Choking' then pin-points the nest site.

Courting **terns** perform a ceremonial 'fish flight', although, often, no fish is carried. Males carry fish and present them to females long before any definitive pair is formed, as well as when properly mated. Unmated male Arctic Terns attract partners to participate by first flying slowly over the colony in a highly distinctive manner (the 'low flight'). If another bird approaches, the male assumes a 'bent' posture with downward pointed beak and tilted cap. Usually, a visitor who shows more than a momentary interest in such a male, is a female. She may then join him in a 'high flight', or, rarely, may follow the male back to his territory where courtship may continue on the ground. Since these low flights are performed only by unmated males, they are probably sexual advertising displays whose function is to initiate pair-formation. The Sooty Tern has a very poorly developed low flight, which may be because it is a pelagic feeder, and also because it carries its fish internally rather than in the beak.

High flights are found in many, perhaps all, terns. For instance, the Sooty Tern high flies much as the Arctic, and the ledge nesting Black Noddy sometimes goes so high that it becomes a mere speck in the sky. As in other terns, the wing movements used in this flight are different from those of ordinary flying, but each species has its own peculiarities. In other words, just as homologous ground displays in, say, gulls, are related but different, so flying modes

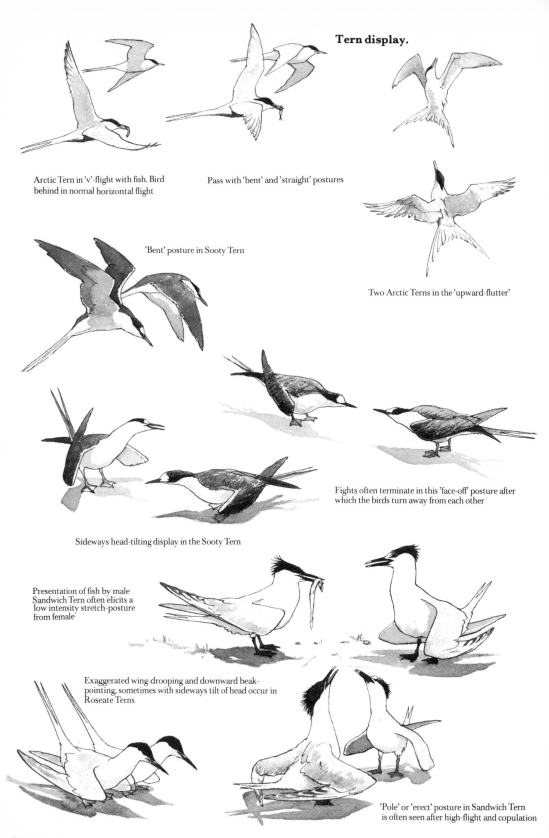

Tern display.

Arctic Tern in 'v'-flight with fish. Bird behind in normal horizontal flight

Pass with 'bent' and 'straight' postures

'Bent' posture in Sooty Tern

Two Arctic Terns in the 'upward-flutter'

Fights often terminate in this 'face-off' posture after which the birds turn away from each other

Sideways head-tilting display in the Sooty Tern

Presentation of fish by male Sandwich Tern often elicits a low intensity stretch-posture from female

Exaggerated wing-drooping and downward beak-pointing, sometimes with sideways tilt of head occur in Roseate Terns

'Pole' or 'erect' posture in Sandwich Tern is often seen after high-flight and copulation

Courtship feeding in the Little Tern. Some form of courtship feeding occurs in all the terns.

in aerial displays of terns are related but different.

The Sandwich Tern has been particularly well studied. These magnificent birds arrive in Europe back from their west African winter quarters in late March. Among the early arrivals are some pairs which have previously bred together, and it may be that Sandwich Terns commonly pair for life. Later arrivals are almost always paired, though in mid-June many unpaired immature birds arrive. An unmated Sandwich Tern 'advertises' by flying over the area with a special flight and call, usually carrying a fish. When he gains the female's attention he adopts the 'bent' posture and the pair may then ascend until they are invisible to the unaided eye. Several 'passes' may occur during the ensuing glide, in which the overtaken bird often 'v' flights. Following the glide, a peculiarly bouncy or dancing display flight may occur.

The ground display is essentially variants of an 'erect pole' or 'stretch' posture, which commonly follows the high flight and includes head tilting, in which the black cap is displayed, wing opening and drooping, and some movement on foot. The Sooty Tern has a comparable ground display, which has been called the 'parade', in which, with head and neck tilted forwards, beak downwards, horizontal or upwards, wings drooped away from body or even dragged and tail tilted upwards, the tern moves with short quick steps towards or around the prospective partner.

There are many more terns, just as there were many other gulls that we could not discuss, but even so it should now be evident that the main tern displays are homologous, as are the main gull displays. With the eye of faith and a great deal of personal experience of many species, one can even see relationships between some displays *throughout* the Laridae. Courtship feeding is probably universal, as is a version of the 'long call'.

Courtship in all **albatrosses** is extraordinarily complex and bizarre. Unfortunately, nobody has yet produced an adequate comparative account and I have had to cobble the following synthesis together from patchy material, my own personal experience being limited to the Waved Albatross of the Galapagos Archipelago.

Albatross courtship is unique among seabirds in that no others perform a comparably sustained and intricate behavioural dialogue. If a pair of Herring Gulls welded all their displays together into a continuous stream, and performed them simultaneously in predictable 'sets', going through them time and again without stopping, we would have something comparable to albatross display. But they don't! One could widen this assertion of uniqueness to include *all* birds, since in those landbirds with complex display courtship rituals, such as lecking grouse, or Ruffs, or manakins on their carefully prepared display areas, only the males display; the females watch, are suitably stimulated and allow copulation, but they do not participate equally in the display as albatross species do.

Albatross courtship, at least in some species, is basically concerned with *establishing* rather than *maintaining* a bond between the two partners and the fact that it occurs communally doesn't alter this. Albatrosses commonly do indeed 'dance' in groups of several pairs and not infrequently, but only temporarily, in threesomes or more. They tend to return to their colony with reasonable synchrony and many

Courtship feeding.

Male Little Tern offering sand-eel to female. Males that feed their females will probably enhance their breeding success. Courtship feeding is common in the Laridae

Male Swallow-tailed Gull about to regurgitate squid for female; female head-tossing in hunched posture

Many Procellariforms do not, so far as we know, show courtship feeding but some species exude oil from their nostrils during courtship-billing, and this maybe a ceremony derived from courtship feeding. Here, Little Shearwaters are billing and calling

No sulid shows courtship feeding but Brown Boobies have been seen to insert their bills into the partner's gape during the mutual jabbing display. This is the way in which the young booby takes food from its parent species gather in loose groups within the general breeding area. Naturally when display begins, there are several pairs ready to dance. Threesomes easily arise when two males are interested in the same female (or vice-versa) and the odd man out may stand nearby and, occasionally, chip in at an opportune moment and 'divert' the female's responses, but this quickly leads to aggression between the males. Again, immature birds may be attracted to displaying pairs and attempt to include themselves in the dance. The effect of several pairs dancing together, with all the movement and the astonishing range of noises which accompany display, must be highly stimulating and doubtless helps to synchronize the subsequent egg-laying. This may be adaptive.

Probably in all albatrosses most of the protracted display is between pairs which are forming or are newly formed, rather than between well-established partners. Such pairs do not breed in the season in which they form, and so there is plenty of opportunity for display, which commonly occurs away from what will become the definitive territory. Richdale emphasizes that Royal Albatrosses arrive at the breeding grounds already paired, and courtship has, indeed, been seen at sea, but this is not true of most species.

Displaying albatrosses often stand facing each other. The display consists of several highly ritualized movements, many of which are common to all albatrosses. Certain of these components are 'linked', in that bird 'A' usually performs movements 'X' and 'Y' in sequence.

Also, certain of them elicit a predictable response from the partner, such that bird 'A' performing action 'Y' will usually elicit action 'Z' from bird 'B'. There is thus a basic pattern to the display, and the cycle of events recurs over and over again.

Perhaps the most basic component in all species is the billing or *bill-circling*, a rapid half-circling of the partner's horizontal bill, back and forth over the top of the upper mandible with close contact maintained throughout. In the Laysan and Black-footed Albatross it is apparently more a gentle nibbling of each other's bill. In all, it is preceded by a distinctive 'look', well named the *gawky-look*, in which the forehead appears flattened and the ridges above the eye become prominent. Commonly, during display oil seeps from the nostrils and maybe billing derives from ancestral courtship feeding, or else the caress of another bird's bill, as of a chick's, elicits incipient 'feeding'.

In the Waved Albatross, a bout of bill-circling is often followed by *clappering* in which with head held low and roughly horizontal the lower mandible is moved up and down so rapidly that it becomes a blur. Clappering, in turn, predictably elicits *flank-touching* from the partner and the flank-touching bird always then skypoints, and 'moos' like a cow (the *sky-call*). So here we see both types of linkage mentioned earlier—that between clappering (bird 'A') and flank-touching (bird 'B') and between flank-touching (bird 'B') and skypoint-and-moo (bird 'B'). Clappering is universal among albatrosses and its noise has been compared to a

Wandering Albatrosses displaying at sea. A bird has been seen to regurgitate food and feed another. Other parts of the display have been observed. It is possible that some pairs may form at sea.

Albatross display.

a Laysan Albatrosses about to begin 'billing'. The bird on the left has the flattened forehead which produces the 'gawky' look.
b Waved Albatrosses billing. Oil seeps from the nostrils.
c Laysan Albatrosses 'skypointing' (one of a series of posture movements in the complex 'dance').
d Laysan Albatross performing the 'scapular action'. It uses only one wing. In the Waved Albatross the wing-action is lost but the associated flank-touching remains.
e Black-footed Albatrosses fan both wings during 'scapular action'.

f The Waved Albatross on the left is about to begin the ritualized 'sway walk' by which a bout of display is often terminated. Its partner is skypointing.
g The 'sway-walking' bird moves off and the skypointing bird flank-touches (the usual sequence). This flank-touching is all that remains of the 'scapular action'.
h The two great albatrosses perform this full-intensity dance, with wings spread, only during the early stages of pair formation. Adults re-uniting do not use it.

football rattle and a drumming woodpecker. It must gain its great effect from resonance within the bill or mouth. The species vary in the orientation of the bill. Clappering may be speeded-up biting or threat-gaping, in which case the flank-touching response could be displacement preening. In many albatrosses flank-touching is accompanied by the raising of either one wing (Laysan) or both (Black-footed), in the so-called *scapular action*, but it is basically the same behaviour. The sky-point is also basic to albatrosses. In the Waved Albatross at least, bill-circling is the theme melody of the display, the base line to which dancers return. Periodically, one bird snaps into a long-necked upright and with widely gaping mandibles calls rapidly 'ha-ha-ha-ha'. This may be the high-pitched 'eh-eh' (double call) of the Laysan, and braying 'haw-haw' of the Black-footed. Both partners may face each other in this gaping posture, which is probably ritualized threat and is, in fact, as one would expect, more frequent in displaying males than in females. The protracted threat-gape terminates with a loud 'clunk' as the mandibles clash together again.

Whilst most albatrosses basically stand facing each other during display, the Royal and Wandering Albatrosses actually step or dance

around each other, moreover with those great wings dramatically outspread, adding a new dimension to the display. Whether this wing spreading is an extreme form of scapular action is unclear. When all this has gone on for half an hour or more, nonstop, the partners have packed much concentrated stimulus into their respective storage systems, but they have by no means finished. The Waved Albatross male leads off in a grotesquely exaggerated *head-swaying walk*, the female following with similar gait. Upon reaching a potential nest-site, both birds crouch forwards and with neck retracted and bill pointing back between their legs, bob rhythmically up and down uttering disyllabic calls before settling down and resting. This call is probably the homologue of the 'yapping' (Laysan and Black-footed, Royal) and 'croaking' (Buller's Albatross). Often, low intensity bill-circling and mutual preening occurs from a sitting position. This *forward bobbing* has its

homologues in other albatrosses. It is the movement closely associated with settling down on the nest-site, or on egg and small chick, and when it occurs before egg laying it probably does indicate the nest-site. After the nest has been built, or the egg laid, display becomes much more desultory if it occurs at all. In fact, in established pairs re-uniting, the male returns first, awaits the female, and mating occurs soon after her return with very little preceding display. This, at least, is the case in the Waved, Laysan, Black-footed, Royal and Wandering Albatrosses. The most protracted display is in established pairs that have not yet bred. At least one albatross (the Light-mantled Sooty) has a synchronous aerial display, reminiscent of the *Pterodroma* petrels.

This extraordinarily elaborate ritual must serve an important function, and the establishment of a strong and permanent pair-bond seems the likeliest. Indeed, Harris noted that some pairs of the Waved Albatross displayed together for two whole seasons before breeding, indicating that it may sometimes take more than a season to establish a permanent bond. Moreover, there is no record, for any albatross, of a bereaved bird re-pairing and breeding in one year. Yet the Fulmar, with its comparatively

poverty-stricken display repertoire, pairs more or less permanently. On the other hand, frigates, which do not pair permanently, nevertheless co-operate adequately throughout a breeding cycle which is even longer than that of the albatrosses. There is therefore still something of a question-mark hanging over the function of such elaborate display.

The **procellarids** have nothing comparable to the albatrosses' ritual. The Fulmar has remarkably poorly developed courtship, consisting mainly of head-waving with thickened neck, cackling, billing and head nibbling, during which the nostrils secrete oil. The partly aggressive motivation of the head-waving, often followed by slight pecking movements, is shown by the obvious withdrawal movements of the partner. The Little Shearwater's courtship behaviour is largely billing (perhaps, the most basic component throughout the entire order) during which the nostrils seep oil, reciprocal head preening and duetting with swollen neck. Though rarely seen other, more nocturnal shearwaters, are probably similar. In addition, there is the presumably important flighting activity, both offshore, and onshore above the breeding colony. The latter is intense on dark and windy nights and is accompanied by much calling. Shearwaters, too, are monogamous and as a rule form life-long pair bonds. How do they do this with apparently so little in the way of behavioural 'cement'? Perhaps it is a valid general rule that strong pair bonds require correspondingly great behavioural investment. It is therefore interesting that, every year, shearwaters spend long periods together in the burrow before breeding. Indeed, like Fulmars and Gannets, they normally spend a pre-breeding season together. During this time a great deal of duetting, billing and preening, goes on. Thus, although they lack the albatrosses', gulls', terns' or boobies' highly ritualized courtship, they nevertheless invest heavily in their personal relationships. The same applies to Fulmars and to many other petrels.

In the **pelecaniforms** courtship displays are often complex. All the boobies, except Abbott's, have a conspicuous sexual advertising display which is clearly homologous throughout. Like the territorial display, it is an excellent example of the way in which, in a closely related group of birds, an ancestral display is modified by each member so that each ends up with a different version. Advertising, however, is only the beginning. Once the pair have come together the ground nesters (Masked, Brown and Blue-footed) parade in ritualized manner, nest-build (functionally or symbolically) and en-

Tasmanian Mutton-birds (Short-tailed Shearwaters) courting on the surface of their breeding ground.

gage in ritualized jabbing or sparring. Some perform aerial courtship ('pair-flighting'). Only two sulids, however, (the Gannet superspecies and Abbott's Booby) have evolved elaborate and intense meeting ceremonies and of these, Gannets, we know, pair more or less for life and Abbott's probably do so. The others are less faithful.

The best-studied pelican is the Brown. Pair formation occurs within the colony. The unmated male, gaily adorned in his highly transient nuptial colours, stations himself on a potential nest site and performs the head swaying display, in which the brilliant head and bill move through a path like a figure eight on its side, against the back cloth of the pelican's grey wings. After a careful study of its form and context, Schreiber describes its message thus: 'I am a male Brown Pelican occupying the site I have selected for my nest. I am apprehensive about this interaction (with the recipient) and am fully ready to defend my chosen site.' When a female approaches after the male has been displaying for hours or even days, it may be a long time before she moves onto the potential nest site. After she has done so, three displays, in addition to further head-swaying, follow in various combinations and intensities, and by both sexes – bowing, head-turning and upright. Bowing is a site-ownership display, as in the Gannet, and is probably a response to the inevitable intrusion of the female. Head-turning apparently indicates a strong tendency to remain together and interact. It has less aggressive

The evolution of a display.

female

Masked Booby male

female

female

Brown Booby male

Red-footed Booby male

Peruvian Booby male

female

This striking display (sky-pointing) – sexual 'advertising' and pair-bonding in function – is homologous in all these boobies, although each species has evolved its own 'style'

female

Blue-footed Booby male

Courtship flight.

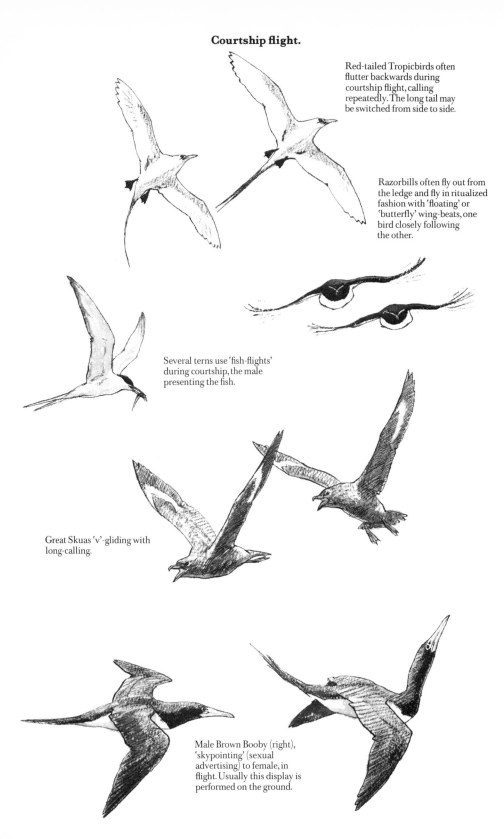

Red-tailed Tropicbirds often flutter backwards during courtship flight, calling repeatedly. The long tail may be switched from side to side.

Razorbills often fly out from the ledge and fly in ritualized fashion with 'floating' or 'butterfly' wing-beats, one bird closely following the other.

Several terns use 'fish-flights' during courtship, the male presenting the fish.

Great Skuas 'v'-gliding with long-calling.

Male Brown Booby (right), 'skypointing' (sexual advertising) to female, in flight. Usually this display is performed on the ground.

potential than head-swaying and more kinship with appeasement, being perhaps analogous to the head-flagging of the Black-headed Gull.

The 'upright' occurs early in nesting, immediately after landing and in response to the arrival of another bird, suggesting to me, ambivalent fear/aggression, with the emphasis on the latter. It occurs less and less as the pair move to full acceptance of each other. An interesting feature of these Brown Pelican displays is the considerable variation in form, intensity and duration and the tendency for them to occur in a complex mosaic. They seem less 'separate' and clear-cut than sulid displays and, indeed, may well be ancestral to them. Yet (I believe mistakenly) some systematists consider sulids to be more primitive than pelicans. It should be added that Brown Pelicans probably do not form long-lived pair bonds and, perhaps, correspondingly, lack a strong pair-maintaining, as against pair-forming, display.

Tropicbird courtship is largely aerial and highly vocal. Groups of Red-tailed Tropicbirds, often threesomes, fly above the nesting area uttering disyllabic calls 'quiv-*ip*, quiv-*ip*'. Periodically they increase the speed of their wing beat and alter its plane, mounting near-vertically and often moving backwards. Commonly, the following birds behave similarly. These group flights are frequent and prolonged in the pre-egg laying stage and probably help to synchronize laying in the small groups in which they often breed. Whilst in many areas there are no strong pressures on tropicbirds to lay at a particular time of year there probably *are* advantages in laying in a synchronized group, thus minimizing interference by conspecifics.

White-tailed Tropicbirds behave comparably, flying in small, tight groups of up to ten birds above the nesting areas and calling 'kek-kek-kek'. Pairs may leave the group and perform a descending glide, or zig-zag, one closely above the other, the upper bird with downbent wings and the lower with wings raised, perhaps for several hundred metres. The Golden Bosunbird of Christmas Island, which is a race of the White-tailed Tropicbird, zig-zags above and sometimes actually within the green jungle, its long tail feathers drooping and jerking as the bird jinks through the canopy – a lovely sight.

Upon meeting at the nest site, tropicbirds briefly touch bills, but the interaction hardly merits the label 'ceremony'. Despite this rather unimpressive display, tropicbirds form fairly permanent pair-bonds. Here, though, the fact that they nest in holes, which are often in short supply, will automatically encourage birds to return and therefore to re-mate.

Frigatebird courtship is one of the most arresting sights in the bird world. The males develop enormous, scarlet gular sacs. During display, they gather in clusters of up to thirty birds, and display in unison to overflying females. The widely-spread wings span well over 2 metres and the silvery undersurfaces are turned skywards. In addition to all this, displaying frigates call 'hoo-hoo-hoo' in a deep, slow voice or a high falsetto warble according to species. This is primarily a sexual advertising display and the displaying male, if unsuccessful, may move elsewhere. When a female joins him, the main interaction is a mutual head waving in which the participants may pass their head over each other's neck. Intermittently, the male may grasp the female's bill but there is no attempt to maintain bill contact, as there is in Gannet mutual fencing or albatross bill-circling. The frigate's display is much less co-ordinated. If a pair forms, usually within two days after the initial meeting, it then builds on the spot. Naturally, the breeding groups which stem from the displaying groups tend to be much more highly synchronized than the colony as a whole, but this does not prevent intraspecific interference with nesting activities, though the culprits are males from outside the group. The pair bond in frigates cannot be considered to be really strong. Very probably it lasts for no more than one breeding cycle, or even only part of it. Once incubation and the first five weeks or so of chick-care have passed, the mates make little contact. Indeed, even nest-relief during incubation and chick-care is often performed without ceremony. One could well conclude that although the display by which the pair is brought *together* is extremely well developed, that which subserves pair-bonding and maintenance is weak. However, frigate display has recently been studied in depth, and some interesting new information is forthcoming.

The many **cormorants and shags** are a fascinating group for those interested in comparative courtship behaviour. Basically, they do not form permanent or even long-lived pair bonds, although some pairs stay together for more than one season. One might therefore suspect that, whatever the pair-forming behaviour, there will be no elaborate pair-bonding display.

The sexually receptive male Common Cormorant advertises to the prospecting female, usually from his nest site, although in some species away from it, with an arresting display using wing-action and head movements (wing-waving, as it is called, is not a good description but will serve). The motion is more a flicking of the folded wings, so that the tips are raised and lowered with mesmeric effect and the action alternately reveals and covers a large white thigh patch. With bent neck and breast kept well down, the male bobs his head (beak upwards and forwards) up and down in opposition to wing movement (wings up, head down and vice versa). The throat and cloaca pulsate in time with the wing action.

There seems little doubt that this display is homologous with the boobies' advertising, and just as, in them, it has given rise to variants, so in the cormorants it varies. The speed of the wing flicks varies. In some the wings are kept closed, or, in the closely related darters, just one is raised. In the Shag, the head is taken much further back and darted more rapidly. In the Pied Cormorant the display (it is called 'wing-fluttering' but is in fact the same thing) is accompanied by a loud, gutteral call whilst in the Common Cormorant it is silent.

The Cormorant seems to have developed a somewhat different version of this display as a greeting ceremony. It is called 'gaping' because the bill is at one stage opened, but it looks much like wing-waving. Unlike wing-waving, but as befits a greeting ceremony, it is performed by both sexes, though the male's movements are more extreme. He droops his wings, cocks his tail and takes his head back through the vertical (when he gapes and calls loudly) until his bill tip touches his tail, when he rapidly rolls his head from side to side and utters a gargling noise before returning his head to the normal position. This display is performed until the eggs are laid but unlike the Gannet's greeting ceremony, does not continue throughout the rearing of the young.

Penguins are essentially non-communal in display, although those species which nest in dense masses ensure, as in Gannets, a high degree of social stimulation. But interaction is strictly between two individuals at a time. Even when nesting in huge rookeries, penguins tend

to return to the site and mate of the previous year. In those species in which breeding is markedly seasonal, external timers ensure considerable uniformity in physiological states and pairs therefore tend to return to the old site at about the same time. Lone males, whether first time breeders, bereaved birds or those awaiting a tardy spouse, have a sexual advertising display. In the Adelie Penguin this is the 'ecstatic' display, which is a perfect example of ritualized behaviour incorporating just about everything the penguin could do. The sky-pointing posture is dramatic, the flippers beat in steady rhythm, the white sclerae of the eyes roll, the crest is raised and the display is accompanied by repetitive sound building up to a climax. Approach by the female is typically followed by a mutual display, 'bowing', in which the birds may walk around the territory. Once again, as so often in sexual encounters, the display (bowing) is often interspersed with an aggressive display, here the 'sideways stare', which is territorial behaviour. This by no means exhausts the Adelie's repertoire of pair-bonding behaviour. Re-union of an established pair is followed by the greeting ceremony or 'loud mutual display', in which with loud calling (individuals' voices are recognized – again a common phenomenon in seabirds) the partners head-wave. They do not attempt to oppose bills or even to keep in phase and often they incorporate other movements such as bending down towards the nest.

Unlike the Adelie, the King Penguin, as a result of its sixteen month cycle and unique habit of breeding twice in every three years, comes into courting condition from October to April. Colonies are made up of penguins at all stages of breeding. Freshly moulted birds of both sexes return to the colony and 'advertise' their presence by means of a special call delivered from a rigid posture, head erect, back concave, neck extended and flippers close to body. This call attracts a bird of the opposite sex, who approaches and 'head flags', the two birds rotating their heads through as much as 120° as they face each other. Birds of the *same* sex as the advertising bird attack it if near enough to do so fairly easily. After a period of head-flagging and calling, one or other partner leads off in a ritualized walk which, like the similar one of the Waved Albatross, is a comically exaggerated version of the normal counterpoise head-swaying. Eventually, leading and following results in the pair becoming isolated from

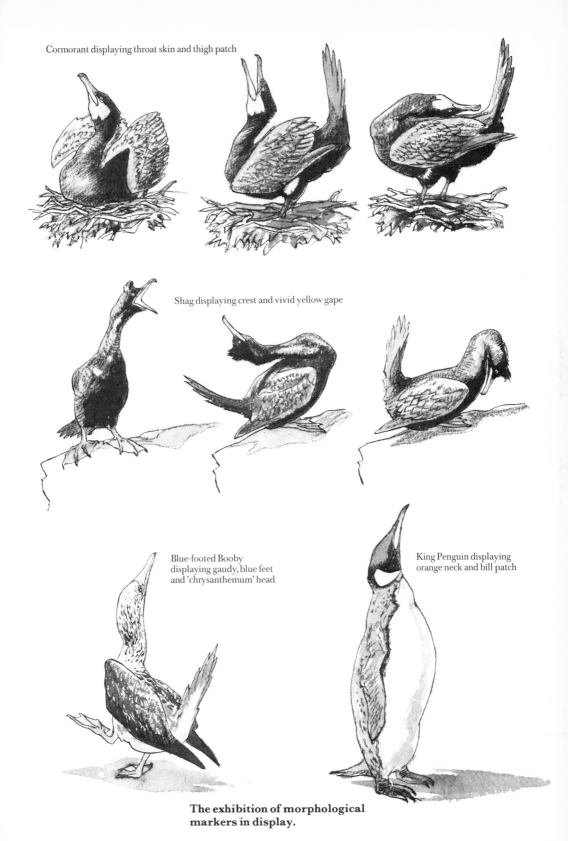

Cormorant displaying throat skin and thigh patch

Shag displaying crest and vivid yellow gape

Blue-footed Booby displaying gaudy, blue feet and 'chrysanthemum' head

King Penguin displaying orange neck and bill patch

The exhibition of morphological markers in display.

Penguin display.

A pair of King Penguins in the 'high pointing' posture

A pair of King Penguins newly come together, 'head flag' through as much as 120°

'Advertising' call of a King Penguin (either sex) newly returned to the colony

During the change-over on the chick, the Emperor Penguin goes through a ceremony. The 'on-duty' bird (a) drops its head and raises its abdominal fold, exposing the chick it then inflates its air-sacs, crows and (b) lunges in all directions

Stages in the ecstatic display of the Adelie Penguin (sexual advertising)

Adelie Penguin in 'bill-to-axilla' posture (see page 69) a threat display which may be given, also, in pair-context

The 'bow' used in pair-bonding

The 'loud mutual' display performed by members of a pair, with calling

A display similar to that of the Adelie Penguin (above) – the 'mutual vertical trumpeting' of a pair of crested penguins

'Vertical head-swinging' in a crested penguin (here the Royal), carrying the head through a wide arc.

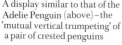

A pair of crested penguins 'bowing'.

Display in some auks.

their fellows. The whole procedure may be repeated many times with different partners before a breeding pair becomes established, and is frequently disrupted, the partners themselves often coming to blows, usually as a result of the intrusion of a third party. This method of pair formation is highly unusual. Rarely does a female 'advertise' more or less on equal terms with a male to initiate pair-bonding and the effect of the advertising call in eliciting attacks from conspecifics of like sex is also unusual, for no territory which another penguin could contest is being proclaimed. Finally, the interaction is initiated from a place which is not the potential breeding site. whereas most advertising is conducted from the advertising bird's territory.

The orange neck patches of the King Penguin are crucial for the elicitation of the following response. Stonehouse showed this by obliterating them, whereupon the advertising bird so treated succeeded in attracting a partner but not in persuading it to follow. As soon as the dye washed off and revealed the patch, it elicited following again.

After the pair has formed, and a site has been established, subsequent display becomes more pair-centred and of less 'interest' to neighbours. The main display, 'high pointing', seems analogous if not homologous to the 'ecstatic' of the Adelie, and develops from the 'advertisement' posture. Frequently, it follows a bout of head-flagging. 'High pointing' is usually begun by the male, who extends his neck and raises his beak to the vertical position, followed exactly by the partner until the pair are standing, often on tiptoe. Heads are waved gently from side to side, sometimes passing over each other's neck. After lowering their heads both birds head flag for a few seconds before relaxing once more. The other main pair display, 'dabbling', seems equivalent to 'bowing' in the Adelie, and is a nest-oriented display.

Clearly, both territorial and courtship display is extremely well developed in this primitive order of seabirds. In some species this may be due in part to the breeding advantages accruing from permanent attachments to site and mate and from the effect of display in hastening gonad maturation and thus reducing the length of the breeding cycle, particularly the pre-laying part. But presumably much more primitive and less patterned display, with excited vocalization, could hasten gametogenesis, so one must conclude that it is important for penguins to achieve the precise communication that a large repertoire of distinctive displays makes possible. Moreover, King Penguins are not notably faithful either to site or mate and yet possess highly ritualized displays, though with little territorial behaviour; most of the fighting is due to contested courtship activity. Our task is to understand why this is *not* so important in some other highly social seabirds, such as auks.

Turning now to the **auks**, one finds that courtship is better differentiated than territorial behaviour. The initial stages of pair-formation are not at all clear cut; there is a great deal of confusing social intermingling and promiscuity, especially on the water. Auks display communally, both on water and land, and (puffins, guillemots and particularly Razorbills) also use a ritualized courtship flight, with distinctive wing positions and wing beat frequency which make it conspicuously different from ordinary flight. Razorbills, guillemots, puffins and Black Guillemots frequently interact in groups on the water, acting as members of pairs rather than members of a group, although some phases of the display become apparently indiscriminate group activity. Association hardens into a pair-bond slowly, after an initial phase of more promiscuous responsiveness, as in many or perhaps all seabirds.

When displaying on the water, Black Guillemots, Razorbills, Common Guillemots and Puffins mix surface display with diving and

1 Pair of Little Auks in (a) courtship walk (male behind). The position of the male (body upright, bill down) is that used in 'bowing' by two individuals facing each other. In (b) the birds are facing each other with rapid side to side movement of the head. They call, and may touch bills.
2 Cassin's Auklets displaying: (a) billing (b) side-to-side head waggle (c) up-and-down head bobbing (d) bowing. The details of function remain to be worked out. After Asa Thoresen (1964).
3 Pigeon Guillemot (a) calling and wing-raising on the water, (b) head-dipping and (c) flipping below the surface ('skittering').
4 Black Guillemot (a) circling on the water during display and (b) wing-flapping (probably a displacement activity). Under water chasing may ensue.
5 Brunnich's Guillemot 'bowing', a display used both territorially and between mates.
6 Greeting behaviour in a pair of Razorbills (see also 'Greeting behaviour').

underwater pursuit, often en masse, which effectively foils the observer's attempts to follow individual pairs. In surface display the male swims around the female, calling (though this is often difficult to hear) and opening and displaying his brightly coloured gape (especially the Black Guillemot's vermilion and the Razorbill's vivid yellow) or beak (especially the Puffin's). He head-nods repeatedly, with variably cocked tail. The female may pivot so as to keep her face to the male, and display similarly. Both birds may displacement-drink repeatedly and wing-flap rapidly, which is another displacement comfort movement. These acts are induced by the tension of the courtship. The pattern formed by the members of the group varies with species. Characteristically, Black Guillemots form foursomes, straight lines or arrowheads, Razorbills and Guillemots swim in lines or form rough rings. Puffin groups tend to be less formal. The Guillemot's 'water dancing' is less formal than that of the Razorbill or Black Guillemot and is confined to mass diving and flopping along the surface. After a while, surface display is followed by diving and swimming underwater. Re-surfacing, Black Guillemots may chase along the surface or take to flight and then, after coming together again, 'bill and twitter', actually touching or even interlocking bills. Similarly Razorbills, Guillemots and Puffins may touch or grasp bills. Puffins, in particular, rub or push hard against each other's bill and also use a 'forward-thrust', slightly down pointing bill as a threat to rival (or initially to partner). The forward-point' as a prelude to sexual bill-rubbing is performed with distinctively quivering bill, whereas the bill point aimed at a rival is stiff. When these displays occur on land the partner receiving the display (probably in all the species mentioned but certainly in Puffin, Guillemot and Razorbill) may crouch rigidly whilst the other is more upright, with cocked tail and drooping wings (particularly Puffin). Puffins, in groups outside their burrows, head-nod in a remarkably concerted fashion. At one moment the group members are standing around without flicking and then, within a minute or two, all have begun to head-flick rhythmically. Little Auks display in groups which (at least in colonies which are not extremely dense) may gather at some distance from the nest sites of the pairs concerned. Once again, these communal displays can hardly serve to initiate pair-formation and must either help to consolidate bonds or serve some other function. Frequently, after communal display, Guillemots, Razorbills and Puffins adopt the upright posture with gape; the head and neck are stretched and the beak upwards and open. This is not thought to be aggressively motivated.

Apparently, Guillemots (and probably other auks) do not arrive, paired, on the ledges. At first, they are less crowded, and pair-formation is probably the result of initially random proximity of male to female rather than special advertising by the male and prospecting by the female, though of course, considerable movement is often possible, and does occur. The pair will then form as the result of females responding differently (than other males) to the male's behaviour but the details have not been worked out. Guillemots, Razorbills, Black Guillemots and Little Auks copulate on land but Puffins on the water, following the displays just described. Greeting ceremonies are ill-defined in the auks, but both the Guillemot and the Razorbill have protracted ones, much resembling aggressive interactions.

The sort of questions to which, perhaps by the very nature of the phenomena, one can give only partial answers, are the following. Why do some groups use intensive bill-contact displays (Gannets, and boobies, albatrosses, petrels and shearwaters) others but little (most auks, frigates, cormorants, pelicans, penguins) and others not at all (terns, gulls). Why do some groups display to subserve functions other than pair-formation and maintenance, or do they? Is it largely true that long-lived pair bonds require commensurate 'behavioural input' in one way or another? Do all species with long-lived pair-bonds have a well-developed greeting ceremony (or equivalent such as mutual preening.)? Of one thing, however, I am convinced; it is that all these bizarre, complicated and energy-costing displays are an integral and essential part of breeding equipment. One should never assume that they 'just happen', or are performed out of some *joie de vivre* or excess of energy, or 'for fun'! Probably, each tiny part of them has been forged in the furnaces of natural selection and is meaningful.

Copulation

Most seabirds mate on land, usually in their territory. Whilst the main function of copulation is hardly debatable, it certainly doesn't follow that insemination is the only thing that matters;

Copulation in the Gannet. No other member of the Sulidae nape-bites the female during mating.

pair-bonding can also be served. Gannets begin to copulate in the dark days of January, though most will not lay until April, and copulation reaches its peak some three weeks before the peak of egg laying. In some species the male grips the female (Gannet but no boobies; pelicans; cormorants) whilst in others the bill is laid alongside the female's head. Male Adelie Penguins 'dibble' with their bill among the female's neck feathers, and 'beat' her flanks with their flippers – all good tactile stimulation. The Gannet, similarly, tramps with his webs, though, boobies do not. The male King Penguin places his beak firmly in the neck feathers of the prone female and uses it as a pivot. Oddly enough, mating males elicit attack from others; even males with established partners may move several metres to attack them. Mating Gannets by contrast arouse no observable interest whatsoever among neighbours. In some, males call during mating (gulls, one sulid only; the Red-footed); in others the female calls (guillemots, shearwaters) but in many, copulation is silent. Gannets may copulate several times in succession at intervals of a few minutes and probably hold the record among seabirds for lengthy copulation. Herring Gulls do even better, remaining on the female's back between succes-sive cloacal applications, although perhaps not all of these result in ejaculation. Burrow-nesters may copulate in or at the entrance to it (petrels, shearwaters) or exclusively on the sea (puffins). White Pelicans too, may attempt to copulate on the water, as do some sea-ducks, though the males of the latter have eversible cloacas to act as a penis. In some species, for instance the Guillemot, there is much promiscuity, but in those in which pair-bonds are important, hardly any.

Care of egg and young

We come now to the more mundane but equally essential behaviours by which seabirds prepare for and incubate their eggs, and care for their young.

Nest-building

In many seabirds the nest is extremely import-ant. So far as nest-building *behaviour* goes, the main points are that fetching and delivering nest material, and, often, adding it to the 'pile' (structure is often too euphemistic a term) are themselves important pair-bonding acts. A male Gannet may bring nest material well over 1000 times in a season, and a Masked Booby may make several hundreds of excursions on foot, each time returning with nothing more than a scrap, a 'symbol', of no structural value whatsoever. But each meeting and 'handing over' is another intimate interaction. Indeed, some species (like the Blue-footed Booby) have evolved highly ritualized behaviour with which to present and place the nest material. Then, too, the nest is a functional focus for displacement activities. Nest-biting, quivering, touching, building, etc. are all acts which commonly are performed when a bird is 'stressed'. These displacement acts are by no means functionless, even though they do not have anything useful to contribute to the nest. They *do* allow the bird time for its sense-organs and nervous system to assess and adjust before issuing further commands.

Functional nest-building behaviour in seabirds is simple. Sideways quivering of the head, whilst holding a piece of nest material, results in crude insertion and interweaving. Rejection of rougher material from the cup (as in the Gannet) results in a 'lining' even if finer materials are not specially selected. Tree or bush nesting species, notably the Red-footed and Abbott's Booby, four of the five frigatebirds and some noddies (the Fairy Tern doesn't use nest material) may have problems in gathering material. Frigates steal most of theirs, either from boobies, which may be one reason why they so often choose to nest in among Red-foots, or from each other. In species that forage for nest material the male brings either most or all of it and the female builds it in. Often, once the egg has been laid and incubation begun, during the ritual of change-over the female may bring nest material. Some species, notably Swallow-tailed Gulls and Cormorants, actually swallow pebbles and the former, at least, may regurgitate them at the nest. Some albatrosses simply rake in material they can reach from the nest site, and scoop out a nest hollow. The Black-footed Albatross chick sometimes builds its own nest near the adults—a development of its instinctive 'sand-kicking' behaviour by which it prevents wind blown sand from burying it.

Guano substitutes for nest material in several seabirds, notably the Peruvian guano trio (Peruvian Booby, Guanay Cormorant and Chilean Pelican) and the African Gannet. The birds retain their excreta until they are at the nest site, rather than voiding it at sea.

Burrowing species, principally petrels but also some auks, excavate with beak and feet, kicking the earth out behind them.

Incubation

The developing embryo needs warmth, controlled humidity and egg movement (turning). It is the function of incubation behaviour to supply these. Most commonly, heat is provided, at the expense of the parent, through the bare skin of the brood patch(es), the number, size and position of which varies with species. All sulids incubate their egg(s) underfoot, transferring heat from the webs which become highly vascularized and hot. The Peruvian Booby can manage a clutch of four, and even species, such as the Gannet, which almost never lay two, can incubate two perfectly well. Cormorants, pelicans and tropicbirds also lack brood-patches and incubate eggs on their webs (or in the case of tropicbirds, which have small webs set far back among the breast feathers). Penguins hold their eggs on top of their feet and snuggle them into a fold of abdominal skin, in this way removing them from contact with the icy ground. All except King and Emperors incubate in a prone position. The brood patch/egg interface temperature in the Herring Gull, during quiet incubation, is about 39.5°C, which is much the same as web-and-egg temperatures in sulids and as interface temperature in the Yellow-eyed Penguin (38°C), Pigeon Guillemot (39.4°C) and many other birds.

Keeping the egg warm is, however, rarely a problem. Gannets on Bonaventure in the Gulf of St Lawrence, sometimes incubating on icy ledges and up to their necks in snow, take only as long as Gannets in the warm south of Wales in Britain. Overheating is often a much greater danger, where incubating birds are exposed to intense insolation. It is commonly, and I think correctly, assumed that eggs are kept cooler if the bird stands over them and shades them rather than sitting on them. The act of rising and loosening the wings may be initially the response of the heat-stressed adult, but the shade which results probably cools the egg. The habit, common to some terns, for instance the Sooty Tern, of flying off the eggs and dipping their feet or underparts into the water before returning may also be initiated by heat stress on the adult, but it results in cooling the egg. In a detailed study of incubation in the Herring Gull, Drent showed that embryos were rarely at risk through chilling when unattended, but that they quickly became at risk through overheating. Even in Holland, with a shade air temperature of only 18°C, an egg in the sun reached an internal temperature of 44°C which is lethally high, within two hours. Again, the egg of the Madeiran or Harcourt's Storm-petrel is remarkably resistant to chilling. One embryo survived twenty-three days without incubation.

The position, central or peripheral, of an egg within a clutch, affects its temperature, and eggs must be constantly shifted, to ensure even distribution of warmth. Also, in unturned eggs the embryo tends to adhere to the shell; turning keeps it 'loose'. An egg has its 'preferred position', to which, after having been shifted, it tends to return, mainly by gravity. Thus, egg shifting and foot movements have a corrective influence; eggs displaced from their preferred position are returned to it. Because of this, the hatching embryo can usually continue to work away at the original 'pipping' point without finding itself emerging into the ground instead of the air. An incubating bird frequently rises, or moves on the egg, and periodically tucks it, using the bill. The rising and subsequent settling movements are of several kinds. The incubating gull, for example, performs 'quivering' and 'tail-waggling'. The former adjusts the fit of the egg against the skin of the brood patch, but without substantially altering its position, whilst the latter involves feet shuffling and tail waggling and causes the egg to rock to and fro. The frequency with which an incubating bird performs nest-settling movements is partly controlled by feedback from the eggs; when things feel 'right', the bird sits quietly for longer. Clutches of three, it seems, satisfy the gull's sensory requirements more than do clutches of two. Birds incubating two eggs are more restless. Furthermore, in several gulls, larger clutches produce more young per egg than smaller ones. Interestingly, the Black-billed Gull, a close relative of the Black-headed, has spread into a new area (New Zealand), to whose ecology it has responded by often reducing its clutch size to two. But it still has three brood patches and 'prefers' clutches of three, and shows it by incubating them with longer quiet spells.

The pattern of incubation differs widely between species and is related to the nature of the social and feeding pattern. In many seabirds, particularly early in incubation, the egg is at risk to predators, especially if the eggs are not incubated continuously. The Herring Gull does not incubate with full effectiveness until about a week after completion of the clutch and is particularly lax during the laying period. This shows up later, when the second egg hatches only 0.8 days before the third, though it is laid two days earlier than it. However, between completion of the clutch and hatching, the Herring Gull attends the eggs for 97.5 per cent of the total time. Once the first two eggs have hatched it tends to neglect the third, some of which die from neglect, even though they have begun to pip.

The incubation of the Kittiwake has been studied by time-lapse photography. Attendance is 100 per cent after the first egg has been laid, until about 25–34 days after hatching, when it suddenly drops to 30 per cent, and then lower still. Work by Coulson has shown that loss of eggs correlates with poor co-operation between mates. Some birds are erratic in their attendance shifts, putting an unfair load on their partner, who eventually has to leave the egg unattended for a period. Such pairs are less successful, and are more likely to divorce, than are normal pairs.

The length of a species' incubation shifts varies enormously, and relates to its feeding methods. Herring Gulls on the Dutch island of Schiermonnikoog incubated for shifts of about 4 hours. Their partners foraged 3–4 hours in every tidal cycle, during which the mussel beds were exposed. The second incubation stint of the Waved Albatross was 19–22 days long. Again, its partner was away at sea, feeding and the length of its absence reflected this species' particular feeding strategy. The Laysan Albatross loses up to a quarter of its weight in one spell of incubation. By contrast, the much larger Royal and Wandering Albatrosses take stints of little more than a week, presumably because they find food more readily than the tropical species. Among smaller seabirds, the Grey-faced Petrel with a weight of approximately 670 grams, which takes incubation spells of 17 days (mean), holds the record for long stints. It loses about 20 per cent of its weight at each stint and if it fails to regain enough during its off duty spell, it either returns late or leaves early. Both cases lead to desertion of the egg.

Even within a species, the length of the incubation shift is related to the local food circumstances. Thus, Greater Frigatebirds on Tower Island in the Galapagos averaged incubation shifts of about 10 days, whereas on the Indian Ocean Christmas Island they were only about 3 days, and from other evidence it is clear that Galapagos waters are considerably more impoverished than those around Christmas Island. Similarly, Sooty Terns on Ascension averaged incubation shifts of 132 hours and fed right out of sight of land, whereas on the Dry Tortugas they averaged 24 hours and fed much within sight of the breeding area. The shortest stints on record are those of the African Skimmers of Lake Rudolph, which, around midday, when the temperature may reach 35.5°C, take stints as short as 4 minutes! Birds whose partners fail to relieve them in time can stand the heat-stress no longer, and fly off to the water. This must often lead to the embryo's death, and in fact

hatching success is very low. The longest incubation shift is that of the Emperor Penguin. The male takes the egg immediately after it has been laid and incubates it for the full period of 9 weeks. Added to the 4 or 5 weeks of courtship, this means that he has starved for 3.5 months during the coldest part of the Antarctic winter.

A few species, which build no nest, have the somewhat odd habit of moving their egg over quite long distances. The Waved Albatross may move its egg up to 40 metres. Several eggs fall into cracks and are lost as a result. King Penguins also move their eggs, but rarely more than a metre. On the other hand some species, for instance the Gannet, will not accept their egg if it is outside the nest at all. Yet others, such as the Herring Gull, may not move the egg, but may build a new nest around it.

Mates can recognize each other, certainly by voice and probably by sight. The process by which partners relieve each other from incubation duty (change-over) varies greatly in nature. In some species, an elaborate ceremony follows re-union at the nest. Abbott's Booby displays spectacularly for several minutes,

A colony of Sandwich Terns at de Beer, Holland. If disturbed they will readily desert a locality and move elsewhere.

whereas frigatebirds appear hardly to notice each other; the outgoing partner simply slips off the nest. In general, change-over displays, although using exactly the same behaviour patterns that occur during pair-formation and maintenance, never reach the same level of intensity.

Change-over in King Penguins involves calling, by which birds locate their partners, but in the process of doing so they may pass their mate and attack it, or be attacked by it, if it is not calling at that precise moment. Eventually, the two calling birds come together and then greet each other; a new arrival, calling as it waddles to the nesting group, electrifies its mate into vocal response. I know of only one clear case in which a highly ritualized signal has evolved with the specific function of co-ordinating the process of nest-relief. This is sky-pointing in the Atlantic Gannet, in which the partners communicate their rising flight motivation by an exaggerated version of the neck lengthening, which precedes flight. If both partners sky-point simultaneously, neither actually departs until it has become clear who is most highly motivated to leave. This discrimination is made on the basis of the intensity of the sky-pointing; gradually one bird increases its display whilst that of its partner wanes. So the egg or small chick is not put at risk, as it would be if it were even momentarily unattended.

Care of young
Once the chick has punctured the air-space, it begins to call and parents undoubtedly hear this. No seabird actively assists its chick to emerge from the shell; indeed, the parents do not even desist from moving the egg when it is pipping but the egg tends to regain its preferred position. Birds breeding for the first time are not always adequate in their responses to the hatching egg or the newly emerged chick. Thus, a proportion of inexperienced Gannets fail to transfer the hatching egg to the top surfaces of the webs. Consequently, they exert too much pressure on it and it caves in, squashing the chick. Comparably, new parents, for example, Shags and Kittiwakes, but doubtless many more, sometimes fail to feed and brood their chicks adequately. This is not because they are inadequate food *gatherers*; rather it is that the relevant behaviour patterns have not all matured. Different behaviour patterns appear in an animal's repertoire at specific periods in its

development and, as in all natural phenomena, individuals vary somewhat around the mean. So it happens that, in some cases, the bird breeds slightly before it has acquired the full machinery. On the next attempt it will be successful, though not because it has learnt how to do it successfully.

The adults respond to the chick's calls within the shell by taking shorter absences, so that the bird on duty when the chick hatches is better able to feed it. The critical period for the chick is the first week or so, after which it is better able to withstand starvation.

Mostly, the empty egg shells are left lying around, but some species, notably some gulls and terns, take them right away. Well-known work by Tinbergen and his co-workers has shown that, in the Black-headed Gull, the empty shell attracts predators (crows and Herring Gulls), so as soon as the chick is dry, and therefore difficult for a predator to swallow, the adult flies off with the shell. Common, Arctic and Little Terns, which when breeding rely mainly on spacing-out and camouflage to avoid detection, remove egg shells, and avoid defaecating near the nest, and attack and distract potential predators. Sandwich Terns, which protect themselves in other ways, for example, by mass desertion of unfavourable localities, don't bother to avoid defaecation at the nest, and they leave egg shells lying around.

The young seabird, like any other, is born with the tendency to seek food from its parents in the appropriate way. The adult American White Pelican has a cherry red nail at the tip of the bright yellow beak. Small, helpless young are presented with the bill tip upside down and peck at the spot. Tinbergen's classical work on the Herring Gull showed that incubator-hatched chicks pecked more often and vigorously at an extremely crude model of a beak, provided it had certain of the key characters of a real bill exaggerated, than at a genuine Herring Gull beak. The most stimulating properties of the adult's beak include the red spot on the yellow lower mandible. Thus, a red and yellow striped knitting needle, which exaggerates this property, is more effective than a real beak in stimulating the chick to beg. But, as in all behaviour, there is constant interaction between innate and learned contributions. The co-ordination and aim of the gull chick improves with age, and rotation of the head, which allows the chick to grasp the adult's vertical bill, and

Methods of feeding young.

The parent albatross squirts a mixture of oil and stomach contents forcibly into the trough of its lower mandible. The chick takes it mainly as it emerges from the adult's throat

The Herring Gull chick pecks at the red spot on the adult's lower mandible and takes the food either as it emerges or after it has been regurgitated onto the ground

The parent tern presents small fishes direct to the chick

All sulids feed their young direct from the adult's throat

Here a chick Cassin's Auklet 'sips' from the adult's bill (these are plankton feeders)

Tropicbirds place their beak into the chick's gape, instead of (as in the sulids) the other way around

is not seen in the newly hatched, appears. At first, the chick will peck at a red spot wherever it is placed on the beak or head, so long as the spot moves through equal arcs, at equal speeds and is at chick's eye level. Later, the chick narrows its preference, and not only chooses a real bill, but responds only to its parents.

Forty-four species of gull in the world have red or black bills, if these are narrow, or red on the narrow portion if the bill is deep. The chicks apparently have an associated preference for a certain range of bill-depth. However in the Kittiwake, which feeds its young directly from the throat rather than the bill, the gape is brightly coloured but the bill is a uniform-yellow, without a contrasting spot. The colour preferences of gulls and terns are mediated partly by a peripheral colour-filtering system consisting of appropriately coloured oil droplets in the cells of the retina.

The ways in which seabirds carry and transfer food to their young is a fascinating subject. Many terns carry one fish at a time in their bills; puffins carry several; plankton feeding

auks carry their concentrated soup in sub-lingual pouches; pelicans carry fish in their huge pouches; boobies in their throats and stomach; albatrosses are veritable oil-tankers. Gulls regurgitate food onto the ground; boobies allow their young to take it directly from their throats; albatrosses squirt a steady stream of oil into the trough of the chick's lower mandible held crosswise in the parent's beak. The various transport methods are closely tied to the adult's foraging techniques. An albatross can remain at sea gathering food for days at a time and the chick will later reap the benefit, whereas a tern has to trip briskly back and forth and so can fish only near the colony. The Sooty Tern, however, is a far-forager and transports its catch in the throat and stomach and feeds its chick by regurgitation. The transfer methods then depend partly on the transport methods, with the additional requirements of economy and nest sanitation. For a sulid to vomit its messy boluses onto the nest would be both wasteful and insanitary. A Herring Gull can do so, partly because it has a large territory and also because the chicks can pick up virtually every scrap.

Adults feed their young because they are wired, as it were, to *need* to feed them. Despite the absence of a pleasurable sensation comparable to that of the female mammal suckling her young, the act of feeding is a reward. A King Penguin, confined, regurgitated quantities of undigested food after three days—not because it was injured or afraid, but because its neural mechanism had inhibited digestion and 'told' it to feed the material to its young (which wasn't there). Anybody who has watched sea-

Australian Pelicans with a crèche of chicks. It appears that the parent birds recognize their offspring by sight.

birds for long must have seen parents return and, almost immediately, upon the first glimpse or sound of its chick, show signs of regurgitating. Of course this is not always so; as parental ties loosen, or if food is scarce, intense stimulation may be necessary and it is here that the chick's begging behaviour becomes crucial to its survival.

Seabirds vary, also, in the rapidity with which they begin to discriminate against strange young. Whilst it appears that no true seabird fails to do so, in effect the practice varies according to need. Thus the Gannet will happily accept foster chicks, even if they differ greatly from its own, *provided* the stranger(s) is substituted, as it were, artificially. A chick attempting to *move* onto a neighbour's nest will be savagely attacked. But if, under cover of some disturbance, it sneaks on, or is placed there, it may well be accepted. This makes functional sense, for it is usually impossible for a chick to swap nests—either the danger of falling, or the barrier of adult beaks, ferociously wielded, inhibit any such attempt. So there is no need to discriminate. In widely spaced, ground nesting boobies, on the other hand, there would be a real chance of strange chicks, especially hungry ones (and tropical boobies are usually hungry) doubling the burden on some adults. So discrimination is practised.

In most cases, perhaps in all, the adult's discrimination is based partly or wholly on the chick's calls. King Penguins will brood and feed *any* chick for the first week, after which they show recognition of their own chick's call. Waved Albatrosses call as they approach the haphazard cluster of chicks, many of whom may be nesting beneath scrub, and their own chick responds by calling and goes to meet its parent. The Sooty Tern nests in such huge, featureless colonies that location of its own chick must sometimes be extraordinarily difficult. At first, parents do not discriminate against strange chicks. In the first four or five days chicks often return to the wrong scrape and are readily accepted and reared by foster parents. After that age, strange young are attacked and may be killed. Again, discrimination appears to be based largely on calls. Until they can recognize their parents (some 42 days), young American White Pelicans are hauled out of the 'pod' or crèche in which they crowd together. It seems that parents recognize their offspring by their appearance, since they have been seen to waddle up to a group of chicks, peer about for a few minutes and then reach right over other chicks to seize a torpid youngster and drag it out of the pod, savage it and feed it! This and other observations contradict the claim that pelicans feed soliciting young indiscriminately, an assertion which ought anyway to be viewed sceptically, since so far as we know, no other species does so. Even among the massed ranks of unattended young penguins, parents locate and feed their young and no other. It appears that young pelicans are unique in requiring to be forcibly induced to feed. Parents persuade them by seizing them by the head or neck, shaking them and sometimes flinging them around roughly. Later, when the young are themselves huge, a measure of retribution occurs when they pursue the parent vigorously, peck at its beak and drag its head roughly down until they can get their bill into the trough.

Unless they are in burrows, small chicks are highly vulnerable to predators, cold and heat. But few seabirds can afford to stand guard over their young for long. A balance must be struck between the advantages of protection and the cost in lost foraging time. Where food is super-abundant, as for the Atlantic Gannet, adults can afford to guard the chick continuously from hatching to fledging. At the other extreme some specialized, plankton-feeding murrelets couldn't cope with the demands of bringing food back at all, and they take their chick to sea two or three days after hatching. But both cases are exceptional. Most seabirds guard their young until the latter can just manage to cope with heat and cold. This, for boobies, is in four to five weeks; for many fluffy young, much earlier. Herring Gulls can thermo-regulate to some extent within a few hours of hatching. Of course, the nature of the nesting habitat also plays a part. Shade, or shelter from rain, can be crucial. Predation cannot be dealt with in quite such a clean-cut way, for whereas there is a more or less definite point, beyond which temperature control is possible, predation is much less determinable.

Young seabirds have several ways of keeping cool. They pant, gular-flutter, and increase the area of bare skin available for radiating heat, by exposing their cloaca, sticking a web out to one side, exposing their eyelid, and hanging their wings away from their body. The African Gannet and probably other sulids, deliberately excrete onto their webs and lose heat by evaporative cooling. And they adopt resting postures which use up the least energy. Young Red-footed Boobies spike their bills into the bottom of the nest and form a resting tripod with elevated cloaca; young Gannets lie prone, wings asprawl; they appear to be dead. As with the egg, keeping warm is less of a problem, except in the extreme case of some penguins. Young Emperor Penguins huddle together in crèches and thus conserve perhaps 80 per cent of the heat that would otherwise be lost. It is essential to keep dry. One patch of wet down can drain a large amount of body heat and it is no wonder that the heaviest weather-induced mortality among young Gannets is precisely when they are still fluffy, but too large to be effectively brooded. Rain can wreak havoc among young terns, gulls and skuas.

Behaviour of young
Unless it is the only chick, the young seabird competes with its sibling(s) for food. Only in the Masked and Brown Booby, however, does the older one, though itself still wobbly, actually kill or drive away its brother despite there being ample food for both. The first-born thereby ensures that it will not be subject to potentially damaging competition at a later stage. Throughout the period before it leaves the colony, the young of these sulids and some others, act aggressively towards intruding chicks. By contrast, the chicks of ground-nesting

pelicans gather into crèches or pods. In the Great White Pelican, these form when the young are 20–25 days old and increase in size from five to one hundred or more. It seems that the behaviour may be concerned with temperature regulation, by mitigating extremes either of cold (at night) or heat (at midday when the pods are largest).

Fledging is one of the greatest hurdles in the life of most seabirds. One could categorize them as fliers, jumpers or walkers, and prevaricators. The fliers are those for whom there can usually

A crèche of young Emperor Penguins, they huddle together to reduce loss of heat in the extreme cold of the antarctic winter.

be no second chance; they must do it properly. Jumpers are those species which, though they cannot fly, nevertheless make their way to the sea by hurling themselves from the cliffs, or walking over flatter ground. Obviously, they face special dangers too. The prevaricators seem to have the best of it as they can take their time in learning to fly.

Gannet juveniles fly straight from their towering cliffs, out to sea. The lucky ones simply jump into space and their flight reflexes take over. Others have to blunder to the cliff edge, attacked on all sides by irate adults. The actual leap is preceded by a period, of several hours, during which the juvenile's internal state is visibly changing as it works up to the flight threshold. One has to remember that, for 13 weeks, the chick's over-riding aim has been to remain securely on its often-precarious perch. It has squatted, face in to the cliff, crouching, gripping, and combating every emergency, such as blundering adults and gusty winds. The major threat to it has been that of falling. Such machinery is not readily reversed.

'Sibling-murder' in the Masked Booby. Chicks hatch several days apart and the older one evicts the younger. Here, their co-existence has been artificially prolonged. Usually eviction occurs within a few days of hatching.

Some fledging procedures in seabirds.

It takes some effort even to imagine the complexity of the neuro-physiological changes that are taking place in the young Gannet as it approaches that climactic moment. What the observer sees, is that the juvenile's pattern of behaviour gradually changes. Its attention becomes wholly centred on the sea, far below. It ignores stimuli which at other times would have engaged its interest. Its neck lengthens and it shows slight intention movements of flight. It swallows repeatedly, probably inflating its air-sacs in preparation for the impact that is to follow. It may go through this repeatedly, between times relaxing, turning back to safety, and responding again to the familiar happenings around it. But, like a puppet on a string, it is jerked back, and proceeds with complete inevitability, towards the threshold which it must cross. Finally with an almost audible click, the switch is thrown, and the Gannet jumps. Within seconds it is actually flying, not merely gliding, and if conditions are good, it may continue for several kilometres. Then it crash-lands in the sea and continues, in this case towards African waters, by swimming. For some time, it is too heavy with fat to rise from the surface.

This introduces the matter of pre-fledging starvation. Despite many assertions to the contrary, young Gannets are not in the least degree starved as an encouragement to fledge. If there is any diminution in their food intake, it is purely because, at the last, they become slightly less interested in food, having laid down a vast fat deposit. But some are fed an hour before leaving. Indeed, aborted-fledgers that somehow manage to stop-off on a neighbour's nest may even solicit, and receive a feed, before trying again. On the other hand, the young of many tubenoses really *are* deserted.

Some Fulmars in Greenland nest up to 30 kilometres inland. Imagine, too, the Manx Shearwaters of the Isle of Rhum in Scotland, high above the Atlantic on the mountain of Hallival, waiting in the dark outside their burrows for the psychological moment. But at least they have almost 1000 metres of height to sit on and better wings than a tiny auk. In fact, such mountainous sites, like the Gough Island colony of the Great Shearwater, may be easier than low, flat islands such as Skokholm off Wales, where many young Manx Shearwaters fail to get down to the sea at their first attempt and must hide up till the following night, or fall to predatory gulls. Golden Bosunbird (White-tailed Tropicbird) chicks scramble out of their tree-holes beneath the green canopy of the Indian Ocean Christmas Island rain forest and somehow weave their way, on untried wings, clear of the lethal entanglement and away to the sea, which may be 3 kilometres distant. Perhaps even more astonishing, the young Kittlitz's Murrelet hatches far inland above the timber line, amidst snow and bare lava on the Alaska peninsula and the Marbled Murrelet in a tree-hole, often far inland.

The jumpers are those species in which the young are incapable of proper flight but nevertheless hurl themselves from considerable, or even colossal, heights and rely on their rudimentary wings to maintain a semblance of direction and trajectory. Often enough they strike projections, or tumble onto boulders, but are capable of surviving hard knocks. Guillemot and Razorbill chicks fledge when about a third grown. They leave the ledges at dusk so as to evade the attentions of predatory gulls, but even so, up to a quarter fall victim. Those most at risk are the ones who strike obstacles or for whom there are no adults waiting on the sea below. The successful ones swim rapidly away with one or two adults (usually, it is thought, *not* their parents) and remain with them for some weeks. Guillemots have been seen feeding young at sea at least two months after the latter fledged. Fledging time is a period of great excitement and in the summer twilights, the July cliffs are alive with the gargling calls of the adults and the urgent chirruping of the chicks. In the confusion, it is not surprising that parents

---

a The fully grown fledgling Atlantic Gannet jumps from the cliff-top. Its parents remain behind and the youngster migrates south on its own. Here, neighbouring adults resent the intrusions as the youngster flounders to the edge.
b The growing Herring Gull chick exercises and practises flight before it leaves its parent's territory. After fledging, it is still fed by them.
c The young Guillemot, only partly grown, jumps from its ledge at dusk and joins waiting adults on the sea below. It may go to sea accompanied by any adult, not necessarily its parent, and is probably fed at sea.
d The young Manx Shearwater is deserted by its parents and starves for a period before going down to the sea at night and commencing its fast and long journey to the South Atlantic or beyond. The fledged young are not fed by adults.

cannot maintain contact with their own young.

Adelie Penguin chicks go to sea unaccompanied by adults. They dive in, one or a few at a time, and apparently lack the anti-predator behaviour of the adults. For instance, they will enter the water even as those who preceded them are being attacked by predators, and will stop to bathe near the shore, where Leopard Seals often hunt.

The obvious advantages of taking part grown young to sea and feeding them there, are that it is safer, and much more economical in effort for adults whose flight is costly in energy and who prefer to feed well offshore by pursuit swimming. It opens up a wider food supply for the young. Nevertheless, it has remained an uncommon strategy, mainly because the above circumstances do not apply to many seabirds. Obviously, species which forage on the wing could not re-locate their drifting chicks. For some of the plankton-feeding auks it is the ideal solution, and as mentioned previously, they hold the record for early fledging.

Most seabirds can practise flying before they finally leave the breeding area. Young boobies exercise vigorously, ride the wind, fly from minor eminences and, if necessary, walk back. Young Herring Gulls jump around crazily, flapping and hopping, and are competent fliers long before they drift away from the colony. Kittiwakes are not in a position to do this, and on their first flight they must be able to regain the nest if they are to survive. Young terns acquire flight gradually and then accompany their parents on journeys of many thousands of kilometres after which they are still together. Some young albatrosses, for instance the Laysan, make their way, flapping or walking, to the beach, where they may take flight from a ridge. They then go to sea alone. Others, such as the Wandering and Royal Albatross, take flight from the windswept slopes upon which they were reared. Young frigates are so light that, once fully feathered, it would simply be a matter of spreading their wings and floating away, but in fact their pre-fledging exercises often lift them from their perches in short practise flights.

The method by which the young seabird acquires its independence is partly a function of the species' feeding ecology. There are four clearly defined strategies: (1) the young bird leaves the breeding area before it is fully grown, is accompanied by its parent, and doesn't return until independent and well on the way to

Guillemot with a chick aged about three weeks. It will fledge in a week or so and be fed out at sea by adult birds.

maturity; (2) it remains in the territory until it is fully grown and capable of flying and then leaves the area accompanied by its parent(s); (3) it remains until fully grown, leaves the breeding area, but for a variable period it returns for handouts, meanwhile becoming proficient at hunting; (4) it remains on the nest or its immediate surroundings until fully grown and then leaves the area, unaccompanied by its parent, not to return until fully independent. All these methods have their own balance sheets. The first entails hazardous fledging and is tied to non-aerial foraging, for a period after fledging, which rules it out for most species. The second is practised by many terns, for example Sandwich and Royal, but to some extent by several gulls. It is essentially an extension of post-fledging feeding (the third method) emancipated from the breeding colony. Young Royal Terns accompany their parent(s) on a migration of more than 3000 kilometres, from North America to Peru and Sandwich Terns fly as family parties from British breeding areas to South Africa. In both species, adults have been seen to feed their young in these winter quarters up to seven months after the young hatched.

Many other terns, for example, the Sooty and the Bridled Terns, feed their young on the wing or on the ground, away from the colony. The third method, post-fledging feeding, is not as common as one might expect. It is practised in all sulids except the Gannets (whose fledging technique makes it impossible); it is found in cormorants and shags and it is most extensive in frigatebirds, where it may last for more than a year. The last, and it would seem the harshest, method, is the commonest. It applies to all the many tubenoses, Gannets, puffins, tropicbirds and penguins. Except for Gannets and tropicbirds, this long list comprises birds that either can readily move into zones of rich feeding (penguins, albatrosses, petrels, shearwaters), even if this means a long, rapid migration first, as in shearwaters, and/or that feed extensively on plankton.

The young seabird's acquisition of feeding skills is a subject about which little is known. Plankton-feeders, extreme examples being murrelets such as Craveri's, which go to sea at the age of 2–4 days, are the seabird equivalent of nidifugous land birds, such as grouse, chicks, or ducklings, which pick at edible particles and quickly become proficient self-feeders. Newly fledged penguins are doubtless easily able to catch their large crustacean prey, which is often abundant, without much difficulty. Pursuit divers, such as guillemots, take somewhat longer; hand-reared guillemots caught fish without parental aid at 25 days, though in the wild they are normally accompanied by their parents far beyond this age. The frigates' acquisition of the technique of surface-snatching seems to pose considerable difficulties; even after six months' subsidized practice, many young Greater Frigatebirds in the Galapagos lost weight and died once their parents stopped feeding them. There is probably little that seabirds can do to teach their young how to capture their prey; it is largely a matter of gradual maturation of the relevant physical and neural skills. However, some adult terns perhaps show rudimentary 'teaching'. Young Little, Common and Roseate Terns have been seen closely accompanying an adult and following all its manoeuvres though always terminating their dives just above the water and never catching a fish. Adult Royal Terns, in winter quarters, give fish to young birds in flight or on the water, after first uttering a series of loud calls (doubtless this is the origin of the terns' courtship fish-flights).

Sometimes adults drop the fish onto the water and the youg bird picks it up. Comparable behaviour has been seen in Elegant and Sandwich Terns. In all cases it is likely that parents feed only their own young, though the effect of the experience on the juvenile would be the same either way. Post-fledging feeding of young, far from the breeding place, is common, also, in Herring Gulls. Apparently playful behaviour, as in so many young animals, plays a part in perfecting the movements used in hunting (young terns pick debris from the surface, Gannets juggle with sticks as though they were fish).

Body care

The juvenile is now on its way. When it returns it will be one of the pre-breeders with which this chapter began. However, it remains to mention one more important category of behaviour, that of body care – preening, oiling, bathing, sunning, scratching, plumage-shaking, stretching, sleeping and various temperature regulating activities. The seabird inhabits a particularly demanding environment, alternating between cold water and cold or hot air. The various comfort movements listed above serve to keep its plumage in good condition to cope with temperature regulation and efficient flight.

Preening takes much time in seabirds, probably on average at least two or three hours a day when at the nest site and considerably more during times of moult. Characteristically, preening shares relaxed time with sleeping and when more urgent demands arise, is easily suppressed. It is not haphazard but tends to follow a characteristic pattern, with more attention devoted to some parts. Although frequently associated with soiled, damp or disarranged plumage it occurs without such obvious external stimuli. Mutual preening is widespread among seabirds (penguins, tubenoses, pelicans and their allies, gulls, auks, etc.) and rarely, indeed I would say never, is it concerned with plumage care. Basically, it is pair-bonding activity with a marked aggressive component. This becomes very evident in 'borderline' situations, where it often grades into pecking, hence the term 'peck-preening'. Feather maintenance activities are an important source of display movements (head shaking, wing-touching, etc.).

The oil (or preen) gland lies above the root of the tail and usually consists of two symmetrical halves. Its orifice(s) often lie on a cone

Comfort and body-maintenance behaviour.

White Pelican regulating its temperature by fluttering gular skin, creating flow of moist air. Evaporation causes cooling. Ambient temperature 44°C

Grey Gull shading its chick in the Peruvian desert. Without shade the chick would quickly die

Gannet rolling oil from the preen-gland, onto its back plumage

Red-footed booby chick conserving energy and losing heat by hanging its head, drooping its wings and exposing cloacal skin for evaporative cooling

'Sunning' posture in juvenile frigatebird. The function of this is not properly known

Black-footed Albatross chick kicking sand backwards. This reflex action prevents the chick from being buried by blown sand or nipple which may be bare or downy and is usually concealed by feathers which are raised to expose it during use. It is probably best developed in the Procellariiformes and Pelecaniformes. The oil gland has the distinction of being the only cutaneous gland in birds whereas mammal skin is, of course, thick with them. It produces an oily secretion, sometimes smelly, which the bird transfers to its plumage either by taking some up in its bill or by rolling the sides and back of the head on it and then rolling it onto its plumage. Oiling, or annointing, typically occurs during a prolonged bout of preening, following bathing or the return from fishing, when the plumage is likely to be damp. The fatty acids contained in the preen oil spread more evenly and rapidly over the feather surface in a film of water, before hardening. Oiling serves to keep the feather waterproof and supple, and so guards against heat loss and breakage. It has been suggested, also, that irradiated preen oil, like the skin pigment melanin in man, is a source of vitamin D. The habit attributed to Ross's Gull, of rubbing crustacea against its plumage, is probably cosmetic (it gives a pink flush) rather than water-proofing.

Sunning is a somewhat mysterious activity which, though somehow concerned with body care, has no immediately obvious function. Frigatebirds are classical exponents. They sit well back on their tails, body nearly vertical and wings outspread to the sun even on fiercely hot days in equatorial latitudes. Boobies sit or stand with wings hanging loosely and crossed at the tips, usually back to the sun. The lowest intensity of this position is with wings just clear of the body, as in heat-stressed birds. Masked Boobies sometimes adopt a prone position, wings drooping. Other species have their own postures. Possible but not very convincing functions include irradiation of the skin and feathers which may produce vitamin D and the discomfiting of ectoparasites which may move and become vulnerable to preening.

Panting, gular fluttering, wing-drooping, feather fluffing, eye-closing, cloaca exposing and excreting onto feet are all used to help regulate body temperature. The panting threshold is reached at body temperatures of 41°C–44°C and panting rates exceed normal respiratory rates by anything up to twenty times or more. In gular fluttering the moist gular area is moved by the muscles serving the lower jaw and the air-currents thus set up cause evaporative cooling. Among seabirds the phalacrocoracids, pelecanids and sulids are particularly prone to use gular fluttering and its effectiveness can be demonstrated by measuring the surface temperature at various points along the pouch. The temperature of feet and flippers of the Galapagos Penguin fluctuate widely both in the water and on land and their use illustrates the dilemma facing seabirds which must maximize heat loss on land whilst avoiding it in water. The strategy is to use the lightly feathered area under the flippers, and the feet, as cooling surfaces whilst keeping them in the shade of the back, body and upper surface of the flippers which are heavily insulated and so do not absorb heat. The flippers are held out at 45° from the body when the penguin is standing, which allows their undersurfaces to radiate heat, and when the penguin is prone they are drooped with tips on the ground, leaving a shady space for convective heat loss but covering the feet. The blood flow to both flippers and feet probably varies automatically with body temperature thus varying the amount of heat available to be lost there.

Temperature regulating behaviour seems not to have been used as the raw material for display in any seabirds. This may be understandable on the assumption that, whereas, for instance, aggression and fear are demonstrably involved in territorial and courtship behaviour, and therefore so, too, are the movements subserving their expression (attack or fleeing), temperature regulating systems are not involved in territorial and sexual contexts and their servant movements are therefore not evoked either.

Much has inevitably been omitted from this chapter, but perhaps it has shown the complexity and diversity of the ways in which, without benefit of 'understanding', seabirds nevertheless cope with the requirements of their social lives. With breeding failure never more than a hairsbreadth away natural selection has ensured that behaviour works well. But—to adapt a simile from Richard Dawkins' *The Selfish Gene*—the instructions for success have had to be included on sheets that contain, also, instructions on many other matters, such as feeding behaviour and choice of habitat. Further, the sheet of instructions has to read coherently; *it* is not just a jumble of unrelated sentences. Perhaps this is one reason why there can be little freedom for behavioural flexibility, or in our terms, experiments with grammar.

Breeding biology
habitats, colonies and strategies

Mammals have invaded the sea more successfully than have birds, insofar as they can reproduce without coming ashore. Birds lay eggs and feed their young and it is impossible to combine these traits at sea. You can do one, as fishes do, or the other, as do whales, but not both. So seabirds must spend weeks or months ashore each year, and since mainland shores are usually unsuitable, they choose islands. Most oceanic islands are small, and a huge number are tiny – mere rocks or fragments of atolls in vast expanses of ocean. The surrounding seas can feed enormous numbers of seabirds, especially because the birds, by evolving many special ways of feeding, have been highly successful in dividing up the various sources of food. Mainly because of their different anatomies, connected with their ways of feeding, seabird species each have their own preferences for nest sites and these, combined with a strong tendency to nest only with their own kind, often lead to a neat parcelling-out of nesting habitat and to some surprising choices of nest places.

Seabird breeding habitats

Most seabirds nest either on cliffs or on or beneath the slopes or flat interiors of small islands. In the northern hemisphere there are innumerable precipitous sea cliffs alive with seabirds. The Atlantic coasts, presumably because of their origin as a crack in the Earth's crust, with subsequent drifting, are particularly well endowed. The North Atlantic coasts, from Maine, via Labrador, Greenland and Iceland, to Britain, are studded with cliffs, stacks, islands and rocks. Probably no cliff-nester in the North Atlantic is limited by lack of nest sites, although there may be local exceptions to this, especially in the high Arctic. Qaerssorsua or Sanderson's Hope in Greenland is 5 kilometres long and

almost 1000 metres high with perhaps a quarter of a million Brunnich's Guillemots nesting on it. Nameless Bay, Novaya Zemlya, held an estimated 1 600 000 guillemots. Bear Island has been described as the finest bird cliffs in the northern hemisphere. Its cliffs rise sheer for almost 500 metres; 'magnificently sinister'. They hold literally millions of guillemots. Siberia, Streymoy (Faroes), Jan Mayen, Spitzbergen, Cape York, Scoresby Sound and many more present towering cliffs to the sea and accommodate huge numbers of seabirds. The Brunnich's Guillemot colonies penetrate as far north as Franz Josef Land in the polar basin. The Canadian Arctic holds an estimated 8.5 million seabirds. Around Britain there are hundreds of islands and mainland cliffs more than 65 metres high. Even on the eastern side, the North Sea supports more than a million seabirds, most of which nest on cliffs.

A cliff face offers several distinct types of nesting site. Gannets prefer broad, flat ledges, from just above the splash zone to the cliff-top. Shags tend to remain in the lowermost 10–20 metres and are ideally suited by broad ledges and low, stepped, flat-topped stacks, which are easy to fly onto with soaked and ineffective wings. They show a distinct liking for gloomy caverns and come nearest to hole-nesting of any pelecaniform except the tropicbirds. The Red-legged Cormorant of Peru often chooses small knobs and ledges despised by the bustling Guanays and Piqueros (Peruvian Booby), but may be forced onto them by their vastly more numerous relatives. Rather than sheer cliffs, cormorants prefer steep slopes with rocky outcrops, although the Pelagic Cormorant chooses narrow ledges and brackets on precipitous cliffs. On the main face of a large, sheer cliff in the North Atlantic the most numerous occupants are likely to be Guillemots and also Kittiwakes.

Division of nesting habitat on a generalised cliff in the eastern North Atlantic. There is considerable overlap between species but broadly typical preferences result in maximum utilization of nesting spaces.

shearwaters

petrels

gulls

Puffins

Gannets

Kittiwakes

Gannets

Kittiwakes

Fulmars

Kittiwakes

Guillemots

Fulmars

Razorbills

Guillemots

Kittiwakes

Black Guillemots

Guillemots

Razorbills

Cormorants

Shags

Gull landing by 'floating down', a manouevre allowed by its low wing-loading

A Guillemot lands by 'underflying', its upward momentum carrying it just past the landing place at a sharply decreasing speed, which is further dissipated by braking wing-beats

10-12 strokes/sec c.120°

7-9 strokes/sec 40°-60°

Gannet coming in to land. Note the fingered
primaries (first emarginated) and spread webs and tail.

Guillemots station themselves in packed rows
along ledges but eschew those which offer few
opportunities for social intercourse. They breed
more successfully when they can cluster together than where ledge structure compels
them to spread out thinly, mainly because they
are less liable to take fright, and thus lose fewer
eggs, in the former situation. Brunnich's Guillemot, which breeds on the same cliffs as the
Common Guillemot in the far north, often uses
small projections which can accommodate only
one or a few pairs, and so reduces competition
with its relative. In this, as in other ways, it tends
to resemble the Razorbill. Razorbills rarely
nest in large groups, preferring cracks, small
ledges or projections, whether or not these are
among Guillemot ledges. Kittiwakes have perfected the art of cementing their nests onto tiny
projections, by trampling mud to form a base.
Sometimes they are too ambitious, and their
nests come unstuck–the commonest cause of
breeding failure. Fulmars readily utilize ledges
but more often nest on steep slopes, cliff-brows

and the tops of small stacks. Terns are mainly
flat ground nesters, but Black Noddies are
highly adapted for ledge nesting. Fulmars and
Gannets are dominant among competitors for
ledge space. Gannets simply prod Guillemots
out of the way and toss their eggs overboard.
They treat the oil-spitting Fulmar with respect,
but usually win in the end, by spending much
more time on the site (the 'in' bird can usually
retain its position). But, due to the different
preferences of each species, there is seldom
serious competition among cliff-nesting birds.

The great advantages of island cliffs are
safety from ground predators, and the provision of wind and air-space, which greatly
facilitates landing and departure. One need
only compare the ease with which a ledge
nesting Atlantic Gannet takes off, with the
laborious procedure forced upon the flat-ground
nesting Cape Gannet, which bounds ponder-
ously along a clear run-way before becoming
airborne. However, cliffs are dangerous for
young birds. The young of the specialist
Kittiwake has several genetically-fixed adaptive traits which a Herring Gull lacks. Its avoid-
ance of the cliff-edge is much better developed;
it has more conspicuous appeasement behav-

African Gannets performing their greeting ceremony at the nest. In this species the strip of black skin on the throat is more than twice as long as the other two Gannets – it probably radiates heat and helps keep the bird cool.

Above left A Fairy or White Tern. A tropical species which lays its egg on bare branches or stumps.

Below left A White-capped Noddy on its nest on North Meyer Island in the Kermadecs.

Below A Sooty Tern colony. These terns gather in breeding colonies which may contain millions of pairs. Note the almost fully grown chicks on the ground.

Top A pair of Swallow-tailed Gulls, these birds have a peculiar snoring, screaming, rattling vocalization unique among gulls.

Above The beautiful Heermann's Gull nests on rocky islands in the Gulf of California. This is a colony on Isla Raza, Sea or Cortez.

Right Kelp or Dominican Gulls mobbing penguins and cormorants to panic them into regurgitating their food.

Top A White-tailed Tropicbird on its nest on the Aride Island, Seychelles.

Above A male Andrew's Frigatebird with a chick on Christmas Island, Indian Ocean.

Left A newly formed pair of Greater Frigatebirds, on the Galapagos. The female has recently landed on the male's display site and the pair-bond will probably be forged in the next two or three days.

A male Abbott's Booby – the world's rarest sulid. It nests only on the Indian Ocean Christmas Island.

Below The Peruvian Booby or Piquero on Guañape Island, Peru. One of the world's great guano producers.

iour, with a special black collar to emphasize the turning away of its head and beak; it begs more passively and it doesn't jump around when wing-exercising, as the Herring Gull does.

Sheer cliff faces are inhospitable, and many seabirds find more congenial nesting sites on slopes, among boulders or scree and on or beneath the tops of islands. Black and Pigeon Guillemots nest beneath boulders or overhangs, in crevices amongst scree or even beneath a thatch of grass or in a hole in a clay bank. The incalculable hordes of the Little Auk, believed to be the most numerous bird within its high Arctic breeding range, are also crevice nesters. In the north Pacific its even more diminutive relative, the Least Auklet, is almost equally numerous. Crested, Least and Parakeet Auklets on St Lawrence Island show little overlap in sites. The first two nest in talus slopes of different rock sizes, and the third in adjacent areas. The shattering effect of intense cold, on rock, is thus put to good use by the talus and scree nesting auks. Among terns, the Bridled Tern nests usually under cover of a boulder, sometimes in a crack, but of all terns, the Inca is perhaps nearest to a true hole-nester. Despite the advantages of cliffs, there are probably more seabirds nesting on or beneath flat ground than on cliff ledges, though, on the world scale, this is largely because there are vast areas of the tropics and of

Antarctica which support seabirds but contain few suitable cliffs. Among northern hemisphere seabirds, only the gulls, terns and skuas colonize flat ground on the surface (the Gannet will do so, but is by preference a cliff nester). In the sub-tropics and tropics, four species of booby, most terns, the tropical albatrosses, and some petrels nest in the open, on the ground. Cory's Shearwater, for example, nests in tremendous numbers on the plateau of Selvagem Grande (Salvage Islands) as well as in the surrounding cliffs. In Peru, the Grey Gull has the unique habit of nesting in the desert, far from water of any kind. By doing so, it avoids the predatory attention of the Kelp Gull. Gulls are notoriously adaptable in nesting, as in feeding. The Black-billed Gull of New Zealand nests in temporarily dried-up river beds, completing its cycle extremely rapidly and, if necessary, moving its breeding areas for successive attempts. In the Antarctic, most seabirds nest either in burrows or on open ground or ice, but even penguins (the Chinstrap) may nest on easy cliffs, using their bills to pull themselves up, and their toe nails to grasp.

Whilst it is evidently feasible for terns, which

Puffins outside their nest burrows. These birds sometimes form colonies numbering many tens of thousands.

can rise easily, to nest on flat ground, or for boobies and albatrosses, which, (man excluded), can usually defend themselves, many seabirds are both too awkward on land and too vulnerable to predation to do so. Therefore they excavate burrows and visit their breeding places at night. Presumably because suitable terrain is limited, the colonies of burrow-nesting shearwaters and petrels occur in strange places and reach staggering sizes. Snow Petrels have been reported nesting 300 kilometres from the coast, at 1500–2000 metres and at 72°S (Queen Maud's Land). But this theory seems weak in relation to the Great Shearwaters of Nightingale Island, Tristan da Cunha, which breed in such huge numbers, estimated in millions, that there are insufficient burrows, with the result that upwards of a quarter of a million eggs each year are laid on the surface, by burrowless birds. Yet there is said to be plenty of suitable, unoccupied land on nearby islands. Social stimulation could hardly require two *million* pairs to breed on the same island, so why do they do so? Probably because, being programmed to seek gregarious nesting, nobody is willing to go off to an uninhabited island! Man is much the same.

Burrow-nesters in general show an amazing ability to recognize their burrows amongst hundreds of thousands of others in the dark, but perhaps even more impressive is the ability of several – for example, Wilson's Storm-petrel, the Antarctic (Dove) Prion, and the Snow Petrel – to locate their burrows even when these are completely buried in snow. Leach's Storm-petrel, it is claimed, finds its burrow beneath a dense fir canopy by landing downwind and scenting its way. Plugging the nostrils and sectioning the olfactory nerve both, apparently, result in loss of homing ability, but I must admit I find it hard to believe.

There is often fierce competition among hole-nesters. On Tower Island (Galapagos) the high nesting failure (77 per cent) among Galapagos Storm-petrels was due almost entirely to intra-specific competition for nest sites, and the Antarctic Prion fights fiercely in competition for nest holes, as do tropicbirds. In general, species which are well able to dig their own burrows may be less prone to resort to severe fighting than species which must compete for a limited number of natural holes. But even the former compete strenuously. In some instances, it seems, burrows are in such short supply that

Snares Island Crested Penguins nest under trees. Here, the pathway from the sea to the colony meanders through *Olearia* forest.

different species use the same holes but at different seasons. The Madeiran Storm-petrel, Little Shearwater and White-faced Storm-petrel, on Great Salvage, apparently do this.

Tree-nesting seabirds may seem out-of-character but most of those that have committed themselves to this habit are highly successful. Two boobies (the Red-footed and Abbott's) are fully arboreal, as are four out of the five frigatebirds (the Ascension Island Frigatebird has to manage without trees or bushes). Among terns, the Fairy Tern is most amazing, incubating its single egg without benefit of any nest, on a bare branch or in a crotch. Black Noddies in the Indian and Pacific Oceans nest in trees, but usually on cliffs in the Atlantic. Brown Noddies usually nest in bushes or trees but also use the ground or cliffs. Genuine tree-hole nesting seabirds are rare. Golden Bosuns (a race of the White-tailed Tropicbird), confined to the Indian Ocean Christmas Island, nest in tree holes on the high central plateau, beneath the thick jungle canopy, one of the most astonishing nest sites one could imagine for a seabird. The Marbled Murrelet is even more bizarre. It nests high in cedar and other large trees, several kilometres inland, in the coastal forests of northern Canada and Russia, and flies to its nest site at night. Imagine the baptismal flight of a young Marbled Murrelet. It may be that tree-nesting in seabirds has evolved to enable its practitioners to avoid competition with more powerful ground or cliff-nesting species.

Few seabirds are utterly restricted to a single type of nest site. Kittiwakes *will* use flat ground if they have to; Red-footed Boobies will nest on walls or even on the ground, instead of in trees; Cape Pigeons will nest in burrows or on open ledges, and so on. But there can be no doubt that seabirds have utilized every niche open to them, and in so doing, become in most cases, highly specialized. The utilization of the several facilities offered by an island is always apparent by examining the composition of the seabird fauna. Usually, regardless of geographical location, there are about ten to fifteen species, which neatly divide up the available living space. The average number of species breeding on the sixty-eight major seabird stations around the British Isles is ten. The greatest number (nineteen) breed on one of the Orkney islands and the least (five) on flat, mainland sand-dune areas of the east coast. The Bass Rock, with nine species, falls near to the average. All but two nest on cliffs, and none of the available niches (broad ledges, small projections, low stacks, steep slopes, flat vegetated top) remain unused. It could accommodate Cormorants, but these usually do not mix with Shags and, in this case, nest on a rock nearby. Skokholm, off the Welsh coast, holds ten species. Here, cliffs are less in evidence and the island's friable soil has attracted tens of thousands of burrowers (shearwaters, petrels and Puffins). Between them, the Bass and Skokholm encompasses half the total number of seabird species breeding regularly in the British Isles.

Christmas Island in the Indian Ocean is one of the few forested and elevated oceanic islands remaining in the world. It holds eight seabird species. Six species nest in trees and one, the Red-tailed Tropicbird, in cracks or holes in the inland cliffs. Although the emphasis has thus shifted right away from cliffs, there is still an obvious sharing-out of habitat. No two species

overlap, except, in places, the Red-footed Booby and Greater Frigatebird, which are so commonly found together in the tropics due to the frigatebird parasitizing the booby. As mentioned the White-tailed Tropicbird's dangerous nesting habitat—holes in jungle trees—may be the result of competitive exclusion from cliffholes, by its more powerful congener.

Of course, the distributional limits of seabirds, determined principally by their food, decides which group of species divide up the habitat. But always, divide it up they do. Rarely is it possible to point to a substantial, unused niche, and usually, ten to fifteen species participate in the carve-up. In the Maldives there are thirteen species, nine of them terns; the Chagos Archipelago holds fifteen species. On Aldabra it is ten, on Tristan da Cunha, fourteen, and so on.

Even in the Falkland Islands, where the dominant, often the only, vegetation is tussock grass, the nesting seabirds divide it up neatly between themselves. Beneath the tussocks occurs the Magellanic Penguin, excavating shallow holes in soft tussock peat; Shoemakers (White-chinned Petrel) and Sooty Shearwaters burrow densely and more extensively; Falkland Diving-petrels use the tussock pedestal; Rockhopper Penguins nest colonially in the edge-growth of the tussock zone; Grey-backed Storm-petrels make a nest hollow, not a true burrow, inside the dead skirt of tussock grass, Brown-hooded Gulls nest between tussock clumps. In the cliff-top and peripheral tussock zone are Macaroni Penguins, King and Rock Cormorants, Dolphin and Kelp Gulls, South American Terns and Falkland Great Skuas, a total, again, of fourteen species. On Signy Island in the Antarctic there are fifteen breeding seabirds. Finally on Bird Island, South Georgia, there are twelve species.

The colonial habit in seabirds

Whatever their breeding habitat, seabirds are, overwhelmingly, colonial breeders, gathering in the avian equivalents of hamlets, villages, towns, cities and metropolises. More than 95 per cent of the world's seabirds nest in colonies (against less than 15 per cent of the world's birds). The matter of colony *size* is distinct from that of colony *density*. One can have 20000 pairs of Red-footed Boobies scattered in clumps of varying density across the 35 square kilometres of scrubby waste of Tower Island or

50 000 pairs of Guanay Cormorants on little more than 2.5 hectares of Guañape Island, in Peru. It is surprisingly difficult to define the term 'colony' rigorously. Definitions like 'a geographically continuous group of breeding birds whose territorial boundaries are contiguous' are obviously unsatisfactory for scattered colonies. It would cover discrete groups within larger aggregations, but that is insufficient. Clearly, the small group of Gannets breeding on the cliffs at Bempton in England is a colony, because each pair is, or at least was, within the behavioural orbit of every other pair (though even so, territories are not contiguous); they see, hear and interact with each other and, potentially, any male could breed with any female. Moreover, the group is physically distant from the nearest other gannetry. But the gannetry of St Kilda comprises the three stacks of Boreray, Stac Lee and Stac an Armin, together holding more than 50 000 pairs. Obviously, none of the criteria which I applied to Bempton, holds true for St Kilda. Nonetheless, it is always referred to as *a* colony or gannetry. The difficulty is even greater in the case of a 'colony' of Guillemots, numbering perhaps millions, and spread along cliffs stretching for several kilometres, and perhaps nearly merging with another such 'colony'. Many workers use the rule that any groups separated by 1.5 kilometres (1 mile) of coast or open sea without an occupied site, rate as different colonies. But why this distance? Clearly, a colony is an arbitrarily defined section of a larger group, which in turn merges into a population; and the definition of 'population' then runs into the same difficulties as 'colony'. However, for practical purposes I find it good enough to think of a colony as a group of potentially interbreeding individuals, *each of which is influenced by being part of the group*. The influence consists of exposure to the sight and sound of conspecifics, to the possibility of benefiting from the transfer of information and to the facilitation of breeding by the reduction of time-wastage. If a bereaved male, for instance, has to wait longer for a replacement mate, because there are fewer around, he wastes time and may miss a breeding season. The transfer of information may include social reaction to the presence of a predator or to communication of the whereabouts of a food source. To be consistent, I would have to use an alternative term for the 'colony' of Sooty Terns on the Pacific Ocean Christmas

Island, for, clearly, several millions of pairs far exceeds the number required to fulfil my definition. Since it is often necessary to refer to such aggregations, I would have to coin a suitable term. But 'colony' is so ubiquitous and entrenched that such a campaign would hardly succeed, so 'colony' they will remain.

The striking thing about seabird colonies, of whatever species, is the huge variation in size. It is difficult to give a typical size for any species. Yet, whilst 100 or 100 000 or even a million pairs of Guanay Cormorants will breed successfully, there is a meaningful, albeit extremely approximate, colony size which is typical of this species and which can be understood in terms of food and nesting space. A million pairs of Guanay Cormorants can breed successfully on Central Chincha, Peru, whereas a million pairs of Common Cormorants on Eynhallow, Orkneys, or of Flightless Cormorants in the Galapagos, would rapidly starve. Chincha is lapped by the Humboldt, with its prodigious reserves of anchovies, for which Orkney and the Galapagos have no counterpart. Flightless Cormorants, indeed, breed in colonies averaging less than ten pairs. So one can typify Guanay colonies as 'huge' and Common and Flightless Cormorant colonies as 'small', and the descriptions, though vague, are meaningful. Much the same could be done for most seabirds.

A few more examples covering seabirds of widely disparate habits will show the range of colony size. The largest colony of Royal Penguins, at Hurd Point, numbers more than 500 000 breeding birds, and the smallest are around 2000 pairs; there were an estimated 2.5 million Rockhopper Penguin nests on Beauchene Island in the Falklands; up to 600 000 pairs of Magellanic Penguins at Punta Tomba (Argentine); 5 million Adelie Penguins on Lawrie Island and a single, almost unbelievable colony of 10 million Chinstrap Penguins on Zavodevski Island in the South Sandwich Islands. Yet all of these species occur, also, in small colonies of a few hundred pairs. As befits birds nesting in huge colonies, they are typically dense-nesters. Fiordland Penguins, by contrast, are but loosely colonial, occurring in small aggregations under cover rather than in tightly-knit colonies in the open. Albatrosses often form impressive colonies. The Black-browed and Grey-headed may number 10 000 pairs in one breeding mass—often mixed. Where, incidentally, two or more colonial species breed in the same small area—as do Piqueros (Peruvian Boobies), Guanays and pelicans, or Herring and Lesser Black-backed Gulls, or Laysan and Black-footed Albatrosses—the species usually occur in separate clumps or masses. I cannot think of a single case in which two or more different species mingle randomly. Among terns, no species approach the Sooty Tern in size of colonies, the largest of which certainly contain several millions of pairs. On the other hand, Little Terns nest in small colonies (usually less than 100 pairs) with well dispersed nests. The Great Shearwater colony on Nightingale, Tristan da Cunha (an estimated 2 million breeding pairs) has already been mentioned and, among burrow nesters, the Puffin comes respectably near, with several 'colonies' estimated to number, or have numbered in the past, more than a million pairs. Guillemots and Little Auks have already been cited.

Colonies of the sizes described above can occur only if their members are far-foragers, ranging over vast areas of ocean, or are near to an exceptionally abundant supply of food. The Sooty Tern exemplifies the first-named condition and the huge concentrations of antarctic krill-feeders, such as many penguins, the second. It has been claimed that the only organism to outweigh the Earth's human population is *Euphasia*, the krill. The arctic concentrations of auks, Fulmars and Kittiwakes are comparable. In between these two extremes lie most of the medium-to-large-sized colonies, such as those of the Atlantic Gannet, and the British colonies of auks, Kittiwakes, etc. Small colonies, with widely dispersed members, such as those of the Tystie (Black Guillemot), reflect the species' nesting requirements and habit of feeding near to its breeding area, on prey which is dispersed and not superabundant. The largest known colonies are on Perret Island, Labrador, and Prince Leopold Island, where more than 2000 pairs nest. In most areas, the number of suitable nest sites may be the factor limiting the size of Tystie colonies. The Razorbill never occurs in guillemot-like concentrations, although it breeds alongside them and eats fish. Presumably, its prey-spectrum differs from that of its relative, although there is considerable overlap.

If the 'typical' colony size can be understood in terms of food (and occasionally of nesting space) it is no less important to stress the fact that colonies range widely in size. And in terms of the definition given earlier, this is readily understandable. For all practical purposes, a species which 'likes' to breed in large colonies can gain all the benefits as well from a colony of 5000, or even 500, as from a colony of 50000 pairs.

However, species are much more prone to stick precisely to their particular *pattern* of spatial dispersal, than to the *size* of their colonies. Gannetries vary in size by a factor of thousands, but wherever topography permits, they nest at the standard density of approximately 80 centimetres, nest centre to nest centre. It is much the same with other species although few are as invariable as Gannets. Fulmars typically space-out at 0.9 to 2.4 nests per square metre; Wandering Albatrosses at 106 nests per hectare but are capable of increasing their density to 170 nests per hectare; Rockhopper Penguins at up to 3 nests per square metre; Gentoos vary between 92.1 and 119.2 centimetres (mean minimum distance between nests at different colonies); Chinstraps range from 80.2 to 90.5 centimetres, whereas Adelies range from 66.9 to 84 centimetres; Guanay Cormorants from 2 to 4 nests per square metre; African Gannets up to 8 nests per square metre; Puffins about 1 pair per square metre, up to a maximum of 2.72 per square metre, on Trenyken (Norway). Perhaps the world record for dense nesting in a burrowing species is held by the gregarious Muttonbirds of Green Island, Bass Straits, which may crowd nine burrow entrances into 1 square metre of surface. Naturally, topography and other factors, such as, in a few cases, the supply of suitable sites relative to the demand, the degree of disturbance (disturbed localities are less attractive), the state of the colony (stable, declining or increasing) all affect the density that one observes at a particular time and place.

All this leads one to ponder the balance sheet for spacing-out. The 'explanations' are of three main kinds: available space; anti-predator device or social advantage.

Shortage of nesting space is nowadays rarely the main factor which causes seabirds to crowd together at their specific densities, but occasionally it does so. The magnificent seabird colonies of southern Africa, in the region of the Benguela Current, form a remarkable parallel with those of the Peruvian guano islands adjacent to the Humboldt. In both cases, several species of seabirds (in Africa, mainly cormorants,

African Gannets and Cape Penguins and in Peru, cormorants, Peruvian Boobies, Chilean Pelicans, burrowing petrels and Humboldt Penguins) live in tremendous numbers, supported by the rich fisheries, and islands are in relatively short supply. Crowding inevitably results. Again, Uspenski has averred that the food supplies in the Barents Sea and off Novaya Zemlya are practically inexhaustible and would permit a considerable increase in birds, especially guillemots, but that all parts of the coast suitable for nesting are already occupied. Careful examination of unoccupied coastal cliffs invariably revealed that for some important reason (the form of stratification, the absence of projections, etc.) the place in question could not be colonized. He considered that an increase in bird numbers would be possible only by increasing the density of existing colonies. But most species have not evolved their nesting-density under such selection pressures. This point is worth emphasizing, for it seems so plausible to attribute dense nesting directly to shortage of space. Yet most seabird colonies and areas are demonstrably under-populated. Of course, it is possible that in the evolutionary past, populations were astronomically greater than now, thus necessitating the evolution of dense nesting which has persisted until now, but this is hardly convincing. Rather, it seems that the availability of suitable nesting islands, cliffs or whatever, has been largely responsible for *creating* the colonial habit, but that something else has determined the *precise nature* of the spacing within those colonies.

To me, it seems that the 'something else' is to be found in the social aspects of colony life. A species will eventually establish the habit of nesting within that range of densities which, under the varying conditions inevitably occurring, leads to the highest reproductive success. The same, of course, applies to colony size, and in fact the two are often related – species that nest densely also form large colonies – and in many cases the advantages of dense nesting cannot be fully realized in small colonies. The essential difference between colony size and colony density, is that the former experiences no upper limits until space runs out, whereas density is usually checked quite independently of space. Evidence is now beginning to show that there is indeed advantage in nesting at the 'right' density. Thus, on the Isle of May off east Scotland, those Herring Gulls which nested at the commonest density started laying earlier than those nesting at higher *or* lower densities, and birds nesting at the commonest density had the highest clutch size, the greatest hatching and fledging success and reared the most young. This is exciting work, but fraught with difficulty in the interpretation, since density itself is in some cases influenced by several factors, such as the age-composition of the colony, the total population pressure in the locality, and the topography of the breeding area, all of which can materially affect the timing and success of breeding.

Social stimulation 'excites' birds, and causes their gonads to develop more rapidly than they would otherwise have done, thus affecting the timing of laying and leading to a greater degree of synchronization than would have occurred *solely* via non-behavioural external timers, such as daylength and temperature. The incredible vocalizations of many burrow-nesters that lack visually-stimulating displays may be essentially social in function. This applies not only to the petrels, but also, for instance, to Cassin's Auklets, which squeal and croak in unison, the whole colony becoming vocal within a few seconds of one bird starting to call.

We now see a seabird colony as a complicated piece of social architecture. It seems that social stimulation helps birds to time their breeding to advantage, reduces interference by conspecifics and stimulates birds to breed, which otherwise might not have been able to do so. Taking these in turn, there is, despite much variability, evidence that the timing of breeding can be crucially important in species that live in strongly seasonal environments, where climate and food can change for better or worse within two or three weeks. Direct measurements of breeding success and post-fledging survival, for several species, have shown that these are *not* independent of laying date. Thus, after allowing for age effects, Herring Gull and Kittiwake production is better in the first half of the season than in the second half; Manx Shearwaters survive better, after fledging, if they have been reared early in the season and the same probably applies to Atlantic Gannets. In Sooty Shearwaters, early pairs are more successful than later ones and so on. Clearly, there are several processes at work in determining this differential success. It may be that early laying produces chicks whose growth period coincides more precisely with a flush of food, or that they grow equally well throughout the season, but early fledgers strike more favourable conditions, as in the case of the Manx Shearwater and the Gannet. Whatever the mechanism, social stimulation is a benefit if it helps to produce earlier eggs and these survive better in the long run. In the White Pelican, the part-grown young group together in a pod or crèche and this event, apparently, causes 'late' adults to desert their eggs or small young and join other 'loafers'. Consequently, all eggs and young less than two weeks old are taken by predators. Again, this penalizes pairs that lay out-of-synchrony, though the mechanism is different from the others that I've mentioned.

In addition, social stimulation affects breeding success by reducing the amount of interference by conspecifics. It may seem surprising that breeding birds suffer from depredations by their own kind, but they do. In Herring Gulls, more eggs and young are lost to other Herring Gulls than in any other way. Even in species which are not cannibals, significant losses can be sustained simply as a result of disruptions, among pairs incubating or tending young, by birds trying to establish territories or attract mates. A colony in which everybody is incubating peacefully, or fully engaged in the demanding task of feeding their young, is a safer place for eggs and chicks than is a heterogeneous assemblage of pairs and individuals, all doing different things. Probably, this is one reason why, even in species which show a wide spread of laying, there is always a measure of synchrony within sub-groups. In fact, I do not know of a single good example of a colonial seabird in which there appears to be no sub-group synchrony. And synchrony is achieved partly by social stimulation, which is one of the benefits of breeding close to one's neighbours. Fraser-Darling suggested that synchronized production of young could enhance success by reducing the period over which vulnerable chicks are available to predators, for these tend to take only the necessary amount of prey, and a thousand chicks available for only two weeks will fare better than a thousand available for four. A study of a colony of Common Terns showed that predation was approximately constant throughout the season, although the available biomass increased a hundredfold. In this particular case, the earliest hatchers fared worst. Darling ascribed synchronization more to colony size than to density, and both factors are involved and often difficult to separate.

Where avian predators are important, and there is communal harassment of them, as by Black-headed Gulls, or Arctic Terns, of crows and Herring Gulls, another potential benefit of synchrony occurs. It is better that everybody should be in the same anti-predator mood, and available to engage in action together.

It is conceivable (though there is no hard evidence) that birds which breed in colonies and forage far afield, sometimes for particular types of prey which may be temporarily here or there, rather than all the time everywhere, may benefit from the inadvertent transmission of information from members who know where that prey is at a particular moment. Synchrony would then be an advantage if specific prey was linked to particular stages of the young bird's development. This general idea, largely attributable to Zahavi, has been applied to several species that roost in flocks and feed at some distance on clumped prey, but it seems unlikely to apply widely to seabirds.

Breeding close to others presumably facilitates pair formation, by bringing large numbers of potential mates into close contact. Moreover, the colony is itself usually a guarantee that the location is a suitable one and the inexperienced young bird, establishing his site, can therefore safely attach himself to an existing colony. Both these functions, also, concern the transfer of information.

The structure of colonies is important. Not long ago, it would have been assumed that the breeding pairs in a colony were essentially alike, give or take normal variability, except that old and experienced pairs were likely to breed more successfully than young, inexperienced ones. Now, thanks perhaps mainly to John Coulson and co-workers, it is known that a colony is a mosaic of pairs of several categories, and moreover a dynamic mosaic, with pairs ascending and descending the ladder of reproductive success, according to circumstances. Breeding success is influenced by age, position within the group and behavioural compatibility of partners and many factors correlate with each other. Thus adults from the centre of the group are heavier, and survive better than 'edge' birds, as well as breeding more successfully, and so on.

When all is said and done, however, we are little nearer to understanding what decides the actual density favoured by particular species. I have suggested that Atlantic Gannets nest as densely as they can, commensurate with their requirements for safe landing and departure and for the accommodation on the site of the large chick and both parents. This density, I believe, confers the maximum social stimulation and helps the Gannet to fledge its offspring earlier than it would otherwise. So the density of its colonies is not to be explained only, or even mainly, in terms of shortage of suitable sites. Similarly, the Adelie Penguin has much to gain from telescoping its breeding cycle and, like the Gannet, breeds in dense colonies, despite an abundance of suitable, unused nesting areas. But does the Kittiwake nest as densely as it could? If not, what determines *its* spacing? And certainly the Herring Gull could compress its territory, so why does it nest at its observed mean density rather than half or twice that, and why, for that matter, is there so much more variability in its spacing pattern than in the Gannet? Why do Black-browed Albatrosses nest 1.55 metres apart and Grey-headed, even when cheek by jowl with Black-browed, nest 1.31 metres apart? Why do Wandering Albatrosses fit only 106 nests into each hectare when they can fit 170 (as shown by an experiment in which eggs were removed one year, thus releasing those pairs to lay again the following year when they would not normally have done so)? We do not know but one guess could be that in the more spaced species, too much proximity could upset the physiological balance of the bird with far-reaching consequences.

Finally, the disadvantages of nesting in colonies deserve mention. Disturbances often lead to enormous losses of eggs and young. Indeed, in at least some frigatebirds, it seems that, contrary to what I have just written, groups which are densest and most highly synchronized show even higher losses than others, though all are subject to extremely high mortality of eggs and young through interference by conspecifics. Predation is, in some cases, made easy. A Fox in a colony of Black-headed Gulls can wreak untold havoc and a colony of skuas or Great Black-backed Gulls can take substantial toll of other colonial seabirds. The 'black-backs' on Skomer ate an estimated 3000 Manx Shearwaters in a season whilst on the sands of Forvie, a single pair of Herring Gulls took 550 Sandwich Tern chicks. At Bird Island, South Georgia, Antarctic Skuas were estimated to account for 10000 Dove (Antarctic) Prions each year. These few examples, which could easily be multiplied, show that colonial birds expose themselves to predation. But, although predation, like unemployment, is 100 per cent for the individual that experiences it, it usually affects only a fraction of the breeding population, most of which experiences the benefits of colonial nesting, and not its disadvantages. At least with hindsight, it is clear that the attainment of a place in a socially adequate part of a colony is of great importance to a prospective breeder.

It has been conventional wisdom to interpret the strong tendency shown by young of the large majority of colonial seabirds, to return to breed in their natal colonies, as the result of selection favouring those who do so, since their own existence testifies to the suitability of their birthplace. But in expanding populations, it may prove difficult to establish a place within a *socially* optimal part of the home colony, and there may be benefit in prospecting for such a place elsewhere. There is, in fact, a great deal of interchange between colonies, almost all, if not all of it, involving young birds seeking to establish themselves and *not* breeders changing their colony. The growth-rate for many gannetries on the west coast of Britain over the last fifty years is clear proof of substantial immigration to each, since the fast growing colonies could not possibly, by themselves, have produced all the recruits. Based on figures for reproductive rate and mortality, around five per cent per year, represents about the maximum possible growth rate for a gannetry, under its own steam, whereas many have grown at rates far exceeding this. So immigration is clearly a normal way in which a gannetry gains recruits. Of course, Gannets are increasing overall, and one cannot necessarily assume that, if the population in the eastern North Atlantic were stable, Gannets would still go to colonies other than the one of their birth. But it seems probable that they would. I picked up a Puffin on the Bass Rock which had been ringed on Skokholm, and Manx Shearwaters have been recovered, breeding, at colonies other than that of their birth. Herring Gulls and Kittiwakes of known birthplace have been recorded prospecting and breeding more than 150 kilometres away. One of the interesting features of this is that, in some species, such prospecting concerns much more than the odd pioneer. It has long been clear, both on *a priori* grounds and by recoveries of marked birds, that a *few* individuals seek pastures new.

But now we must think of large, floating populations of young birds wandering from colony to colony, until one of them provides the right stimuli, which include social features as well as topography. A young, foot-loose Herring Gull will not be attracted most strongly either to the densest or the sparsest colony, or part of a colony, but to the one with 'right' spatial and social texture. So, paradoxically enough, culls designed to *reduce* Herring Gulls may end up by creating such attractive spatial and social textures that recruits flood in preferentially, and nullify the cull. I have observed, over many years, that the Bass Rock gannetry increases in bulges. One area begins to attract recruits and the effect snowballs. This is probably due to a behavioural phenomenon which one could call peer-attraction. A growing point in a colony, or a growing colony as a whole if it is small enough, has a particular behavioural 'badge' which is different from the 'badge' of a stable group or colony. And prospectors are attracted to the part with the right badge. This, it seems, would obviously be sensible, if birds could think, so instinct does it for them. Young birds are, perhaps, more likely to get into their own peer group, and then to acquire a mate and to synchronize with their neighbours. Sometimes, birds breed far away from their natal colony. Sandwich Terns from the Farne Islands off Britain's east coast have been recorded breeding in the Black Sea, Gannets from Ailsa Craig off Scotland, in Norway, Red-footed Boobies from Kure have been recovered on other Central Pacific islands over 1000 kilometres disant. If young, unestablished birds happen to encounter a socially stimulating colony, they are liable to respond to it.

Breeding strategies in seabirds

Timing of breeding
Seabirds nest in small, dispersed groups or large, dense colonies, according to the nature of their feeding behaviour. If they live near to super-abundant food they can nest in large colonies, and if sites are scarce, or other advantages accrue, they will do so. On the other hand, even if they live in less productive tropical waters, but have evolved the habit of foraging extensively, they are still able to nest in large colonies, as do Sooty Terns, Masked Boobies and Greater Frigatebirds. The millions of Great Shearwaters on Tristan da Cunha have much of the South

Atlantic open to them, and so do not run into direct competition for food. But if a species is restricted to a severely limited feeding area, it is likely to form small colonies, like those of the Flightless Cormorant, the Common Shag and the Tystie or Black Guillemot. Broadly speaking, the size of the colony is predicted by an equation whose main factors are foraging distance and the nature of the food supply, which includes abundance and dispersal; one can have the same biomass per 1000 square kilometres, but the optimal feeding strategy is different for clumped than for randomly dispersed food.

Basically the same considerations apply to a seabird's breeding season. The time of year at which it lays its egg and rears its young will be determined mainly by the balance between the cost of these activities, their success, and the food available to meet the cost. The cost, for instance, could be met either by dipping into capital, or by relying on interest. An adult seabird could accept significant stress, thereby shortening its reproductive life, or it could restrict its breeding activities to periods in which it suffered no strain. Success can be approached either by having a high proportion of eggs give rise to fledged young, or by accepting a high pre-fledging failure but enhancing post-fledging survival. Breeding strategy involves these and other considerations.

A bird's breeding season is that period of a calendar year during which it is engaged in breeding, and 'breeding' means *all* the activities which are necessary for reproduction. It does not mean merely the period between laying the egg and producing the fledged young. In the northern hemisphere, north of the tropics, seabirds breed once a year and each species lays its eggs at more or less the same time each year, though not necessarily, or even usually, the same time as other species. The more closely all individuals of a species cluster around a mean laying date, constant from year to year, the more one can be sure that that particular date is advantageous. In temperate and arctic northern latitudes, seabirds lay in spring and rear their young in summer, but within this general framework there is considerable variation. Some examples follow, arranged in the regional sequence: northern (temperate); tropical and sub-tropical; antarctic.

The Atlantic Gannet's breeding season runs from January to October. The mean annual date for egg laying varies with locality, from about mid-April to mid- or the third week of May. On the Bass Rock, the mean date falls around mid-April every year, whilst on Bonaventure in the Gulf of St Lawrence it is about three weeks later. Both the general period within which the mean laying date for the Gannet always falls, that is between mid-April and mid-May, and the differences which exist between colonies, can be understood in terms of the Gannet's relationship with its food. Thus, all Gannets rely largely on Mackerel upon which to feed their young. Mackerel are abundant in inshore Gannet waters, on both sides of the Atlantic, from June to September, which means that they become readily available just when the young are growing rapidly and requiring large amounts of food. But, one might well ask, why is there so much regional variation in the time of laying? The Gannets of Bonaventure, have to face barbaric climatic conditions when they return to their ledges. Indeed, they cannot even use the cliffs until April, because these are still locked in ice and snow. Moreover, until early April, fishing is difficult in waters within foraging distance of the colony. Under these circumstances it is amazing that they manage to come within striking distance of the mean laying date for colonies such as the Bass Rock, and they do so by telescoping the pre-laying activities. This, incidentally, is a fine illustration of the effects of social stimulation. The Bonaventure Gannets are forced to stay away until the ledges become habitable, by which time they are ready to occupy them *en masse*. So the season starts with a bang, with breeding behaviour into top gear almost immediately, and everybody exposed to a frenzy of territorial and sexual activity. By contrast, things build up more slowly on the Bass Rock. So Bonaventure Gannets partly recover the time lost as a result of their exclusion from the ledges and fishing grounds.

Each colony has its own set of conditions. Ailsa Craig Gannets lay a fortnight or so later than Bass Gannets, probably because they face a different set of feeding conditions. Other seabirds show comparable differences between colonies. The Puffins of St Kilda, for example, lay three weeks later than those of the Isle of May on the eastern side of Scotland.

The timing of breeding is determined not only by the needs of the young in the nest, but also by their requirements for survival after fledging. Gannets which fledge early survive better than later ones, because they are less likely to encounter adverse conditions on their southward migration. This should have the effect of advancing the mean laying date until something halts the process. In the Gannet's case, the limit is likely to be set by at least two factors. Early in the year, when days are short, Gannets cannot afford to spend too much time on their sites, and laying date depends, in part, on the amount of time spent at the colony beforehand. It is during the prelaying period that males, at least, are under most stress, and lose weight. Short days, meaning little time for fishing, limit the amount of energy which they can put into attendance and display. Second, they probably need to produce their young to coincide with the summer access of the Mackerel shoals.

Like the Gannet, the Manx Shearwater lays at the same time each year—on Skokholm regularly between the 6th and 10th of May. Also like the Gannet, there is considerable spread. This spread has to be explained. It is not the same thing as the variability *between* colonies for, obviously, it cannot be explained on the basis of regional differences in food. There are at least two contributory factors. First, the age of the females (young birds lay later); second, the genetically controlled variability maintained by natural selection. In a variable environment, variability in organisms will be maintained, whether in physique, physiology or behaviour. In some years, females laying later will do better than those laying earlier, and in proportion to the frequency with which this happens, their genotype will be preserved. If early females *always* fared best, then late layers would be eliminated from the population, and the only late laying would come from the young females. Clearly, one would not expect all species to be subject to the same degree of variability in environmental pressures. Manx Shearwaters make an extensive flight, of some 9000 kilometres, to South American waters. They must therefore cope with the weather *en route*, and, at least for the first leg, this is certainly not going to be narrowly consistent from year to year; in some years there is considerable mortality. The same applies to the Gannet. The Muttonbird (Short-tailed Shearwater) shows a constant laying date but less spread than the Manx Shearwater, but it is difficult to assess the amount of environmental variability with which it must cope. In the Manx

Shearwater, though not in the Gannet, an important factor determining the date of laying may be the energy cost of the egg. At 15 per cent of the female's weight, even the single egg of the shearwater is a significant cost; the Kittiwake's clutch of three represents 36 per cent of the female's weight, whereas the Gannet's egg is but 3 per cent. Species with high production-costs benefit from timing their egg-laying to follow a period of good feeding, which may impose seasonal restrictions. The pre-laying exodus of shearwaters, petrels, albatrosses, etc., is to help meet the energy cost of the egg, by uninterrupted feeding. Thus, prior to laying, female Manx Shearwaters, (at least from Skokholm) spend a fortnight feeding on sardines in the Bay of Biscay. An example of the effect of food on the timing of breeding is to be found in the auks of Langara Island (Canada). Ancient Murrelets and Cassin's Auklets, mainly plankton feeders early in the season, lay much earlier than the fish-feeding Marbled Murrelet, Pigeon Guillemot, Rhinoceros Auklet and Tufted Puffin. The plankton becomes plentiful before the fish.

In the strongly seasonal environments of the north temperate region, then, breeding is strictly correlated with season, and therefore occurs only once each year. Northern seabirds lay as early as they can, so as to give their young the best chance of survival both in the nest and after fledging, but they have no chance of completing two breeding cycles in one year. The seasonal shutters come down so smartly that even an extra week or two, gained early on, has survival value. The annual, seasonal breeding cycle is not, however, universally appropriate.

In the tropics, selection pressures and breeding strategies are completely different. Some tropical seabird stations lie in climatically seasonless zones. Food tends to be highly unpredictable; sometimes there is plenty, but at others there is so little that foraging efforts have to be greatly increased. Under these conditions, a range of options are open to the seabirds. Since food does not vary annually, there is no point in breeding annually. They can breed annually and 'seasonally', annually and non-seasonally, at intervals of less than a year, or of more than a year. Which strategy is chosen depends on a host of other factors, as the following examples show.

Annual, seasonal breeding is shown by the Waved Albatross of Hood Island, Galapagos. The mean laying date is early in May, and 50 per cent of eggs are laid in the first half of this month. This surprisingly seasonal breeding could be related to seasonal changes in food in the albatross's foraging area, which may be far south of the Galapagos. The Masked Boobies of Hood and of the other Galapagos Islands are also annual breeders, but much more loosely timed. There is scarcely a month of the year in which it is impossible to find Masked Booby eggs on one island or another, and on any island, the spread of laying covers several months. The mean annual laying date is almost certainly not very consistent. Yet, they tend to breed once a year, and at roughly the same time each year, on the same island.

Annual, non-seasonal breeding may seem paradoxical. It can occur where a successful cycle and the recuperative period total about twelve months, but an unsuccessful cycle can be followed by another attempt after a short interval. For example, and disregarding more or less immediate replacement eggs, a Gannet which loses its egg in June will not lay again until the 'proper' time next year—that is, in April—but a failed Masked Booby on Ascension Island may lay again within less than a year. If then successful, it will cycle along at roughly twelve monthly intervals, but its laying month will now be different. Several failures could result in the same female, during her lifetime, laying in most months of the year.

Yet, also on Ascension, the Brown Booby has adopted a different strategy. If successful, it breeds approximately once every nine months, which effectively eliminates seasonal breeding. It remains more or less in a state of continuous readiness to breed. The triggering factor, apparently, is food. Soon after the economic climate becomes favourable it initiates a new breeding attempt. In this way it fits more attempts into, say, ten years than does the Masked Booby, and even if the same proportion fail, it rears more young. Elsewhere in the tropics, as for example on the Indian Ocean Christmas Island, the Brown Booby breeds annually and broadly seasonally; the Ascension Island strategy is a special response to those particular conditions. The great merit of laying when food is relatively plentiful is that the pair court, mate and the female lays her eggs whilst well fed, and since there is no way of ensuring that food will be plentiful for the chick, the adults may as well take advantage of a favourable period in this way. Several tropical seabirds do much the same thing, fitting in as many cycles as possible, and moulting inbetween–for example, out of the seventeen seabird species breeding in the Galapagos, eight breed at non-annual intervals and are probably breeding as often as possible, using the intervals to moult. Since I have mentioned Galapagos seabirds a great deal, it is worth summarizing the spectrum of breeding strategies found in these islands. Two species (the Waved Albatross and the Hawaiian Petrel) have a rigidly fixed annual cycle; five species have a much less well-defined annual cycle, in some cases with considerable variation in timing between islands (Galapagos Storm-petrel, Madeiran Storm-petrel, Red-billed Tropicbird, Red-footed Booby, Masked Booby); eight species have a shorter-than-annual breeding cycle (Audubon's Shearwater, Brown Pelican, Blue-footed Booby, Lava Gull, Swallow-tailed Gull, Brown Noddy, Flightless Cormorant and Galapagos Penguin); two species have a longer-than-annual cycle (Greater Frigatebird and Magnificent Frigatebird; the Red-footed Booby, at least on occasions, also takes more than a year to complete a cycle). The Sooty Tern also breeds there but its cycle length and breeding frequency are unknown. In terms of breeding frequency, seven species breed once a year, eight breed more than once a year and two breed less than once a year (three if the Red-footed Booby is counted). Thus, non-seasonal food has allowed eight out of seventeen to breed non-seasonally, and a further seven to breed only loosely-to-very loosely seasonally. Only two are tied to a fairly strict seasonal (and annual) regime.

Such opportunistic breeding is not the only method of increasing the number of breeding cycles. Sub-annual breeding can also cycle regularly, rather than opportunistically. Thus the Sooty Tern breeds annually over most of its range, but every 9.3 months on Ascension and every 6 months on the Phoenix and Line Islands. It nowhere breeds at irregular intervals as the Brown Booby on Ascension does. The Bridled Tern lays every 7–8 months.

On Ascension, some species breed seasonally and annually (Fairy Tern and Madeiran Storm-petrel); some at less than annual intervals (Sooty Tern, Black Noddy, Brown Booby) and some breed annually but non-seasonally (Red-billed and White-tailed Tropicbirds).

Even in the Seychelles, which have a much more seasonal climate than the Galapagos, or Ascension, four kinds of breeding cycles are in evidence: non-seasonal (Fairy Tern, White-tailed Tropicbird), annual and loosely seasonal, or extended annual (Brown Noddy, Black Noddy, Audubon's Shearwater); annual and seasonal (Sooty Tern, Roseate Tern, Wedge-tailed Shearwater) and restricted, sub-annual (the Bridled Tern with its eight-month cycle). Where sub-annual breeding occurs in regular cycles, breeding can be synchronized just as readily as in the more conventional annual cycle. But opportunistic sub-annual breeding inevitably weakens synchrony, since the breeding population is, as it were, scattered all over the reproductive globe. Of course, synchrony in a sub-annual breeder can be local rather than overall. Thus, the Swallow-tailed Gull of the Galapagos breeds every 9–10 months in sub-colonies which are synchronized within themselves, though over an entire island breeding may be staggered. Breeding at 6-monthly intervals makes double-broodedness feasible, and besides the Sooty Tern, of the Phoenix and Line Islands, Cassin's Auklet and the Silver Gull of Australia and New Zealand rear two broods per year, the latter being the only gull to do so.

The non-seasonal environment also opens the way to breeding at intervals of a year and a fraction. The Red-footed Booby of the Galapagos often requires more than a year to complete a breeding cycle. Like the Brown Booby of Ascension, it appears to commence a new cycle when food becomes plentiful. Its breeding could therefore be characterized as opportunistic supra-annual.

A few seabirds breed at two year intervals, among them the frigatebirds (which are tropical) and one booby–Abbott's Booby of the Indian Ocean Christmas Island. This, however, need not make them a-seasonal breeders, and in fact Abbott's Booby is quite markedly seasonal, laying mainly in May and June but not completing the cycle until July or August of the following year. However, Greater Frigatebirds in the Galapagos are only loosely seasonal. Although the main egg-laying period on Tower Island is in the first quarter of the year, eggs can be found up to September. On Aldabra (Indian Ocean), it lays principally in August and September and its laying shows less spread. Similarly, on Christmas Island (Indian Ocean) it lays mainly between April and June. In both these latter areas, the climate shows much more seasonal variation than in the Galapagos, and laying is correspondingly more seasonal.

All these breeding strategies of tropical sea-birds are correlated with feeding. The extreme case of the biennially-breeding frigates is a good example. Frigatebirds snatch their prey from the surface or the air whilst on the wing. This, in the impoverished tropical areas in which they live, often imposes lengthy foraging trips. One of the necessary adaptations to infrequent feeds is slow growth of the young, and frigates carry this to extremes, taking almost six months between hatching and fledging. They are then fed by their parents for a further six months or more. The result is a breeding cycle which far exceeds a year in length. Frigatebirds do not moult whilst breeding, and this probably requires some months. Breeding is thus limited to once in two years. In theory, such a biennial cycle need not be tied to a-seasonal environments. It is possible to lay seasonally but once every two years. But it does (in the frigate's case) require that the young are fed for an *entire year*, which means that food has to be available all year round, within foraging distance of the breeding place. It doesn't require food to be plentiful, and indeed the fully grown young often suffer severe starvation and many die. The same happens to the young Abbott's Boobies in the much more seasonal climate of Christmas Island. But obviously enough young survive, to make biennial breeding, (successful, not merely attempted) with its long dependency period, feasible. Biennial breeding is extremely rare among seabirds, and apart from the five frigatebirds and Abbott's Booby, great albatrosses are known to breed so, although two or three others may do so and the King Penguin breeds only twice in three years.

Departure from normal, annual and reasonably seasonal breeding has several consequences in addition to affecting productivity. Frigatebird populations, for example, are divided into two portions, breeding in alternate years. These are by no means equal, since around three-quarters or more frigate pairs fail in their nesting attempt and many of these try again the following year. Nevertheless, the biennial breeding system means that it is impracticable for frigatebirds to acquire a permanent site or mate, since their old site might have been taken over in the meantime, and without a fixed meeting place it becomes impracticable to maintain a permanent pair bond. This leads to modifications in the behaviour which serves territorial and pair-bonding. All these changes emphasize the fundamental role of food and feeding methods in determining many of the details of breeding ecology and behaviour.

Another aspect of non-seasonal breeding which deserves mention is that it provides a means of partitioning resources. If nesting sites are limiting, as they may be in the case of hole-nesting tropicbirds or burrow-or-crevice-nesting petrels, two 'populations' can use the same resource each year. On Plaza, of the Galapagos, for instance, two populations of Madeiran Storm-petrels breed, one in the hot 'season' and one in the cold, whilst on Isla Pitt, the Madeiran Storm-petrel breeds only in the hot season and the Galapagos Storm-petrel uses the same sites in the cold season. In theory, too, such a device could spread the load on the local food resources. A comparable effect could be achieved by staggering the laying dates of closely related species breeding on the same island. For example, where two eudyptid penguins share a breeding station, the larger species arrives before the smaller and lays first. At Macquarie Island the earlier breeding of approximately 2 million Royal Penguins results in their chicks leaving for sea one month before the 500 000 or more Rockhopper Penguins. Staggering the breeding seasons ensures that two vast hordes of young birds are not thrown upon the food resources simultaneously. But, in many instances, it is far from certain that competition for food *is* limiting.

In the sub-tropics, disregard for seasonal breeding is less marked than in the tropics but greater than at higher latitudes. The petrels illustrate this well. Several of the gadfly-petrels, which feed mainly in the sub-tropics, breed partly in winter (this number includes the following members of the *Pterodroma* (gadfly-petrels): Grey-faced Petrel, Bermuda Petrel, Black-capped Petrel, Soft-plumaged Petrel, Bonin Petrel, Atlantic, Solander's, and Kermadec Petrel). They breed in the winter, despite the general rule that, outside the tropics, petrels lay in spring or early summer, when marine production is high, (thus, for example, of the twelve petrel species with which the Grey-faced shares its various breeding islands, ten lay between September and December). The Grey-faced Petrel is enabled to lay in winter by virtue of its exceptionally long pre-laying absence of one to two months, which presumably helps it to form the necessary food reserves. This is itself facilitated by the petrel's ability to lay fertile eggs two months or more after copulation. The total length of the breeding cycle is extended to 9–10 months, significantly longer than in summer-breeding relatives, and the Grey-faced has to complete its moult in the 2–3 months which remain.

Comparably, on Tristan da Cunha, of fourteen breeding procellariforms, seven lay between October and March, when the seas are warmer and poorer, and the others lay in summer. The former benefit by producing young which fledge at the time of maximum abundance and the latter by courting and egg-laying when food is plentiful.

The antarctic, south of the antarctic convergence, is an extremely rich and highly seasonal zone and holds incalculable numbers of seabirds. As one would expect, the further south one goes the more restricted is the breeding season available to birds. Birds in general have only a limited number of strategies which they can deploy, and the penguins have two main methods of coping with the short antarctic season. Like the seabirds of tropical regions, they can either extend their cycles, or (though by quite different means) effectively shorten them. The pygoscelid penguins complete their breeding cycles during the three or four months of summer, but the Emperor and King Penguins are too large, and therefore grow too slowly, to achieve this, and they run into the severe problem of beginning or continuing breeding during the antarctic night. Emperors occupy the antarctic coastline as far south as the sea extends (Kings have a different range; they breed on the islands and shores of the sub-antarctic region). As in arctic and north temperate waters, the Antarctic Sea varies in richness, in a consistent manner, from month to month, and the Emperor's solution is to produce young which become independent just when there is rich feeding, so that they can fatten up for the ensuing winter, and when the sea-ice has broken up, so that the young do not have to walk long distances to reach open water. To achieve this, it has evolved the 'eccentric' habit of laying its eggs in mid-winter (in May or June). At this time, when the stress of intense cold and blizzards has to be endured, it is more economical for one sex to perform all the incubation than for the birds to trek back and forth over the ice to effect nest-relief. So the males incubate. To conserve heat, they huddle tightly together, and Stonehouse has estimated that they save 80 per cent of the heat which a single bird would lose. Huddling has meant abandoning territorial behaviour, and Emperors are notably unaggressive (adult King Penguins do not huddle, although their chicks do). The female, presumably under physiological control, returns around hatching time and feeds the chick for the first three weeks after hatching. After about five months, when about three-quarters grown, they moult (King Penguins do not moult until full size and ten or eleven months of age) and may float away on the ice as it breaks up. Presumably they achieve independence, after a period of starvation, some six or eight weeks before the level of plankton falls and summer ends. The Emperor's breeding strategy is thus to lay in winter and meet its chicks' maximum demands during the spring, when food is abundant, and to leave its chick to mature in autumn before food falls away. So it can rear its chick within the one year. The King Penguin's solution makes an interesting contrast. It lays during spring and summer, brings its chick to full size during the autumn whilst plankton is still plentiful and keeps it alive, though at starvation level, throughout the winter. The chick then fattens during the summer and completes the moult. Consequently, Kings cannot rear a chick every year. By laying at different times in successive cycles, alternately early and late, they fit two cycles into three calendar years—the only seabirds known to do so. As in the frigatebird, though no contrast in conditions could be greater, the disruption of annual, seasonal breeding has resulted in disruption of the pair-bond, which is impermanent in the King Penguin.

Adelie Penguins meet the seasonal demands of their extreme antarctic environment (they breed within 1400 kilometres of the South Pole in McMurdo Sound) by breeding to a very tight schedule (and arctic birds do exactly the same). They head towards their breeding colonies in October, whilst these are still in the grip of winter. They may walk 80 kilometres across sea-ice, and take up nest sites which are still buried in snow, at a temperature which may reach −15.5°C. Their large fat deposits, as in other penguins, are crucially important in tiding them over the first weeks, during which they approach the physiological limits of weight loss, which appears to be about half their initial weight. Unlike the Emperor and King Penguins, the Adelie has reduced the length of its incubation period and, in addition, its chick grows fast. At the time the young are growing most rapidly, the Antarctic Ocean is 'red with euphasids and as productive as the richest farmland; . . . a thin endless consommé with two or three particles of rich food (larval fish or euphasids) suspended in every cubic yard [metre]' (Stonehouse). Before winter begins in early April, the chicks have moulted their down, grown their feathers and fattened up. Their parents, likewise, have moulted and fattened before the sea-ice drives them northwards. Late chicks are abandoned and thus sacrificed in mid-February, when their parents begin their pre-moult fattening. So tight is the schedule that to care for them would jeopardize the parent's moult and therefore its life.

Penguins with a considerable latitudinal breeding range show a corresponding range of breeding seasons, generally laying later in more southern latitudes. Their laying date is closely correlated with mean annual sea-temperature. The Rockhopper lays around 1st December on Heard Island (mean sea-temperature 1°C) and around 25th September on Tristan da Cunha (15°C). Only the Fiordland Penguin, among the crested penguins (eudyptids) lays its eggs in the winter and therefore has to rear its chicks during spring.

Possibly the most abundant seabird in the antarctic is Wilson's Storm-petrel. This tiny bird returns from its winter quarters in the topics and the northern hemisphere, where it has been recovered as far north as New Jersey, U.S.A., to its breeding grounds in the far south, on the antarctic peninsula. It well illustrates the difficulties faced by a small, weak bird with insignificant fat reserves, in breeding in Antarctica. Wilson's Storm-petrel cannot scrape away snow and ice from its nesting crevices and so cannot return as early as the larger antarctic petrels. This allows scarcely enough time to fit the breeding cycle into the short summer. Under such circumstances one might imagine that every pair would be under strong pressure to begin breeding as early as possible, and therefore synchronously. But egg laying is in fact spread over six weeks in some years (late December until early February). This is largely due to variability in the time taken to form the egg. This would presumably not be allowed by natural selection if late layers were *consistently* penalized, but heavy snowfalls in mid-season, in some years, kill the newly hatched chicks of early breeders.

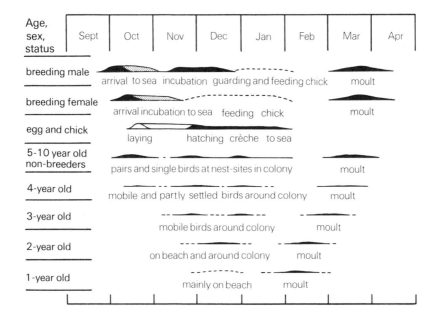

Annual cycle of Royal Penguins on land according to age and breeding status. After Carrick (1972).

Length of breeding cycles

This patchy survey of breeding seasons and frequency has already touched upon the length of breeding cycles. As we have seen, some seabirds have extended the length of their breeding cycle so much that they cannot complete it within a year, or cannot moult in the remaining time. An equally small number manage to fit two cycles into one year. Others complete one and part of another cycle in a year. All of these non-annual cycles, short or long, occur in the tropics or in the antarctic; elsewhere, the annual cycle reigns. Thus each species deploys its breeding energy in its own way. It may put a lot of effort into the pre-laying part of the cycle, or into the egg (or clutch) and incubation, or into the pre-fledging growth of the young, or the post-fledging period. Rarely, it may even invest considerable energy in the post-breeding period, attending and displaying on the site even though the young have gone. Occasionally, there may be basic differences even between closely related species, as in the Gannet and boobies, the former being the only sulid whose young are not fed after they have fledged. Or again, the Grey-headed Albatross has a cycle longer than the Black-browed's by one month, and breeds less than once per year, whilst the Black-browed breeds annually. Yet the two species form mixed colonies. Clearly, the main factor determining a species' strategy will be the nature of its food and feeding method, as the following examples show.

The pre-laying period, between return to the colony and egg-laying, has been somewhat neglected in seabird studies. It is a busy and exacting period, during which the site is established or re-established, the pair formed or re-formed, the nest site prepared and the female helped to reach egg-laying condition. Extremely few seabirds pair at sea, before entering the colony. Usually, the male arrives first and takes up his station. In the Adelie Penguin, for example, in 97 per cent of pairs the male arrived first, and the same is true for albatrosses, Gannets, gulls, auks and many others. In some species, especially those in which climate and food allow the pair to spend considerable time at the site before laying, and there is keen competition for sites, the pre-laying period is extensive, for example three months in Gannets in the eastern Atlantic. Some tropical sulids, on the other hand, must usually take advantage of the temporarily favourable food supply as

Brown Booby with a chick about three weeks old.

quickly as possible, and their preliminaries may occupy no more than the three weeks or so, which is about the minimum for establishment of the territory, formation of the pair, and the development of the egg. Similarly in some auks, for example, the Guillemot, at lower latitudes, attendance at the breeding cliff begins many months before the egg is laid, although this period may be punctuated by lengthy absences. At higher latitudes, where the breeding season is greatly restricted, the pre-laying period is as short as possible, for it is more readily compressible than incubation or the chick-rearing stages. In the Adelie Penguin, for example, the mean return date was 7th November for females, and the mean egg-laying date was 15th November. In 'crested' penguins, the time between arrival of the female and the laying of the egg is just over two weeks. In penguins with considerable variation in the laying date, as the Little or Fairy Penguin, at lower latitudes, the pre-laying stage is both more variable and longer.

Continuous occupation of the breeding site, so that, in effect, the pre-laying period stretches from the end of one cycle to the next laying, is known, so far as I am aware, only in one population of one species—the Brown Boobies of Ascension. In a less developed form, however, it may be much commoner, for several tropical seabirds attend their colonies loosely and sporadically throughout the year.

The honeymoon period, a device to meet the energy cost of egg production, is best developed in the procellariforms, though suspected in some other species, for instance the Little Penguin and possibly some auks. Its precise role varies. In the Wandering Albatross, the male always returns first and waits continuously at the site, for (on average) 27 days. The females come ashore only two or three times, and relatively briefly, for copulation. The male must be there, especially since the site is relatively mobile and other males are keen to copulate with the females. The Royal Albatross, which nests about a month earlier, has a pre-laying period of about 34 days. In the smaller procellariforms, in which the egg is a much greater fraction of the female's weight, the honeymoon period may be more marked. It must always be related to the species' ecological circumstances. The female Dove Prion goes off for 7–14 days, but the male visits the hole daily, to keep it free from snow and possibly to maintain ownership. Similarly the male Manx Shearwater occupies his burrow nightly whilst his mate is away. The Madeiran Storm-petrel, often breeding in unproductive waters or foraging far afield, may take up to three weeks. The Fulmar is away for about ten days.

The incubation period is related mainly to the size of the egg, which means principally its amount of yolk and hence the extent to which the chick develops before hatching and the amount of yolk reserves with which it hatches. Some procellariforms have the longest incubation periods and the largest eggs, both in absolute terms and as a proportion of the female's weight, of any seabird. The Royal Albatross's egg requires 79 days incubation, which is the record, (the Wanderer takes 78.4) and no albatross drops much below 60 days: Waved Albatross 60, Laysan Albatross 64, Black-footed 66 (the two latter often breed together in the tropics, and the difference in their incubation period, as in their cycle-length, is statistically highly significant), Black-browed 68 days, Grey-headed 72 (these two species also breed together in the antarctic, and again show significant differences). The egg of the Wandering Albatross, despite its weight of between 380–530 grams, is only 5 per cent of the female's weight, whereas that of the Manx Shearwater is 15 per cent, incubation period 51 days, and that of the Black-bellied Storm-petrel no less than 26 per cent of the female's weight, with an incubation period of 38–44 days. At such weights, the value of the pre-laying feeding period can readily be appreciated. The Grey-faced Petrel incubates its egg for 55 days, and even the tiny British Storm Petrel, whose minute egg (7 grams) is 26 per cent of the female's weight, has an incubation period of 41 days. In all these cases, it is important that the young bird should be able to withstand long periods without food at an early age, and should be able to regulate its body temperature, releasing the parents for foraging as soon as possible. Because of their unique method of manufacturing oil rather than merely feeding young on regurgitated stomach contents (the latter view is held by some, but opposed by many), the procellarids tend to have long foraging stints and thus to feed their young rather less frequently than most seabirds. Penguins lay proportionately smaller eggs than procellarids, but they are unusually heavy birds, having been released from the need to fly. For example, the King Penguin's single egg weighs only some 460 grams, or 2 per cent of the female's weight and takes only 54–55 days to hatch. The Adelie Penguin's egg weighs about 5 per cent of the female's weight, with an incubation period of 35 days, and the Magellanic Penguin's clutch of two averages 8.5 per cent of the weight of the female's weight; the first egg average is 129 grams or 4.3 per cent of the female's weight and takes about 43 days to hatch. Thus the penguin's incubation period varies very much less than the size and weight of the adults. But penguins either feed their young extremely frequently or, if they hatch before this is feasible, as in the Emperor, the adult can produce food from its own reserves for about three weeks at a time.

Seabirds whose young may have to face a period of immediate starvation tend to produce large eggs and thus to have long incubation periods. The frigatebirds are all extremely light, weighing less than half as much as one of the smaller albatrosses despite out-measuring them, but they lay eggs weighing about 6 per cent of the female's weight. This, for a pelecaniform, is considerable, and is an adaptation to this genus' long foraging stints. Again, Abbott's Booby, the slowest grower in the entire family, lays the biggest egg (up to 7.6 per cent of the female's weight) and has the longest incubation period (55 days) whilst the Red-footed Booby in the Galapagos, where food is notably erratic, lays larger eggs and has longer incubation periods

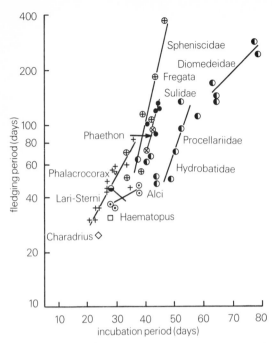

The relationship of incubation period to fledging period. From Lack (1967).

bility, resistance to starvation); and on the nature of the chick's growth. The development of the chick, from the point at which the ovum is fertilized by the sperm, right through to the achievement of maturity, is a continuum; a long incubation period is followed by slow development.

The period between hatching and fledging, where the latter is defined as flying, or in some other way leaving the site or territory, is commonly called the fledging period, and it is usually the longest component of the breeding cycle. Not surprisingly, very few seabirds take their newly-hatched young to sea with them, and in none at all are the young wholly able to feed themselves, as the young of gallinaceous birds do. The plankton feeding murrelets of the Northern Pacific take their small young to sea but they probably feed them there. The Little Auk is also a plankton feeder, but it feeds its young in the nest hole until these are well grown, bringing food in its throat pouch, which can be greatly distended. Presumably the smaller auklets would find it impractically costly in energy to fly back and forth over relatively long distances with the small amount they could carry.

Female Abbott's Booby with a chick about two months old. Note the similar pattern of plumage of the adult and chick.

than the Red-footed Booby on Christmas Island, which enjoys a more reliable, seasonal food supply. The Gannet, which has an assured and abundant food supply, lays an egg weighing only 3.4 per cent of the female's weight and taking 43.6 days to hatch, whilst the Red-foot's egg, which is much smaller in absolute terms, nevertheless takes 45 days.

Most auks produce down-clad young, and this trait is, in birds in general, associated with longer incubation periods than that of producing naked young, but auks do not commonly face early starvation threats. The Common Guillemot's egg is large (103 grams or 10.2 per cent of female's body weight) and the incubation period is about 28–30 days in the southern race and a little longer (up to 34 days) in the northern. Brunnich's Guillemot, with its more northerly distribution, lays a slightly larger egg than the Common. Similarly, the Black Guillemot's incubation period is about 30 days in Britain but longer in the Arctic.

In sum, the amount of energy devoted to the egg and incubation, in seabirds, depends mainly on factors affecting the female's energy-budget when forming the egg; on the nature of the environmental demands made on the chick when it hatches (temperature regulation, mo-

The longest fledging periods are found in those seabirds which forage far from the colony, in many cases finding difficulty in gathering enough food, and therefore feed their young relatively infrequently. Size, as such, is not the main factor in determining growth rate. Since generalizations are prone to exception, and often frustratingly abstract, I will try to make the main points by specific examples. The longest fledging periods occur in King Penguins, frigatebirds, the great albatrosses and Abbott's Booby, but for very different reasons. The King Penguin chick has to sit through the winter, having failed to grow and moult in time to get away. Its cycle thus lasts 14–16 months, of which 10–13 months is occupied by the fledging period. The decisive factor, here, is the restricted period during which it is possible for adults to feed their young adequately. To achieve annual breeding, the related Emperor, it will be recalled, had to incubate its egg in winter. The King has 'chosen' to let the chick tackle winter survival on starvation rations. Other penguins, which squeeze their breeding cycle into a summer, fledge more quickly, for example Adelie Penguin around 50 days; Little Penguin 56–70 days; Rockhopper Penguins 67–72 days (other eudyptids average around 75 days). Frigatebirds take 5–6 months to fledge, as an adaptation to periodic starvation, or, at best, a low level of feeding, though on a non-seasonal basis. Abbott's Booby takes the abnormally long period of about six months to fledge. This is a particularly intriguing strategy because Christmas Island, where this booby breeds, is not in an impoverished ocean zone. Moreover, the climate is seasonal and there would appear to be every advantage in getting the young away before the monsoon rains and wind arrive in November or December. It seems that, partly because Abbott's Booby forages far from the island, its chick shows the slow growth usually associated with this habit. In addition, the unusual habitat (the canopy of tropical rainforest) compels the young bird to remain in the nest until it can fly properly. A fall would be fatal. Since the incubation period is also unusually long, the young Abbott's cannot fledge in time to become proficient before the onset of 'winter'. Judged by the infrequency with which adults return to feed their still-dependent young during winter, it must be relatively difficult to find food, so, presumably, it would be a poor time to launch newly-fledged young. These,

therefore, have to sit it out in their jungle trees. More than 90 per cent of them starve, and the survivors, severely underweight, pick up again during the following summer before fledging more than a year after hatching. It is as though, having taken the path which ensures the ability to resist starvation, this particular adaptation becomes part of the physiology of development from the egg onwards. The consequently protracted growth period, which lands the chick into winter before it is properly equipped to face it, just has to be borne. It may be *because* the balance between recruitment and mortality is so fine that a series of bad years can seriously decrease numbers, that the population is so small. Within the same family, the Atlantic Gannet provides a telling contrast. Despite feeding well away from the colony, it has the shortest fledging period of any sulid (13 weeks), made possible by its abundant food. The latter enables it to grow and to deposit enough fat to fuel its transition to independence without any recourse to post-fledging parental feeding. Cormorants and Shags do even better, in that their fledging periods (49 and 55 days respectively) are achieved even though the parents have to feed two or three instead of the Gannet's single young, a feat enabled by their inshore feeding, which allows them to feed their young several times daily. Pelicans, though huge, also fledge their young in relatively short time (for example, 65–77 days in the White Pelican) and for much the same reason. Wandering Albatrosses require between 263–303 days, which is on average about 44 days longer than the Royal, to fledge their single chick. Its growth is retarded mainly before the primaries erupt. After that, the two species both take 100–120 days. Possibly the Wanderer uses more energy for thermo-regulation. These fledging periods far exceed those of any other seabird and may be ascribed to the combination of large size and the far-foraging feeding method of the adults with which is normally associated slow growth and resistance to starvation. The crucial importance of the latter may be inferred from the ability of the Wandering Albatross chick to survive without food for the fantastic period of 81 days (though if this information resulted from a deliberate starvation experiment, it is to be thoroughly deplored). Other albatrosses show prodigious resistance without going quite so long; 30–40 days is probably within the compass of the large and well fed young of all albatrosses,

A Southern Royal Albatross feeding an almost fully grown chick (on left), Campbell Island.

and has been demonstrated for the Laysan and Black-footed. One Wanderer fasted 'naturally' (that is the parents left it, or died) for 51 days, losing 44 per cent of its weight, and then flew away! Because of the long cycle, Wanderers breed in alternate years. The young of one season are still present in the colony when the adults of the next season come ashore to begin breeding, and this, it has been suggested, may account for the fact that young Wanderers have black backs. This serves to distinguish them from adults, and prevents them from disrupting the latter's prelaying procedures. Royals apparently manage to breed annually, although some authors state that they are biennial breeders.

The smaller antarctic albatrosses have considerably shorter fledging periods, for example Black-browed 116 days; Grey-headed Albatross 141 days, whilst those of the tropical albatrosses of comparable size are longer again, (Laysan Albatross 165 days, Waved Albatross 160–180 days). But even the small procellariforms have extraordinarily long fledging periods compared with other seabirds, for example: Storm Petrel 63 (56–73) days: Black-bellied Storm Petrel 65–71; Wilson's Storm-petrel 60; Galapagos Storm-petrel 110–118; Manx Shearwater 70 (62–76); Fulmar 46 (41–57) days. The long fledging period of the Galapagos Storm-petrel compared with most other small petrels is because,

like most Galapagos seabirds, its parents either travel further for their food or take longer to gather it so it is less well fed. The gulls have relatively short fledging periods, usually around 35–45 days, although once again the tropical gulls such as the Grey Gull, the Lava Gull, the Swallow-tailed Gull, etc. have extended fledging periods. The tropical terns, too, take a longer time to fledge than do temperate species–for example 56–63 days in the Sooty compared with 23–28 days in the Common and Arctic Terns.

Some auks have substituted care at sea for care on land. Thus the chicks of Cravieri's and Xantus's Murrelet fledge at the age of 2 or 3 days and are accompanied to sea by adults. The Common Guillemot chick spends 18–25 days on the ledge, according to locality, before it makes its dramatic twilight jump-flight, or glide, down to the sea. It is a further three weeks or more before it can make a sustained flight. The chicks vary greatly in size at fledging time, according to locality, but all are similar in plumage density and feather length. It has been claimed that adults accompany their own chicks to sea, but by colour-ringing, Tuck showed that, adults other than the parent accompany it to sea and feed it there, just as they contribute to brooding and feeding it on the ledges. Communalization of parental care is highly unusual among seabirds but it must effectively circumvent the difficulty of locating one's own chick in the frantic, twilight shrouded melée which occurs when hundreds of chicks make their leap from the packed ledges high above the sea, to land among the adults milling around at the base of the cliffs. In any case, a young captive Guillemot unaided, caught fish when 25 days old, so adult assistance may be of limited importance. Puffins, which fledge at night and without attention from adults, have a fledging period of 46–53 days, which is more than twice as long as the Guillemot's, probably because the Puffin has to fend for itself after fledging and therefore needs to be more advanced. Similarly, it appears that adult Cassin's Auklets do not accompany their young to sea and these, too, have a long fledging period (mean 45 days).

Whilst it is, in some cases, artificial to separate the period spent caring for the chick between hatching and fledging, from that spent after fledging, the two strategies, that is to continue feeding the young for an extended period after it can fly adequately or to leave it to cope unaided, are quite distinct. Mostly, the two traits split along family (or ordinal) lines, but there are notable exceptions, reflecting the divergence in feeding habits which occur within families and which then affect breeding strategy. There is no seabird order in which *all* species show post-fledging feeding.

No procellariform has evolved the habit of feeding its young after this can fly, and, indeed, some do not even feed it right up to the time of fledging, (the Manx Shearwater chick fasts for 2–18 days (average 8.5) and loses some 36 per cent of its peak weight, before fledging). No penguin, so far as is known, feeds its young after the latter has taken to the sea. In both cases, this is probably partly because the young birds do not face enormous difficulties in feeding themselves. The incredible abundance of euphasids in antarctic waters must make feeding straightforward for penguins, compared with the task which young frigatebirds face. Similarly, young albatrosses may find squid abundant enough to tide them over initial difficulties.

Within the pelecaniforms, the largest family, the cormorants and shags, continue to feed their fledged offspring for several weeks (5–6 in the Common Cormorant, between 9 and 14 or more weeks in the Common Shag). The sulids grade from no post-fledging feeding at all, to more than six months. In this family, the influence of the environment shows clearly, both between

and within species. Between species, one may contrast the Atlantic Gannet and Abbott's Booby. The young Gannet *cannot* enjoy the benefits of post-fledging feeding because, when it fledges, it is too fat to fly properly and could not possibly return to its ledge. The Gannet has taken full advantage of its abundant food by producing fat young as quickly as possible, thus getting them away, well fuelled, before seasonal deterioration of weather. Abbott's has met *its* particular problems by slowing down, rather than speeding up, the development of its single chick, and this culminates in a long period of post-fledging dependence. This is Abbott's way of beating a food regime which does not allow it to get its youngster away in one season. Within a species, the Brown Booby demonstrates the effect of environment on post-fledging feeding. Where food is reasonably dependable, it has the normal sulid habit of feeding its young for a few weeks after fledging. But on Ascension, where food is often drastically scarce, it may prolong this several-fold. The frigatebirds, feed their fledged youngsters for 6–9 months, occasionally even longer, until they have acquired the ability to forage and feed for themselves. And in some harsh environments, as in the Galapagos at times, even young

Free flying juvenile Greater Frigatebird enters the females mouth for food – often a bolus of flying fish.

which have had several months of parental subsidy starve to death once they have to fend for themselves.

The pelicans, however, do not feed their fledged youngsters, although the White Pelican has been said to do so, and Schaller saw them being fed when they were beginning to be capable of flight. Although the Brown Pelican plunge-dives, the others feed mainly by scooping, which may be less dependent on the acquisition of skilled and experience-modified coordination. The tropicbirds, however, go straight off to sea and fend for themselves, and they are plunge divers, often in highly impoverished tropical zones. In their case, the 'explanation' may be that hole nesters never return to their holes or burrows, once fledged. Perhaps, once having made the startling venture into the outer world – a transition which must have an unimaginably great impact on the young bird's senses – it is impossible for it to return. The step is behaviourally so momentous that it is irreversible. Things are obviously quite different for a chick developing in the open air. This seems to me to be the only factor which all hole-nesters have in common, and until a hole-nester which *does* have post-fledging feeding is discovered, it is all I can offer.

The gulls and terns are another family in which post-fledging feeding is important. Even the omnivorous and scavenging Herring Gull not only feeds its juvenile in the breeding territory, for five or six weeks after it can fly, but in many cases feeds it away from the territory, and has been seen to do so for seven months. The terns are all inveterate post-fledging feeders. Yet the tern's plunging cannot be more difficult than the tropicbirds!

Deferred maturity and 'rest-years'
There remains another major aspect of breeding strategy. This concerns the age at which seabirds first breed and the occurrence of 'rest-years'. Both of these have generated considerable discussion among seabird people, for both are potentially important determinants of recruitment rates and therefore of populations, and they are susceptible to fundamentally different interpretations. By husbanding strength and avoiding harmful stress, they may be considered to be devices which *maximize* the number of offspring which an individual produces in its lifetime. Or they may be means by which the recruitment rate may be *varied* in

response to the current state of the population in relation to whatever resources may be limiting; usually food or nest sites. Theoretically, stress could be important, because in a long-lived species, and most seabirds can live more than twenty years, a slight enhancement of adult mortality has a marked effect on further expectation of life, and therefore on the number of offspring that can be produced. With an adult annual mortality rate of 4 per cent, an individual has a further expectation of life, at any time, of 24 years, but at 8 per cent mortality, which after all is fairly low, life expectancy is only 11.5 years. And stress could be imposed by the demands of feeding young, and of establishing the territory and forming the pair.

At first glance, there seems no obvious pattern to deferred maturity. The Wandering and Royal Albatrosses breed for the first time at the age of 10 years, or more; the Laysan Albatross at 8 years or more; the Waved Albatross usually 4 to 5; the Fulmar 7–11; Manx Shearwater 4–6; female Short-tailed Shearwater at 5 to 7 but the male at 7 or 8 years; Leach's Storm-petrel at 4 or more; Royal Penguin at around 10 years, Adelie Penguin at 4–6 years; and the Greater Frigatebird at between 7 and 11 years (suspected). The slowest maturers among seabirds are to be found in the families instanced above. Atlantic Gannets breed first at 4 or 5 years but Cape Gannets at 2 or 3; White Pelicans at 3 or 4; Shags at 3 or 4; Cormorants at 4 or 5, occasionally 3; Herring Gulls at 3, 4 or 5 according to the nature of the colony; Red-billed Gull at 3–5, occasionally 2; Kittiwakes at 3–8 (mostly 4 or 5); Common and Arctic Terns at 3 or more usually 4 years; Sooty Tern at around 6 years (4–8, or possibly even 10); Antarctic Tern at 2 years; Guillemot at 2 or 3; Razorbill at 5 or 6, occasionally 3 or 4; and Puffin at 4 or 5. In general, seabirds take much longer than landbirds to mature. There is no relationship between size and the length of deferred maturity. A tiny petrel requires longer than a pelican and a Sooty Tern longer than a cormorant. Among the important determinants, one might expect to find the following: complexity of feeding method and/or sparsity of, or degree of competition for, food; complexity of social organization; longevity and fecundity. The general pattern of deferred maturity accords to some extent with the complex of feeding factors, in that all the groups with really long periods have to contend with one or more of the following: a highly specialized feeding technique (though this is always a dangerously subjective judgement); the need to acquire extensive 'lore'; the need to compete with other individuals.

Taking these in turn, some feeding techniques do seem simpler than others. It must be more difficult to acquire the skills of diving after strong, swift prey than swimming through a thick soup of euphasids with an open mouth, or to snatch flying fish in mid-flight than to sit on the sea, or submerge superficially, and scoop up squid from the surface layer. Some species probably require much time to learn the location of different prey species, at different seasons and under various sea and weather conditions (quite a different thing than acquiring physical skills). And such 'lore' could be critically important. Finally, if young birds have to compete with old ones, for food, there could be a premium on age and experience.

Frigatebirds score highly on difficulty of feeding technique, but not so well on 'lore', since it would often seem difficult or even impossible to acquire knowledge of favourable feeding locations. Many frigates forage widely, in mid-ocean, where availability of prey is often erratic, presumably due to fluctuations in oceanographic conditions. Nevertheless, there *are* locally food-rich areas (convergences and upwellings) in the open ocean and though these often move with the season, it may be possible to acquire useful experience of them. Also, social factors may be important (see below). Albatrosses may rely on extensive foraging journeys to known and far-flung feeding areas. There is a hint of this to be gleaned from the superficially surprising fact that, in the great albatrosses, mortality during the years of free wandering is low, but in the year in which they begin to attend the colony systematically, it suddenly shoots up. The inference may be that they have no difficulty in sustaining themselves when they have nothing to do but feed, but once they have to spend much time at the colony, 'lore' becomes extremely important, and those that have too little, die. And in albatrosses, too, there is complex social behaviour; several species are known to spend two or more seasons at the breeding colony before attempting to breed. It seems understandable that Herring Gulls should have a relatively short deferred maturity, since their omnivorous feeding habits open up many more food sources than most seabirds enjoy.

One could proceed through the remainder of the species whose deferred maturity period I have just listed, but the essence of the argument remains the same; most seabirds take several years to acquire feeding technique and 'lore'; a few take an exceptionally long time and these are difficult to explain in terms of acquisition of feeding skills.

Intraspecific feeding competition certainly occurs in many species. Adult Herring Gulls, when scavenging, dominate immatures and are highly aggressive to each other; some gulls have 'feeding territories' (stretches of coast) which they defend outside the breeding season. Carrick suggests that in Royal Penguins, young birds are unable to breed because, for some time, they are dominated by adults in the important feeding area that lies within foraging distance of the colony. Outside this, they can feed as much as they want to, but that is no good for breeding purposes. And adults that fail to reach a certain weight by the beginning of the breeding season have no chance of breeding. Whilst, no doubt, further cases could be adduced, I do not believe one could construct even a remotely convincing case for direct intraspecific competition as a sufficient factor to enforce a probationary period of many years.

Sparsity of food is also a nebulous proposition. If (as in the tropics) food is often scarce, it could only enforce long-deferred maturity if it acted differentially on young birds, and it seems next to impossible that, once adequate motor skills have been acquired, it could do so. Out of all this, therefore, only the acquisition of lore emerges as a possible cause of long deferred maturity, though motor skills might account for a year or so.

What about social factors? Could some seabirds require several years to perfect their perception of, and response to, social signals? It seems unlikely, and in any case to explain differences between species in these terms one would have to embark on a quite unjustifiable comparative exercise, interpreting one species' display as more complex than another. Why should a Herring Gull's display repertoire be considered less difficult to acquire than a frigate's?

In sum, the 'stress factor' – young birds being unacceptably stressed by breeding – does not, of course, exist as such. It is stress in feeding, stress in territory establishment, etc. Feeding stress in turn must be based on competition if it is to differentiate between age classes.

Taking the quite different line, that seabirds which live a long time do not 'need' to start breeding early, one is really suggesting that productivity is geared to population. When there are plenty of birds in relation to some limited resource, usually food or nest sites, the argument goes, productivity is scaled down, and one way of doing so is to increase the age of breeding (See population chapter).

'Rest' years, in which an adult, experienced breeder refrains from breeding, without prior loss of site or mate, are susceptible to the same two 'explanations'. Either they mitigate stress, or they control recruitment. Most of the intensively-studied seabirds appear to breed every year (or their equivalent cycle-length) under normal circumstances. But non-breeding years apparently do occur in Masked Boobies, several petrels and shearwaters, some albatrosses, auks, gulls, penguins and probably others. The trouble is that it is usually difficult to distinguish between pre-breeders, failed breeders and 'resting' breeders. At many petrel and shearwater colonies, up to 80 per cent of the birds are unemployed. In a New England colony, 20 per cent of the resident Herring Gulls had no nest, and, among gulls that returned to breed over more than four years, six females between them missed seven out of thirty-four possible breeding seasons and four males missed three out of twenty-eight. *All* of those birds nested again after the 'missed' seasons, during which they were absent from the colony. The proportion of non-breeders in a Black Guillemot colony varied from 9–33 per cent over twenty years and seemed independent of the numbers actually attempting to breed whilst in 1970, and judged by the absence of a gular pouch, 27 per cent (40000 birds) of the Cassin's Auklets on Farallon were non-breeders and had never bred. Field observations of Adelie Penguins suggest 20 per cent non-breeders at a rookery and if one assumes a stable population, this agrees closely with the figure calculated from known productivity and mortality rates. But, whilst it is true that, commonly, 20 or 30 per cent of pairs in a gannetry are non-breeders, observation of colour-ringed pairs shows that, virtually without exception, these *attempt* to breed every year. Nevertheless, it seems that 'rest-years' do occur in some species. We have no evidence about why they do so, and any

proof that breeding adults lose weight must be carefully judged against control, non-breeders, before stress is assumed, for whilst Laysan Albatrosses lose 10–15 per cent of their weight by the end of the breeding season, former breeders and immatures show a similar decline. Changes in weight in birds is often hormonally controlled as an adaptation to migration, moult, or perhaps other phenomena. In some species, the normal pattern of breeding may well be disrupted if birds fail to reach good enough condition before the breeding season and this may in fact be the commonest cause of non-breeding amongst experienced adults. But probably most of the non-breeding population are young, inexperienced birds. There are now several seabird species for which the age-structure of a breeding population is known, and also the frequency with which its members breed. One of the very best documented studies is Harvey Fisher's, on the Laysan Albatross, in which records for 13 849 breeders, observed between 1963 and 1972, showed 10 per cent 8 years old or less (these were first-time breeders), 37.9 per cent between 10 and 14 years, and 51.2 per cent over 15. No less than 31.5 per cent were over 20 years old. Fisher shows, also, that in 212 experienced pairs in which the pair bond remained intact for the several years of the study (up to 12 years for some pairs and never fewer than 10 years for the others), breeding was attempted, on average, on about 84 per cent of the years available. But the most interesting thing was that in some years everybody, without exception, bred (for instance, in 1960, 61 and 62 100 per cent, 100 per cent and 99 per cent of the 82 pairs under study, bred) whilst in others, as few as 40 per cent did so. This probably indicates the great influence of the current food situation. Fisher's fascinating data also includes an analysis of the effect of mate-changing on breeding frequency. With an unbroken pair bond the mean frequency, as just mentioned, is 84 per cent. With one change it drops to 71 per cent over the 10–13 year period of the study, whilst with two changes it is 64 per cent and with 3, only 57 per cent. The mean frequency of breeding in their first five breeding years (starting as inexperienced pairs in breeding year one) was 59 per cent – i.e. about half of them bred in any one of these five years.

So, in many, or most, seabirds, there is, in each breeding season, a significant proportion of experienced pairs that do not breed.

Moult

The replacement of feathers consumes much energy (3 per cent of body weight per day in some penguins) and seabirds, according to their differing energy budgets, have evolved several variations on the general theme. Penguins feed heavily after breeding, and then remain ashore fasting during moult, shedding everything in 3 or 4 weeks. Their core temperature rises, indicating intense metabolism, and they choose sheltered, sunny spots to reduce heat-loss. Guillemots, soon after breeding, go to sea and drop all their flight feathers within a few days (as, also, do Razorbills) and then take about 63 days to grow a new set. They are flightless until their new primaries are about three-quarters grown, which takes 40–50 days (this is highly variable, but, in general, higher latitude birds of the same species, complete their moult faster than do those from lower latitudes). Cassin's Auklet begins moult at *any* stage of the nesting cycle but may suspend it whilst rearing young. By contrast, Gannets moult three or four primaries each year, suspending their moult when they commence the breeding cycle and *resuming* it soon after the chick hatches, thus giving themselves the joy of long foraging flights with incomplete wings! The big gulls commence moult towards the end of the breeding cycle, whilst feeding large young, and take about 4 months to complete it.

Many, perhaps most, seabirds moult when free of breeding activities, or, if migrants, after completing their journey (as in the case of several shearwaters). But there are many exceptions. Most surprising, perhaps, is the habit common to several tropical species, even including some populations from impoverished areas, of moulting whilst breeding. Some Galapagos petrels moult wing feathers whilst still rearing a chick and may not complete moult until shortly after their return to the colony for the next breeding season. This spreads the load over a long period. Ashy Storm-petrels start body moult when the egg hatches, then after another 40 days begin to moult tail feathers, and 30 days after that, primaries and secondaries. Moult takes so long (257 days) that most birds are still moulting the last two or three primaries at the beginning of the next breeding cycle. Leach's Storm-petrel follows much the same pattern, but differs in the intervals between moulting the several parts; it

shows little overlap between moult and migration, and between primary moult and breeding, whereas the Ashy shows considerable overlap. Correspondingly, as Humphreys has pointed out, Leach's is a long-distance migrant, largely in the open sub-tropical ocean and the Ashy Storm-petrel is a short-ranging, sedentary species of sub-arctic coastal waters, and its moult is apparently unique among the storm-petrels so far studied. Similarly, Bridled Terns finish their primary moult just before beginning a new cycle and start again when the chick hatches. Aububon's Shearwater on the other hand begins to moult immediately after a breeding attempt, no matter whether failed or successful, and begins a new attempt once it has completed moult. Galapagos Red-footed Boobies may moult some primaries whilst feeding young, but frigatebirds apparently never do. Tropicbirds have a complete annual moult which stops during breeding. In Sooty Terns breeding semi-annually, some replaced all primaries in the interval between breeding attempts whereas others replaced only some. Successful, annually-breeding Sooty Terns were absent for 6 months after breeding, during which they underwent one complete moult and started a second, before suspending it at the beginning of the next breeding attempt. Similarly, the Fairy Tern moults only when not breeding, and one complete replacement occupies 5.5–7 months whilst the bird is at sea. In an a-seasonal environment, Fairy Terns can begin a new breeding cycle whenever moult has been completed, much as in Audubon's Shearwater. There are thus all sorts of variants and there probably is no general explanation for overlap in breeding and moult in areas where food is scarce (where it is super-abundant there is no problem).

In general, birds at higher latitudes speed-up moult because this is often favoured by selection pressure. The three auks, Guillemot, Razorbill and Puffin provide an instance, for Guillemots often return early to their ledges and this depends on completion of moult. Razorbills return later (even though remaining further inshore than Guillemots) and Puffins later still, and the two latter take longer to complete their moult. But there are several other selection pressures in addition to early return to the colony.

The moult of body feathers is often subject to different selection pressures from the wing moult and may take the form of a pre-nuptial moult which produces the breeding plumage.

Breeding biology
eggs, clutches and mortality

We have now discussed habitats, colonies and general breeding strategies; it remains to consider eggs, clutches, breeding success and mortality.

The egg and clutch

Seabird eggs vary adaptively in size, shape, shell-structure and colour or markings. The largest eggs are laid by species which forage far from the colony and/or breed in impoverished zones and produce downy young; as a proportion of the female's weight, some procellariforms, at 26 per cent, lay larger eggs than any other bird. The smallest seabird eggs, in proportion to female weight, are laid by large penguins, followed by pelicans, cormorants and Atlantic Gannets, all of which are heavy birds. Shape is probably not usually of great significance. Most seabird eggs are more pointed at one end than the other, and this is carried to extremes in the Guillemot, where it has value in reducing the tendency of the egg to roll off the ledge; instead, it is more likely to pivot, although many do roll off.

Colour and markings in seabird eggs has two possible functions: individual recognition and camouflage. Individual recognition might be important in species which nest densely and have little or no nest, but from the 'selfish gene's' point of view, it would be a clever ploy to let somebody else rear the chick, always provided that the foster parent did not prejudice the chick's chances of survival by caring for it less well than the real parent. In any case, all we know is that Guillemots appear to recognize and prefer their own eggs, and so do Royal Terns. Razorbills, by contrast, nest more solitarily and apparently do not discriminate against strange eggs. Camouflage is not usually important, except in some of the ground-nesting terns, especially those, for example the Little Tern, with widely scattered nests on a background (such as pebbles) which eggs can simulate. Hole-nesters usually have white eggs, or (as in the Puffin) these retain vestiges of the markings which occurred in the open-nesting auk ancestral to the Puffin. Storm Petrel eggs are mainly white with a few reddish spots at the large end, and shearwater eggs are white. But many open-nesters have white or pale, plain eggs, for example, Fulmars, albatrosses, Gannets, shags and penguins. In all these, camouflage is unnecessary, and the presumably primitive colour of the egg has been retained.

Egg-shells vary in structure and thickness in the different orders of birds. Usually the shell comprises 10–12 per cent of the fresh egg weight. Gannet eggs have exceptionally thick (though not unusually dense) shells, to withstand the pressure exerted by the heavy adult as it stands on the egg to incubate it underfoot. In cross-section, however, there is no obvious difference in structure between the shell of an albatross egg and that of a Gannet; both have simple, round shell pores, with funnel-shaped openings. Most pelecaniform eggs are unusual in that the shell has a thick limy cover. But in addition to differences between species, egg-shell thickness varies within species, according to locality, for it is affected by the amount of mineral salts obtainable by the female. When calcium, phosphorous and magnesium are short, shells are thinner. Apparently, the shells of Brunnich's Guillemot eggs from the Murman coast are only half as thick as those from Novaya Zemlya. This example shows the complexity of adaptations, for it seems that the guillemot nest sites in the former area are predominantly soft, whereas those of the latter are bare rock, the inference being that thin shells would perhaps often break. The contents of the egg also vary between groups. Birds with downy and/or starvation-resistant young have proportionately more yolk. Some idea of the importance of the yolk as a food reserve for the chicks may be gained from the fact that they hatch with half the original yolk still available as food.

Where clutches of more than one egg are laid, there is often a marked difference in size. Usually, as in Brown Boobies, cormorants, gulls and terns, the first egg is larger than subsequent ones, but in the eudyptes penguins the second egg is markedly heavier than the first—in the Macaroni Penguin the second egg averages 71 per cent heavier than the first. Except in the Rockhopper, the first egg is usually lost before it hatches and may be rejected by the adult even before the second egg has been laid. It appears to be functionless and is presumably a relict. Times have changed but the penguins haven't. It sometimes hatches, but the chick does not survive beyond the guard stage. The Yellow-eyed Penguin also normally lays two eggs, but they are not markedly dissimilar in size, and experienced adults usually raise two chicks. In the Brown and Masked Boobies the second egg is a valuable insurance against the loss of the first chick, and usually hatches. The smaller chick is then ejected by its brother. Similarly in the Antarctic Skua, two eggs are laid but rarely are two chicks reared; hunger causes the first-born to attack its sibling.

The commonest clutch among seabirds is the single egg. Two egg clutches are commoner than three and only two boobies, shags, cormorants and occasionally pelicans, some terns and some gulls, lay three or four. So in comparison with many landbirds, seabirds lay small clutches; only some of the sea-ducks, for example the eider ducks, lay large clutches but in them, the young are merely shepherded by the adults, much as in gallinaceous birds which also produce large clutches.

A basic aspect of clutch size is its relation to foraging. As David Lack showed, birds which tend to feed far from the nest lay smaller clutches than those which feed nearby, and this relationship is especially evident in seabirds. All the procellariforms lay but a single egg and with two exceptions, which in a sense are not valid since they later reduce the brood to one, no far-foraging tropical seabird lays more than one egg (Red-footed Booby, tropicbirds, Sooty Tern, Swallow-tailed Gull, etc., etc.). Within families or genera, this same trend, namely to reduce brood size to the minimum if feeding frequency

Female Gentoo Penguin at nest with four chicks. This unusually large brood must be due to the adoption of two strangers.

is low, is evident. In the sulids the Peruvian Booby lays the largest clutch, (two to four, usually three) and is exceptional in having the multitudes of anchovies in the cold upwelling which bathes the shores of Peru. Next comes the Blue-footed, which lives on the fringes of productive areas, and lays one to three eggs, usually two. The three tropical boobies (Masked, Red-footed and Brown) either invariably lay one egg (Red-footed) or lay two, but reduce the brood to one. Either way, they have only one chick to feed. The remainder of the family also lay single eggs and in each case this habit can be related to feeding. Thus the Gannets are committed to rapid growth and the laying-down of large fat reserves which (at least for the African and Australasian Gannets) would be difficult with more than one chick, and, at the worst time of year, Abbott's Booby finds it extremely difficult to feed even one chick. In this entire family, therefore, brood size is unquestionably determined by the number of young that the parents can support.

In penguins, the King and Emperor, which are the only penguins to lay single-egg clutches, obviously could not support two youngsters through the leanest periods in their cycle—as it is, the King chicks are kept at starvation level and the Emperors have to moult whilst part-grown and living on fat, in order to achieve independence at a propitious time. In gulls, it is the Swallow-tail of the tropical and often impoverished Galapagos waters, that has reduced its clutch. The Grey Gull of the arid Peruvian desert, which has to fly long distances to the coast to feed, sometimes lays only a single egg (it often lays two, but it is thought to be in the process of evolving a single-egg clutch). In terns, the inshore feeding Arctic or Common has two chicks, but the pelagic Sooty Tern, only one. Nor can I think of any species which forages far from the nest and brings infrequent feeds, but nevertheless lays clutches of two or more eggs. Perhaps the nearest approach is the Ancient Murrlet, which is a relatively offshore feeder (incubation shifts are unusually long, for an auk, at 72 hours) but lays two-egg clutches whereas the inshore-feeding Marbled Murrelet, nesting on the same island, lays one-egg clutches. It seems that the Ancient Murrelet's food is patchy in distribution and may require fairly long trips to locate.

Clutch size is certainly affected, too, by the amount of food available to the adult female, but this factor does not determine whether a species lays one egg or more; it merely determines whether the clutch size is larger or smaller than average. In other words, there probably is no seabird which lays only one egg but which could rear two or three young if only the female could find enough food to form the eggs. Many landbirds far outstrip any seabird in the weight of their clutch as a proportion of female weight. But the effect of food on clutch size was nicely shown, in the Red-billed Gull, by massive egg-loss. This led the birds to replace their eggs, and relaying coincided with the flush of euphasids which normally greets the newly hatched chick. As a result, 25 per cent of replacement clutches were larger than the first clutches. Similarly, in the Long-tailed Skua, clutch size is related to the abundance of the lemmings upon which it feeds.

Some nest sites clearly would be incapable of holding two young. This applies to most holes or burrows, but presumably, if the more important factor (food) allowed, larger burrows could be dug. This would not apply to natural holes, such as tropicbirds use, which are often in short supply even though small ones suffice, and would be much shorter if only large ones could be used. But again, food is the factor which determines their clutch size, and the choice of hole follows. Guillemot chicks are very susceptible to chilling for the first ten days or more, and adults could not adequately brood two. Whether, however, they could make enough flights to and from their feeding grounds, to sustain two young, is in any case doubtful.

Both the egg (where it is single) and the clutch, are affected by the age of the female and by her status and condition. Eggs become broader as the female grows older and they also increase in volume until the female reaches middle-age, after which they begin to decrease. Similarly, clutches become larger as the female grows older, and then become smaller. Four-year old Adelie penguins, for example, lay clutches of one egg, whereas six-year olds lay clutches averaging 1.92. But, although older females are more successful than those breeding for the first-time (indeed, in some species, such as Guillemots, first eggs are rarely if ever successful), the difference is probably not due to egg size. The smaller eggs of *old* females are probably as successful as the ones she used to lay.

Gulls, at least, incubate the normal clutch better than any other seabird, it is therefore interesting that the Western Gull, which lays three eggs, has been shown to have the highest hatching success at this figure (it was tested with clutches of one to seven eggs). Similarly, the Herring Gull hatches fewer chicks per egg from smaller than from larger clutches. Apart from the effect of clutch size on the efficacy of incubation, there is evidence that, in the Herring Gull, it is specifically the third egg of the clutch, which is 11 per cent smaller than the first egg, that suffers heavier mortality than the others. It also suffers heavier mortality after hatching, but *only* during the first week of the chick's life. It is during this week, anyway, that over half of all the post-hatching mortality occurs, which shows that pressure is most intense then. The third egg is simply less able to withstand this pressure. This is, at least, partly because it hatches last. If it is transferred to a foster nest in which it hatches first, it suffers less mortality than otherwise. But survival of Herring Gull chicks on Skokholm was closely related to hatching weight. Chicks dying at *any* age were previously lighter than those that survived. Similarly, early mortality in the Kittiwake and Shag may be due to the size and quality of the yolk. Much of this detailed and fascinating work on the Herring Gull has been carried out by Jasper Parsons, on the Isle of May, Scotland.

Clutch size varies adaptively. The Shag, for example, lays on average 3.07 eggs, but on Lundy, in the Bristol Channel, the average clutch size varied annually by up to 0.4 of an egg. On the other hand, in the Farne Islands, the average clutch size of the Shag and the Kittiwake did not vary between 1955 and 1972. Presumably this reflects feeding conditions prior to egg-laying. Clutch size varies, too, on a seasonal basis. Almost always, later clutches are smaller than early ones. The Kelp Gull averages 2.3 throughout, but there are more one- and two-egg clutches as the season progresses. The Kittiwake's clutch also shows a seasonal decline, and, although that of the Shag does not, its egg volume decreases (a compensatory effect). In other words, where clutch size varies markedly with season, egg volume varies little, and vice-versa. In the Kittiwake, at least, one reason for later females laying smaller eggs is that they are smaller, lighter birds and therefore probably in poorer condition than the early birds. Similarly, in the Grey-faced Petrel, there is a strong relationship between the weight of the individual female and the weight of the egg. In the Laughing Gull, successive eggs in the clutch are lighter, probably due to the female's decreasing food reserves. On the other hand, in the Shag the first egg of a clutch of three is the smallest, the second is largest and the third intermediate. Clutch-size, egg size and shape, are to some extent hereditary, which gives natural selection the chance to favour advantageous genes.

The chick

When discussing breeding strategies, I tried to show how the rate of development is closely related to the species' feeding ecology. Some chicks grow rapidly, others slowly; some lay down enormous pre-fledging fat deposits, others do not. It must be added that young seabirds vary enormously in the pattern of growth. Rarely, if ever, do all the parts (bill, wings, tail, feet, etc.) grow at the same rate. The feet may grow extremely rapidly, as in the murrelets that go to sea at the age of two days, or the bill may grow to adult proportions more slowly than the wings. There is usually a fairly obvious advantage in the adopted pattern of growth. For example, the wings of tropical boobies continue to grow at the prescribed rate regardless of fluctuations in food, whilst the bill does not. This enables the young bird to fledge without delay, thus furthering its chances of augmenting its food supply. Most penguins reach independence with feet and flippers almost fully grown, but adult body weight is achieved during the first year and in the Snares Island Penguin, the large bill is developed later still. In the Double-crested Cormorant, the growth of feet and legs slows down after the first week whilst the bill and particularly the forearms grow most rapidly late in the nesting period. The bird's viscera do not necessarily grow in parallel with its weight. The digestive organs, as one might expect, grow particularly rapidly in the first week, when the length of the alimentary tract triples. After that, it takes thirty more days to double.

The peak-demand period, so far as food is concerned, is usually just as the feathers are growing and the chick is exercising its wings. Soon afterwards, its weight typically declines from the peak. In the Double-crested Cormorant, food intake peaks at four weeks and a pair of adults with an average brood must exert twice the effort of a non-breeding bird to secure enough food. In species such as the Manx Shearwater, which lay down much fat, the chick may at one stage weigh almost twice as much as the adult.

Young seabirds, especially if fed irregularly, have an enormous capacity for food and an equally great resistance to starvation. For much of their growth period, they can fluctuate from twice the average weight for a given age, to about half of it. The ability to withstand 2, 3 or even 4 weeks without food is not uncommon among large seabird young, and some species can fast far longer. In a fluctuating environment, this can be extremely useful. The frequency with which young are fed is determined by the nature of the species' food and foraging behaviour. Seabirds which travel far, whether or not their food is dependable, can feed their young less frequently than species which hunt locally, and those which must gather plankton cannot shuttle back and forth as rapidly as fish-eaters foraging the same distance from base. Even within a species, local conditions can be important, and the following examples are merely an indication of the scale of differences. Young Atlantic Gannets are fed about twice per day; Kittiwakes just over three times; puffins, guillemots and Razorbills between three and

Sooty Tern

Red-tailed Tropicbird

Atlantic Gannet

Abbott's Booby

Herring Gull

The development of the adult plumage in seabirds (simplified into downy chick, feathered chick and adult). Usually feathered young differ markedly from adults.

158

Kittiwake

four times; Little Auks more than five times; tysties (Black Guillemots) at least a dozen times and in some places, two dozen; Common, Arctic and Sandwich Terns feed each chick about once per *hour*; Black Terns as often as fifteen times an hour; Wandering Albatrosses once each 3.5 days; Manx Shearwaters 1.7 times per day and King Penguins two or three times a day. Obviously, the growth characteristics of the young, and hence the breeding strategy of the species, depend on their food, and some of these links have been explored elsewhere.

Most seabird chicks are born somewhat intermediate between the fully nidifugous state (in which they are downy, extremely active and usually competent feeders) and the nidicolous state (naked and helpless). Gull chicks are downy and active but totally dependent on adults for food. Albatross, petrel, and shear-water chicks are downy, but may be totally inactive (within the burrow) or able to walk only to a very limited extent, as in albatrosses. The only downy pelecaniform chicks belong to tropicbirds; the remainder are essentially naked. One of the major hazards is chilling or overheating, and in most species the adult must provide either warmth or shade for two to four weeks after the chick hatches. The tropical Laysan and Black-footed Albatross chicks achieve the ability to control their temperature at the age of 18–20 days; tropical boobies between 20–30 days; frigates 23–35 days. The lethal body temperature is extremely high–higher than in even the best-adapted desert

Little Shearwater feeding chick at night in its burrow amongst rocks.

mammal. A chick of the Grey Gull recovered from a body temperature of 45°C, but at 47°C it died. Again, if this was done deliberately, I would much rather do without the information.

Productivity and mortality

I must now say something about the balance sheet of breeding. How successful is it in terms of young reared, and where and how does the mortality fall? It must be stressed that the figures I will quote cannot always be taken as typical for the species in every locality and every year, but they are broadly comparable.

Birds vary greatly in the number of young reared per 100 eggs (or equivalent) laid. Disregarding, for the moment, the relationship between productivity and population regulation, it is easy to illustrate the large differences that occur between species in breeding success and productivity. Taking breeding success as the proportion of eggs that give rise to independent young (not a completely satisfactory definition but the best simple one), one may cite the Atlantic Gannet, with a breeding success of 75–85 per cent, and, in the same genus, Abbott's Booby with one of less than 10 per cent. But such a comparison could be seriously misleading since, when they fledge, young Gannets still have their major risks to face and most will die, whereas when young Abbott's Boobies finally leave the nesting area, the few survivors may be relatively safe. So, in order to embrace the topic of breeding success, one must consider hatching success (chicks hatched from eggs laid), fledging success (chicks fledged, that is free-flying, from those hatched) and success to independence (independent, viable young produced, from eggs laid). In the example of the Gannet, I am strictly correct in calling the fledged youngster independent, but would be incorrect in implying that it is viable, even though the word 'independent' is often taken to mean this. So it is difficult to define, satisfactorily, the 'simple' matter of breeding success.

Hatching success can reach more than 95 per cent in a particular year and can remain consistently in this region. The Atlantic Gannet has achieved 96 per cent, and remains around 90 per cent year after year, but most species fall below this (for example: Manx Shearwater 80 per cent, Fulmar 52–73 per cent, Giant Petrel 57 per cent, Shag 69–73 per cent, Snow Petrel 50 per cent, Cape Pigeon 52 per cent, Wilson's Storm-petrel 50 per cent, Wandering Albatross 72 per cent, Grey-headed Albatross 54 per cent, Black-browed 39 per cent, Double-crested Cormorant 60 per cent, Herring Gull 56–92 per cent, Black-Headed Gull 75–78 per cent, penguins around 80 per cent [that is, hatch at least one egg from the clutch of two], Sooty Tern 75 per cent, Common Tern 60–80 per cent plus, Razorbill 36–69 per cent, Brunnich's Guillemot 84 per cent, Cassin's Auklet 77 per cent, Little Auk 65 per cent, Greater Frigatebird about 35 per cent).

The causes of egg loss are: interference by birds of the same species; inadequate physiological condition of a parent; adverse climatic or economic conditions; predation; accidental loss; infertility. Interference by conspecifics is to some extent inevitable in colonial nesters; there are always altercations between neighbours and rivals, and in some species, notably frigates but also boobies and some petrels, such as the Galapagos Storm-petrel, and probably others, unemployed birds, particularly males, can create a deal of havoc in a breeding colony by attempting to usurp the nest-site, or to interact with incubating females. Even in non-colonial species, such as the Carrion Crow, interference by conspecifics was found to be a significant cause of nesting failure. Synchronized breeding probably reduces the likelihood of interference.

Undoubtedly, the internal state of the breeding adult affects its incubation behaviour, but beyond this self-evident fact it is hard to go. We know that young, inexperienced birds often incubate fitfully and ineptly, and that, if we can generalize from Shags and Kittiwakes, 'poor-quality' birds (lighter) are less successful at hatching their eggs than good-quality birds. It seems reasonable to suppose that these birds are hormonally or metabolically less adequate than the others, and that they are simply less good at everything including incubation. Probably, successful breeding demands absolute fitness and, as in the Royal Penguin, a small deficiency in fat, and therefore energy, can defeat a breeding attempt. On the other hand, it could be that a specific hormonal deficiency, part of the internal control of reproductive behaviour, is sometimes responsible. Anybody who has watched seabirds intently must have noticed the difference between the committed territory-owner and the desultory one; the strongly-bonded pair and the weaker one; the bird intent on incubating and obviously 'soaking-up' the stimuli flowing from the nest and eggs, and the slightly bored incubator. And, in comparable fashion, some birds are better parents to their chicks. These things are all indicative of the underlying state of the bird, but it is hard to make the idea of 'breeding drive' clear-cut and rigorous. Detailed measurements of behaviour and assessment of physical condition is relevant here. Coulson and his co-workers have shown for the Kittiwake that 'fitter' birds rear more young, but, notwithstanding this extra effort, these parents survive better than poor-quality birds outside the breeding season.

The breeding effort can be totally disrupted by climatic and economic adversity. For example, in the high Arctic, in bad ice years, Guillemots go through the preliminaries of breeding but, in the main, fail to nest. In the Antarctic, burrowing species too fragile to scrape away drifted snow and ice (for example, Wilson's Storm-petrel and the Snow Petrel) can suffer heavy loss of eggs or young. Many petrels leave their eggs unattended for quite long periods, during which this may happen. Of 82 Wilson's Storm-petrel eggs laid in marked burrows on Signy Island, in the Antarctic 53 failed to hatch; 17 were drifted over with snow and subsequently deserted; 13 chilled due to interruption of incubation; 11 were deserted by adults for reasons other than snowfalls (perhaps failure to feed adequately, or low breeding 'drive') and 12 disappeared without trace. This shows the hazards of this particular environment. In the tropics, the sudden withdrawal of food, due to oceanographic changes, not uncommonly leads to the wholesale desertion of eggs. The adult will incubate for two or three times as long as its normal stint, but then deserts. This happened to the Red-footed Boobies I studied on Tower Island in the Galapagos, to the Blue-footed Boobies on Hood, and to the Brown and Masked Boobies on Ascension Island.

Predation can be a significant cause of egg-loss. Few species are cannibals, but among them, the Herring Gull takes many eggs and chicks in some colonies. Frigates, too, can be notable predators. In one Sooty Tern colony on Christmas Island (Pacific) an estimated 20000 eggs were laid in the last week of May, and by 12 July only 12 chicks and 248 rotten eggs remained. Frigates and cats were responsible, but mainly in the chick-stage. On the island as a whole, hardly any young were reared from the estimated 3.5 million eggs laid in one breeding season. Guillemots and other auks lose eggs to Herring Gulls; Peruvian Boobies to Turkey Vultures; Black-headed Gulls to Carrion Crows and so on, whilst many tern, gull and auk colonies are vulnerable to mammalian predators. On Atpatok Island, fourteen foxes lived off one guillemot colony. But, with a few, perhaps, notable exceptions, I believe it is easy to over-estimate the significance of predation on seabird eggs. Except where man has introduced pests such as pigs, rats, cats dogs, mink, etc., predation is usually insignificant. Only a small number of 'specialist' robbers are involved and in most species, such as Puffins, Little Auks, petrels and penguins, that are well known to suffer from the attentions of skuas, great gulls, Giant Petrels etc., it is the adults or young, rather than the eggs, that are important prey items. Furthermore, a false picture can easily be obtained by witnessing predation which, basically, is the result of interference or disturbance by man and his associates.

Accidents and infertility together account for only a fraction of the total loss. Guillemots lose thousands of eggs due to adults flying off the ledges in alarm, taking eggs with them, or knocking them off, but they are exceptional in laying eggs on narrow ledges without a nest. Infertility appears to account for, at most, around 5–10 per cent of egg loss. Few workers can give precise figures, and most tend to lump genuinely infertile eggs with those killed by chilling (or heating), which, again, can often be artefacts due to disturbance.

Moving now, to fledging success, that is, the proportion of young that achieve free-flight, or its equivalent, from those *hatched*, one finds that it is often extremely high. Gannets fledge, on average, about 92 per cent of chicks that hatch. The tropical boobies show much greater variation, from, in the Brown Booby, with 81 per cent success on Christmas Island (Indian Ocean) and Kure Atoll (Pacific) to 25 per cent on Ascension (Atlantic Ocean), though these are not all average figures over a run of years. Cormorants and shags are highly successful, for example, Common Shag 90–95 per cent, Double-crested Cormorant 95 per cent. Albatrosses usually do very well (around 80 per cent for Grey-headed and Black-browed, 81 per cent for the Wanderer and 50–80 per cent even for the Waved Albatross of the Galapagos). The

Giant Petrel achieves about 75 per cent, Manx Shearwater 95 per cent, Short-tailed Shearwater over 90 per cent, and Fulmar 60–86 per cent. The small petrels usually do less well. Over three years, Wilson's Storm-petrel on Signy fledged only 45 per cent of eggs hatched, and these were all in one year, leaving the other two years totally unsuccessful for the samples studied; the Snow Petrel was no better. In the Galapagos, the Dark-rumped or Hawaiian Petrel fledged less than 5 per cent of eggs hatched, but here, Black Rats were probably responsible. Sometimes, figures are given merely as 'breeding success' (fledged from laid), and this is so in the following cases (all procellariiforms): 26–59 per cent in Audubon's Shearwater, 39–58 per cent in the Southern Fulmar, 33–65 per cent in the Cape Pigeon and 30 per cent in the Madeiran Storm-petrel.

Adelie Penguins had a fledging success of 62 per cent up to the crèche stage, but Chinstraps had 84 per cent fledging success on Signy. King Penguin chicks suffer considerable mortality – probably as high as 75 per cent in some localities. Some gulls are extremely successful. Kittiwakes have the highest fledging success, at 90 per cent; Black-headed Gulls fledged 50–74 per cent of chicks hatched on the Ribble salt marshes in England but less than 10 per cent in some years at Ravenglass; Herring Gulls fledged 31–41 per cent on Skokholm, but as low as 20 per cent in New England. In the Seychelles, Sooty Terns fledged 73 per cent, whereas on Ascension it was only a fraction of this. Arctic Tern chicks in Spitzbergen suffered 75 per cent mortality due to apparent food shortage (1970); Common Terns fledged 34 and 55 per cent in 1971 and 1972, the low figure being due mainly to the chilling of chicks by rain, but elsewhere, terns often do much better, for example on Coquet Island, the Common Tern had an overall breeding success, in 1967 (the best of a three-year study) of 71.3 per cent whilst the Arctic, Roseate and Sandwich achieved 79.4 per cent, 92 per cent and 91.1 per cent respectively. Sandwich Terns vary enormously from year to year, due to their drastic reaction to disturbance. Among the auks, the Pigeon Guillemot averaged 62 per cent fledging success (54–74 per cent) over four years; razorbill 36–61 per cent on Skokholm; Brunnich's Guillemot 94 per cent on Prince Leopold Island, Cassin's Auklet 66 per cent, Little Auk in Greenland 77 per cent, Tufted Puffin 66 per cent and Rhinoceros Auklet 62 per cent. Most of these are average figures, and are subject, in some species, to considerable variation from year to year. An intriguing cause of failure in the Rhinoceros Auklet, one year, was its habit of feeding its young on fish, Pacific Sauries, which were too big! Usually, massive failure is due to shortage of food due to unusually bad weather.

Juvenile Ascension Island Frigatebird seizing Sooty Tern chick. Frigate depredations can account for colossal numbers of tern chicks in a large colony.

I believe this list, tedious as it may be, is necessary in order to convey the extent of mortality among young seabirds. As with egg loss, its causes are many: predation; starvation; climatic and even parental inadequacy.

Many more chicks, than eggs, are lost through predation. On Christmas Island (Pacific) between 6–11 July, daily, there were between 50 and 100 frigatebirds snatching chicks in one small area of a Sooty Tern colony. By 30 August, from an estimated 600 000 eggs laid in the entire group, only 25 chicks survived. Clearly, this is not a representative case, and in fact cats and humans were also involved. Gulls and skuas are notorious predators. One pair of Herring Gulls took some 550 tern chicks on Forvie Sands (Aberdeenshire) in one year, and on Manan Island (Maine) Herring and Greater Black-backed Gulls took between 0.48 and 1.2 chicks *per pair*, from Arctic and Common Terns. On Dun, St Kilda, 34–40 pairs of Greater Black-backs took some 2700 Puffins in one year, but on North Rona, 1800 pairs of Black-backs took only 400 Puffins from the large colony there. Guillemot chicks are vulnerable to gulls when fledging, which is why they do so at dusk, and partly, perhaps, why they synchronize their fledging. On Bear Island the frequency of predation was lowest, per chick, at peak fledging time, due to a swamping-out effect on the gulls, etc. Even burrow-nesting auks may be at risk if the burrow is short. Gulls have been seen dragging out young Cassin's Auklets. Antarctic Skuas are feared by all the small petrels of the Antarctic and penguin chicks are much at risk from them and from Giant Petrels. Carrick indicates that, among Royal Penguins, any chicks late in joining the crèche are doomed. Whilst Spurr recorded 45 per cent of Adelie Penguin chicks lost to skuas. But as in most cases of direct predation, the effect on the productivity of the colony is negligible.

Starvation in the nest is not usually a threat to young seabirds. After all, their breeding strategies have evolved especially to ensure that the young can be fed. But there are exceptions, principally but by no means entirely, among tropical seabirds. Directly, food shortage kills many young frigates, boobies, tropicbirds, Sooty Terns etc. in some impoverished areas, and indirectly endangers more, by requiring both parents to forage, thus exposing chicks to risk from predators and possibly extremes of temperature. Even in less demanding regions,

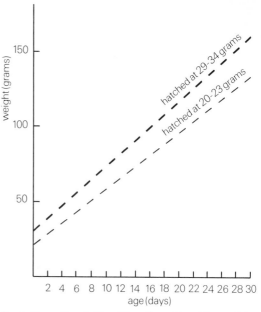

Sooty Tern, Seychelles. The effect of hatching weight on subsequent growth. After Feare (1978).

there is often little margin between enough and insufficient food, and large-scale failure and even desertion has been recorded in some auks, the Australasian Gannet and others. Experienced parents, in many species, are able to rear more young than are inexperienced adults. Royal Penguins aged 5–8 years reared only 5.6 per cent of 390 eggs, and almost every intensive study reveals that inexperienced parents have a lower breeding success. For example, three, four and five-year old Common Terns were less successful than six-year-olds; three-year-old Arctic Terns are generally unsuccessful; young Kittiwakes and Gannets are less successful than older ones and so on. But not all of their failure is due to inadequate food-gathering. Indeed, in the Gannet, none is so due. Parental inadequacy can work in other ways (see below). Most of the chick mortality, in almost all species, occurs in the first week or so after hatching, when the young are least resistant to starvation, and, often, unable to cope with heat or cold.

Highly seasonal and synchronous breeders are sometimes subject to heavy chick mortality as a result of bad weather. Young terns are susceptible to chilling from rain and young Gannets too big to be brooded, but still downy, sometimes suffer heavily.

Parental inadequacy is perhaps the most interesting and least expected cause of mortality among small chicks. As with incubation, the behaviour patterns associated with care of the chick take time to mature, and young parents simply perform the requisite behaviour imperfectly. The requirement may be transferring the chick to the top of the webs, as in the Gannet, or feeding the young chick 'skilfully', or brooding it properly. Whatever it is, the chick suffers for the parent's ineptitude. Usually, though, the exact nature of the inadequacy is not known. Nor is it merely that inexperienced birds are lighter and less fit than older ones. Even heavy five to six year old Royal Penguins do not usually succeed in rearing their chick, though thereafter, weight becomes crucially important.

The female's nutritional status clearly influences the weight of her egg(s) and therefore the chick's survival, but the male, too, is important. He has to share in feeding the young, and in some species his performance during courtship-feeding influences the weight of the female's eggs. This applies to the Red-billed Gull and also to the Common Tern (and probably others). Nisbet has made the interesting suggestion that the male tern's performance could even be used by the female as a predictor of his future performance as a parent. If he feeds her well, he is likely to feed the chicks well, too.

Parental adequacy in chick care obviously involves the same reproductive 'drive' that I mentioned when discussing incubation. Internal and external stimuli are involved in producing the state, or motivation, that one may call 'drive'. It is therefore not surprising that colonial seabirds are influenced by the level of social activity in the colony. If this is low, an important contributory factor is correspondingly weak. This, I believe, is partly why breeding success is relatively low in small colonies. For example, the Grey-headed and Black-browed Albatrosses nest on Macquarie Island, but in very small numbers, and in one colony of twelve pairs, only one young was reared in five years. One could multiply instances, but unfortunately there are usually factors other than simply colony size which could be influential and which are difficult to disentangle.

Fidelity to site and mate

Many seabirds are faithful to the same site and mate in successive breeding attempts. For example, in the Gannet, the male (if alive) returns to last year's site in 94 per cent of cases, and moves site in only 6 per cent, whilst the female returns in 88 per cent and moves in 12 per cent. Kittiwakes are similarly faithful to site and mate, and so, among others, are Fulmars, Manx Shearwaters, Puffins and most albatrosses. Boobies (except, probably, Abbott's) are less faithful. The Masked Booby, in some localities, usually does not return to exactly the same site. Of a group on Kure Atoll studied by Cameron Kepler, 90 per cent of the members moved a mean distance of 19.8 metres from their previous site. But in the Galapagos I found over 80 per cent fidelity to site in two successive years. On Ascension, Simmons found that 90 per cent of Brown Boobies with favourable sites remained faithful to them. Fidelity to site is proportionate to the effort that is involved in acquiring it, that is to the value of the site. One would hardly expect a Gannet to endure the stress and trauma of battling for a new site every year. Similarly on Ascension, the Brown Booby has to be in constant readiness to start a new breeding cycle, and once a favourable site has been acquired it is an advantage to stick to it. Burrow-nesters remain faithful to their sites because it is an effort to dig one, and often there is considerable competition for holes. The same applies to natural-hole nesters.

But some seabirds show little or no site-fidelity. They are usually species with unlimited nesting habitats and (often a corollary) small colonies. Waved Albatrosses, making no nest but simply laying their egg on the bare, boulder-littered ground, have no precise territorial ties. Indeed they often move even whilst incubating, shuffling along with their egg between their tarsi, for many metres. This leads to appreciable loss of eggs. On the other hand, the Laysan Albatross, which does build a nest, remains largely faithful to it or the site. Terns move localities readily, and so cannot become strongly attached to precise territories, which, anyway, are usually plentiful. Cormorants often change sites, or even the colony, which is usually only small. Shags are less prone to do so and are more faithful to their nest sites, perhaps especially where (as on the Farne Islands) there is a shortage of good sites. Guillemots return to the same ledge, but not the exact site, which, anyway, shifts somewhat under pressure; the bird moves its egg. Frigatebirds are often unable to keep the same site from one breeding attempt to the next because they build where their display has led to pair-formation, and displaying birds move around.

Similarly, the permanence of the pair bond varies widely between species. The Flightless Cormorant of the Galapagos often changes partners for successive breeding cycles, which are usually within twelve months. Frigatebirds almost certainly do not usually re-nest with the same partner and Tony Diamond has some evidence that, half-way through a breeding cycle, the male Magnificent Frigatebird of the Caribbean leaves his part-grown chick to be cared for by the female and starts a new cycle with another female. Comparably, simultaneous polygamy has been recorded for the Shag; Potts estimated that on the crowded Farne Islands, 3–5 per cent of males had two partners and nests at the same time. King Penguins do not keep the same mate in successive cycles. Nevertheless, seabirds differ from most landbirds in that strong pair bonds, often lasting for several years, are common, if not the rule. A pair of Buller's Albatrosses is known to have remained together for twenty-three years, and of fulmars for 27 years. I know of several pairs of Gannets that have remained together for ten years or more. Among species which usually keep the same mate in successive cycles are most boobies, most albatrosses, most penguins, whether colonial or solitary, most gulls, skuas, probably most shearwaters, many or most of the small petrels, and some auks. In long-lived birds, a strong pair-bond is probably the norm, provided there are no special circumstances. For example, it is impracticable for a King Penguin to meet up with his mate because their unusual breeding frequency (twice in three years) and highly variable cycle-length, makes it difficult for them to reach precisely the right breeding state simultaneously. But seabirds that breed annually, at a fixed season and in the same territory each year, are easily able to maintain their pair bond. Coulson has shown that, in the Kittiwake, there is an advantage in staying together. Pairs that split-up, even if they re-mate with a bird as experienced as the discarded partner, show slightly depressed breeding success for a year or two thereafter. But on the other hand it is clearly better for incompatible pairs to split up and try again, and since incompatible pairs tend to fail in breeding, it is no surprise to find that in Kittiwakes and Gannets, to name but two, failed pairs tend to change partners more than successful pairs. Nevertheless, there remain anomalies. For example, on Kure Atoll, Kepler found that of 42

pairs of Masked Boobies that attempted to breed in 1964, 23 remained together in 1965 and 19 split up. Of these 42 pairs, 32 were successful, but 13 (41 per cent) nevertheless split up in 1965. Yet it seems they would have done better to remain together, for the 23 pairs that remained together in 1965 had a 74 per cent breeding success but 17 re-mated pairs (from the 19 that split up) had only 47 per cent breeding success. It may be that a longer run of years is needed before one can judge the merits of fidelity and divorce in this species and locality.

So, annual, seasonal breeders stay together but non-annual, a-seasonal (or very loosely seasonal) birds usually do not. Successful breeders stay together but failed breeders tend to divorce, perhaps to try for greater compatibility. If you wonder how bird partners *could* be incompatible, it may be mentioned that co-operation in taking properly timed incubation and chick-guard spells, and at times of nest-relief, and in feeding the young, can all mean the difference between success and failure.

Mortality rates

Seabirds are long-lived. I believe the record for fully authenticated longevity belongs to a Laysan Albatross, now 53 years old. Other records of wild, exceptionally long-lived seabirds are: Royal Albatross 46 + years, Fulmar 41 +, Herring Gull 31, Buller's Albatross 30 +, Ring-billed Gull 29, Caspian Tern 26, Manx Shearwater 23 +, Atlantic Gannet 23 +, Masked Booby 23, Little Penguin 17, Razorbill 23, Fairy Tern 17. Of course, these records are probably far from the upper limits, depending as they do on the chance recovery of single birds, but they illustrate that comparatively great ages actually are reached. Thus, from the annual adult mortality figure for Buller's Albatross it can be calculated that the oldest bird should theoretically reach an age of 47 years (mean expectation of life 8.5 years), so the observed 30 years is comfortably exceeded. From the statistics of reasonably large numbers of colour-marked adult individuals seen in successive years, one can calculate the annual mortality and, from this, the expectation of further life. The latter figure is necessarily a minimum, since some birds lose their identifying marks and are wrongly assumed dead, and a few emigrate. That this may introduce a gross distortion can be shown by comparing the 4–9 per cent annual mortality for Herring Gulls of two years or more, obtained from a knowledge of the age structure of the population and its rate of increase, with 25–30 per cent mortality derived from ringing data. However, mortality rates obtained from direct observation are doubtless broadly representative, and are vital components of life-tables, which give a species' population balance-sheet. A few examples of annual adult mortality rates follow (where two figures are given they represent different authors' estimates, usually based on direct observation of marked birds): Cape Pigeon 5–6 per cent; Snow Petrel 4–7 per cent; Kittiwake 14 per cent (female); Herring Gull 4–10 per cent; Glaucous-winged Gull 10 per cent, 19 per cent (male); Caspian Tern 12 per cent; Arctic Skua 11–12 per cent; Great Skua 7 per cent; Antarctic Skua 6 per cent; Southern Fulmar 7 per cent; Atlantic Fulmar 3 per cent; Black-browed Albatross 7 per cent; Grey-headed Albatross 7 per cent; Buller's Albatross 11 per cent; Laysan Albatross 5–6 or >8.6 per cent, according to author; Waved Albatross 5 per cent; Royal Albatross 3–9 per cent; Wandering Albatross 4.3 per cent; Manx Shearwater c. 9 per cent; Adelie Penguin 15 per cent (female), 22 per cent (male) (higher in some years); Royal Penguin <14 per cent; Yellow-eyed Penguin 13 per cent; Razorbill 8–11 per cent;

Guillemot 9–13 per cent; Puffin 5 per cent; Cormorant c. 10 per cent; Shag 13 ±9 per cent; Gannet 11 per cent (male) and 9 per cent (female) but thought to be between 4–6 per cent, the difference due to ring-loss.

The mean expectation of life may be calculated from the formula $(2-m)/2m$ where $m =$ percentage annual adult mortality. Species with around 3 per cent annual mortality have a further expectation of life, at any time, (assuming that older birds do not have a higher death rate than younger ones, which seems to hold for most species, at any rate until they become quite old) of about 30 years, and about 5 per 1000 could theoretically reach more than 80 years of age. It appears, too, that in some species, the sexes are not equally at risk; usually males appear to suffer slightly greater mortality than females (Kittiwake, Gannet, Atlantic Fulmar), but in the Shag, Yellow-eyed Penguin and Adelie Penguin, for example, males survive better than females. Higher male mortality may be due to the longer period spent ashore and their greater involvement in territorial disputes, whilst females may suffer greater stress from breeding. In some species, for example the Laysan Albatross, mortality in both sexes rises when breeding begins.

As yet, we have really detailed figures for the pattern of mortality for only a very few species but it is worth citing two. Dick Pott's intensive

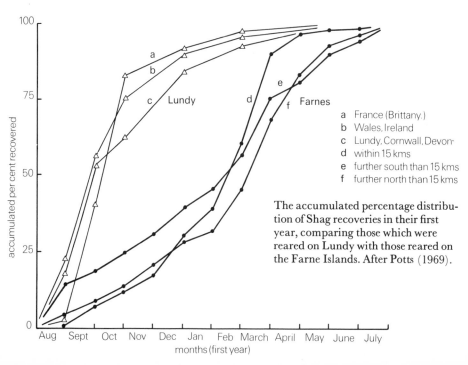

a France (Brittany.)
b Wales, Ireland
c Lundy, Cornwall, Devon·
d within 15 kms
e further south than 15 kms
f further north than 15 kms

The accumulated percentage distribution of Shag recoveries in their first year, comparing those which were reared on Lundy with those reared on the Farne Islands. After Potts (1969).

work on the Shags of the Farne Islands, for which observations and recoveries stretching over many years are available, show the pattern of survival for the different age-classes in both sexes. Of females aged 3 years, 20 per cent die; aged 4, 22 per cent; aged 5–6, 18 per cent; aged 7–9, 21 per cent and aged 10–15, 21 per cent. The figures for males are: aged 3, 17 per cent; aged 4, 15 per cent; aged 5–6, 17 per cent; aged 7–9, 12 per cent and aged 10–15, 16 per cent. This series shows that older birds survive as well as young ones, even after the latter have had several years of experience.

Young birds are of course at considerable risk, and in nearly all species show a much higher mortality than adults. They are especially likely to die in their first year, when they have to perfect their feeding behaviour, polish their anti-predator responses (which often means learning to treat man warily!) and become physiologically resistant to various stresses. After the first year, they are almost as likely to survive as adults and after two or three years, fully as likely, with the exception that increased mortality may attend the onset of breeding. From the point of view of recruitment, the important figure is not the crop of youngsters produced, but the proportion that survives to breed. A few examples will show the patterns that occur. Among the highest figures for mortality in the first year of life are around 70 per cent (Atlantic Gannet), 70–75 per cent in the Brown Pelican, 70 per cent in the Wandering Albatross, about 70 per cent in Manx Shearwaters (at least, 26.7 per cent of young ringed on the surface prior to fledging were estimated to be alive two or more years later), among penguins, the Adelie has an approximate first-year mortality of 48 per cent, Yellow-eyed 52 per cent, and Royal Penguin 33 per cent or less. The young Waved Albatross, on the other hand, appears to have an inexplicably high first-year survival rate. Of young birds ringed in 1966, 94 per cent are said to have survived to 1970 but this figure is almost unbelievable.

The proportion of any year's production that survives to breed depends, among other things, on the length of the pre-breeding period. About 10 per cent of Gannets survive to breed; 18 per cent of Razorbills, 17–28 per cent of Guillemots, 10–16 per cent of Puffins, 20 per cent of Glaucous-winged Gulls, 7–15 per cent of Royal Penguins. Even from these limited figures, and additions to them would not materially alter the trend, it can be seen that for seabirds with single-egg clutches, a long breeding life is essential if the population is to remain stable, or increase. The main difficulty in producing life tables from breeding and mortality data, which allow one to see if the population 'should' be increasing or decreasing, is that of obtaining a reliable figure for pre-breeding mortality. Emigration could lead to significant over-estimation of mortality. A further difficulty in calculating the productivity of a colony or population of seabirds is that of estimating the number of non-breeders. As mentioned earlier, the picture presented by the life table is highly dependent on the figure for adult mortality. A small difference in annual mortality greatly affects life-expectancy, and hence the number of young produced and the number that must survive if the population is to remain stable. The following simple table illustrates this point, using a range of mortality rates and productivities which cover those occurring in most seabirds. Thus the Wandering Albatross, at 3 per cent annual adult mortality, a clutch size of one and a breeding success of 50 per cent, would require a pre-breeding mortality of 87 per cent to maintain a stable population, whilst a Herring Gull with an annual adult mortality rate of 10 per cent producing 1.8 young per pair per year would need a pre-breeding mortality of 89 per cent.

Probably the commonest causes of death among free-flying seabirds are starvation and bad weather, often in concert, and accidents. Seabirds are well adapted to survive shortage of food for long periods. They can readily lose 30–50 per cent of their weight, as indeed some do as a normal event during breeding, but most of this is fat. It is a different matter if a lean bird is subjected to prolonged starvation. After exhausting their fat, they use liver lipids and begin to show stress symptoms, amongst them malfunction of the kidney with the accumulation of metabolic waste products. The bacterium *Eschericia coli*, and others, may then cause trouble whereas in a fit bird they would not do so. Storms at sea sometimes cause spectacular 'wrecks' of seabirds, amongst which Little Auks and the small petrel species are prominent, but which may involve other auks, fulmars, albatrosses, shearwaters, prions, penguins, terns and probably many other species. But even here, the predisposing factor is sometimes food failure. This appears to be so in the case of the Little Auk wrecks, which occur after easterly or

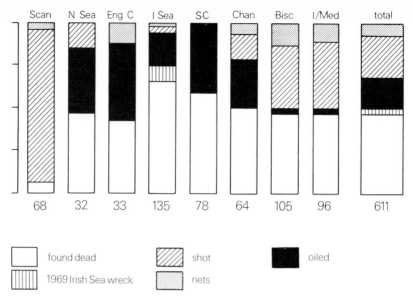

Scan	N Sea	Eng C	I Sea	SC	Chan	Bisc	I/Med	total
68	32	33	135	78	64	105	96	611

found dead   shot   oiled

1969 Irish Sea wreck   nets

Bar charts showing recovery method by locality for Razorbills. After C. J. Mead (1974).

north-easterly gales in winter. It seems that high winds disturb the surface waters and as a consequence the plankton does not rise so far and the auks cannot feed. But wrecks occur in the southern, not the northern limits of the bird's range, even though storms are as common or commoner in the north. Possibly the birds are driven south by bad weather and then, if they meet prolonged gales, which they are too weak to resist, are wrecked en masse.

The most famous example of mass starvation is that of the Peruvian guano birds, principally boobies, cormorants and pelicans. In some years, with a vague periodicity of around seven years, the cold upwelling off Peru and Chile, fails, and warm water invades the coastal waters. The anchovies, upon which these hordes of seabirds are utterly dependent, are driven into the deeper layers and are inaccessible to the birds. Because a contributory (but relatively unimportant) factor is the southward extension of a warm-water current from central America, usually around Christmas time, the whole phenomenon has become known as 'El niño' (the child). It is not commonly appreciated that minor 'niños' are a frequent, indeed a usual, occurrence. It is only in severe cases that the effect is catastrophic. In such cases, the birds die by millions. It is not uncommon for a population of about 20–30 millions to be reduced to around 1–2 millions in a few weeks or months.

So far as unfavourable weather, as such, is

concerned, examples affecting dependent young are legion (flooding of terneries, blockage of burrows by snow in Antarctica, drifting sand, cyclones devastating tree-nesting boobies, etc.) and even adults may be affected. There are numerous records of Guillemots trapped by quick-freezing sea-surfaces, and perishing, and gales occasionally drive even healthy adults ashore. Recently, over 100 000 Guillemots were found dead on the Alaskan peninsula. They were starved, but not polluted.

Accidents are common among seabirds at their breeding places. Each year, on Ailsa Craig, several hundreds of adult Gannets kill or injure themselves in landing accidents. Among albatrosses, injuries are relatively common. Their long, narrow wings are built for gliding in gales, not for touching down neatly on the ground. Even terns, the epitomization of aerial grace, suffer accidents. Of fifty adult Sooty Terns found dead or incapacitated, 62 per cent involved broken or dislocated wings. Possibly these result from aerial collisions in the vast dense masses around the breeding colonies.

Disease can be important. The 'peste' (a poisonous bacterial condition of the sea) kills huge numbers of seabirds, for example Sooty Shearwaters off Ecuador. Off the Farne Islands, in May 1968, 80 per cent of the Shags were killed by poison produced by dinoflagellates. Many diseases have been recorded in seabirds, among them psittacosis (in some procellariforms and the Emperor Penguin), puffinosis (sometimes kills large numbers of shearwaters and is found in Shags), botulism (which killed 2000 Herring Gulls in northeast Britain in June 1975), influenza (the virus has been discovered in the Wedge-tailed Shearwater and anti-bodies in Lesser Noddies), Newcastle disease (Gannet and Shag), aspergillosis (African Gannet), salmonellosis, etc. Infestation with various internal and external parasites is common. Seabirds harbour nematodes, tapeworms, acanthocephalid worms, flukes, mites, ticks, lice, fleas and flat flies. Debilitated Shags are subject to heavy infestation with mites beneath the skin. But all of these are probably unimportant in well-fed birds, as in animals in general. A porcupine, fit and fat, was found to have 20 per cent of its weight made up of tapeworms!

Man is undoubtedly the main disaster so far as many seabirds are concerned. His activities are food for another chapter, but it may be mentioned here that his waste oil is a major hazard, especially for auks, whilst his nets take an estimated 20000 auks in Galway Bay (Ireland) alone, each year, and the annual toll of Brunnich's Guillemots taken by drift nets off Greenland is around 0.5 million, many of which have dependent young; altogether, an estimated 1.5 million guillemots die at man's hand each year. This is more than the population can withstand. Shooting or trapping can be an important cause of death in some seabirds. Ten per cent of Farne Island Shags recovered, had been shot; most of the Black-browed and Grey-headed Albatrosses recovered had been captured or killed by fishing boats, 21 per cent of Caspian Terns recovered in the Great Lakes area had been shot, whilst of recoveries made beyond the southern United States 57 per cent had been shot!

Even within a species, the causes of mortality differ according to area. Razorbills, for example, tend to be shot in Scandinavia, Biscay and the Mediterranean but not in British waters; south coast birds tend to get oiled but this is not an important cause of death in Scandinavia, Biscay or the Mediterranean, and so on. Inexperience is linked with mortality not only through starvation but through shooting; first year birds of most, if not all, species are more vulnerable.

Natural predation accounts for only a small fraction of total deaths. Skuas are formidable predators and, together with Giant Petrels, take their toll of Antarctic seabirds. The nests of skuas on Bird Island (South Georgia) were littered with remains of Antarctic Prions and diving-petrels and these predators were estimated to account for 10000 prions each year. They are caught on the ground, where they are vulnerable. The big gulls will take auks, shearwaters, etc. Sea-eagles could have been significant predators, locally, when they were more numerous. Of 1044 prey items taken by sea-eagles in Norway, 62 were adult Shags. Peregrines take Craveri's Murrelets in the Gulf of California, some Sooty Terns on the Dry Tortugas, some Kittiwakes and auks off British cliffs.

Large fish take seabirds, but it is impossible to judge how many. Cod and angler fish take a few Shags and Cormorants and sharks may be significant predators in tropical waters. One 5 metre Grey Shark had thirteen juvenile Laysan Albatrosses in its stomach plus feathers belonging to many more. Among mammals, sea-lions take a few Guanays and a whale stranded near the Farne Islands had seven Shags in its stomach. Grey Seals may take a few birds, but there is no northern hemisphere equivalent of the Leopard Seal. These are serious predators of penguins against which they have evolved several behavioural ploys. Bernard Stonehouse gives a memorable description of King and Gentoo Penguins' reactions to seals. After winding in a crocodile through the tussock grass, the birds form a jostling mob at a favoured place of entry into the sea, 'the leading birds standing with toes in the water, the rest surging gently from behind'. The sudden appearance of a dark head in the surf sends them scuttling back up the beach. They may wander back and forth for an hour. Often, after the birds have entered the water, they panic, and leap ashore again. The sound of clapping, like a flipper smacking the water, is a signal to which they respond like magic. Nevertheless, despite the inbuilt fear responses, one worker, at least, concludes that Leopard Seals have a negligible effect on penguins. Introduced animals are much more serious enemies of seabirds than 'natural' mammalian predators, of which there are very few. Occasionally they are disastrous pests on islands unfortunate enough to become infested. So, directly and indirectly, man's influence on seabirds is largely baleful and exceeded, in magnitude, only by the long, slow changes in climate and oceanography that have shaped seabirds throughout evolutionary time.

Movements and distribution

Seabirds migrate for the same reason as land-birds, namely to move from an area in which it is, or will shortly become, difficult to subsist to a more favourable one. In strongly seasonal regions seabirds breed when food is most plentiful and then move out. In a-seasonal environments there is no need to do so. Shearwaters move out of the Mediterranean in winter and Sooty Terns desert the Caribbean for the east tropical Atlantic, to say nothing of the more extreme cases of antarctic and arctic/boreal species, some of which migrate deep into the opposite hemisphere. But migrating seabirds have an easier time than landbirds, for they can rest and feed on the way. A 7 gram Willow Warbler's crossing of the Mediterranean and Sahara in one hop is more impressive than a 23 gram petrel's transequatorial sea migration. Probably, most seabirds suffer much less mortality during migration than do most landbirds, even though they must often cross vast areas of unproductive seas. But many features of bird migration apply equally to seabirds and landbirds: for instance, there are similar effects of locality; birds (of the same species) born in certain areas migrate to specific wintering localities; in some cases there is comparably rapid migration over great distances; the underlying physiological and navigational mechanisms are probably similar; inexperienced individuals can migrate successfully without adults; there is both broad and narrow front migration; movement is often associated with definable meteorological conditions (birds tend to move north when pressure is high and winds southerly, and south in north-westerly air-streams whilst in advance of approaching low-pressure systems they tend to settle or appear inshore) and so on. But whereas landbirds commonly migrate at great heights seabirds appear to migrate low over the water.

True migration is not always readily separable from other types of movement such as dispersal and nomadism. Indeed, like most categorizations, these are essentially artificial devices, useful for handling ideas but by no means cut and dried. Migration results in a clear seasonal shift in the centre of population, from locality A to B and back again. British Sandwich Terns, for example, migrate to south-west Africa and Manx Shearwaters to Brazil. In migration the distance and direction of the target area appears to be innate. In dispersal movement, it is more random, at least with regard to distance, but not necessarily with regard to direction, though preference for a particular direction is, in fact, often weak. Since in dispersal the distance moved 'falls off' (more birds stay near to their place of origin than move far from it) a simple model can predict, from the rate of fall-off, the farthest distance that the birds would be expected to go. This cannot be done for migration for there is no such fall-off. Nomadism may perhaps be distinguished from dispersal in that nomadic seabirds keep on moving, perhaps randomly but sometimes along broadly defined routes that eventually lead them back home. Dispersing seabirds tend to find a suitable area, at a highly variable distance from base, and stay there for a period. However, there are instances which fall between the two. Nomadism is essentially an adaptive response of seabirds to the vast areas within which they must seek local concentrations of food. Eruptive movements are a form of dispersal and vagrancy is weather-induced wandering into areas far from those which the species normally visits. Few seabirds are genuinely sedentary and most of those that are belong to the Phalacrocoracidae. Even penguins may swim more than a thousand kilometres from base.

The more complex and demanding phenomenon of migration presumably arose from dispersal. In post-breeding dispersal the vastly augmented population spreads itself over a greater area. This would be clearly adaptive whether the environment was seasonal or not for in the former case the climate, worsening in winter, would affect food and cause movement whilst in an a-seasonal environment dispersal would ensure the best use of scarce resources. Nomadism and continuous migration effectively tap food which would otherwise remain unused, and they enable seabirds to exploit to the full the patchy distribution of food in the ocean. It is not surprising that convergences and upwellings attract and concentrate large numbers of many species which in impoverished areas are widely dispersed or absent. Nomadism is the life for which many seabirds are adapted and the fetch and carry existence which breeding enforces is the alien mode. In fact, the long-deferred maturity of so many seabirds, especially the more pelagic ones, encourages full use of the sea's scattered resources. Instead of staying around home waters or hurrying to a well-defined nursery area the randomly nomadic or

Brown Pelicans flying in a distinctive 'v'-formation.

the continuously migrating young seabird, pelagic for extended periods, battens where it may before returning to tackle the demands of breeding.

Many tropical seabirds, not surprisingly, disperse without strong directional bias and without a clear target area. This probably applies to tropical boobies, frigatebirds, tropicbirds, tropical albatrosses, Sooty Terns, Fairy Terns, etc. It is not known whether post-breeding adults stay within a radius of a few hundred kilometres of their breeding areas or disperse more widely, but young birds certainly travel considerable distances. Many frigatebirds and boobies have been recovered up to at least 6000 kilometres from their place of origin in the first year after independence. There is some evidence from the thousands of boobies ringed in the north central Pacific that dispersal does have a directional bias. Immature Red-footed Boobies tended to move mainly south whereas adults moved both north and south. But no doubt the same species behaves differently in different localities. During

171

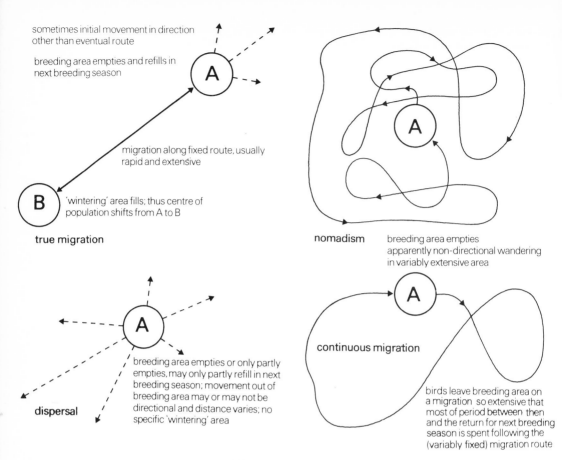

sometimes initial movement in direction other than eventual route

breeding area empties and refills in next breeding season

A

migration along fixed route, usually rapid and extensive

B

'wintering' area fills; thus centre of population shifts from A to B

true migration

A

nomadism   breeding area empties apparently non-directional wandering in variably extensive area

A

breeding area empties or only partly empties, may only partly refill in next breeding season; movement out of breeding area may or may not be directional and distance varies; no specific 'wintering' area

dispersal

A

continuous migration

birds leave breeding area on a migration so extensive that most of period between then and the return for next breeding season is spent following the (variably fixed) migration route

Different types of dispersal.

their dispersed or nomadic phase boobies and frigatebirds, at least, establish temporary bases on islands far from home. Some remain there to breed, and dispersal obviously leads to extension of breeding range. Even in generally productive sea areas there are local concentrations, often remarkably precisely demarcated and caused by underwater topography or other factors, which the nomadic bird can find and exploit. Such nomadism has no real counterpart among landbirds.

In the temperate and sub-polar regions dispersal, or perhaps variably extensive nomadism, is the habit of auks, penguins, some albatrosses, petrels etc., some pelicaniforms, and many gulls. Among the auks, Puffins appear to disperse widely—in fact it is surprising how little is known about the winter movements of this common and popular species—and Guillemots show highly variable types of movements, depending on area. Those of the eastern North Atlantic, especially the adults, are generally

fairly sedentary. Norwegian birds, for example, remain off the coast or in the fiords; British Guillemots return, to their ledges, albeit transitorily, as early as November. Some young birds from Britain, the Faroes, the Baltic, and elsewhere migrate to Norwegian seas although others move south, possibly as far as Iberia or even Morocco. Guillemots of the eastern Canadian Arctic, the coast of Labrador, the northwest coast of Greenland and the Pacific sector of the polar basin may undertake long annual migrations to the south after an initial post-breeding movement northwards (chicks from Funk Island reach Labrador by early August and begin to move south in early October). The Newfoundland region, including the Grand Banks, is the main wintering area for most of the Common Guillemots in the western North Atlantic. Some cormorants disperse—indeed this type of movement seems fairly typical of the group, but with considerable differences between and within species. Of the

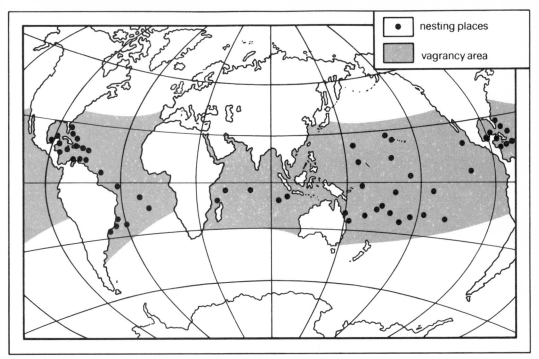

Distribution of the world's frigatebirds. A tropical family. The dissemination of frigates to the Atlantic has probably taken place through the Panama Isthmus and around southern Africa.

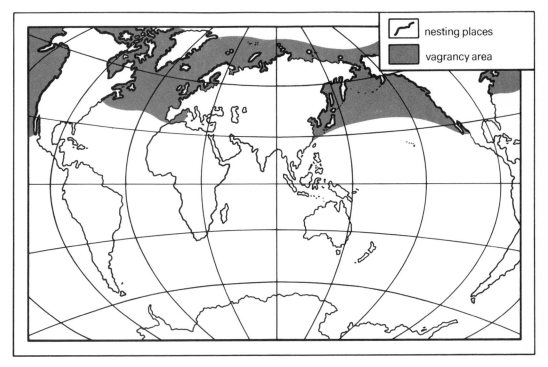

Distribution pattern of the Alcidae. A northern hemisphere family. Their dispersal took place essentially in a latitudinal direction, probably coming to the North Atlantic in the Oligocene or beginning of the Miocene period. Figures on pages 173 to 175 after V. P. Shuntov (1974).

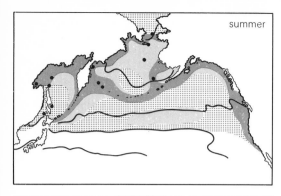

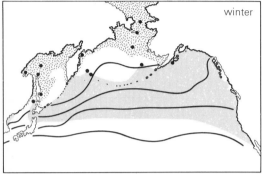

Distribution of the Tufted Puffin in the Pacific Ocean.

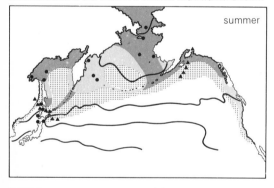

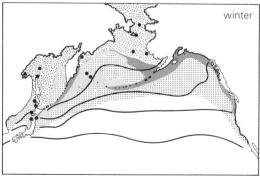

Distribution of the Common and Brunnich's Guillemot in the Pacific Ocean (triangles indicate southern boundary of the Brunnich's nesting area).

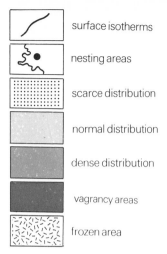

surface isotherms	
nesting areas	
scarce distribution	
normal distribution	
dense distribution	
vagrancy areas	
frozen area	

Key to maps

five cormorants in south Australia, none move far, though one (the Black Cormorant) disperses as far as Tasmania and Macquarie Island. The Black Cormorant disperses, also, to inland waters, possibly to avoid competition with the Pied, which is the most sedentary of the five – a suggestion supported by the observation that in North America the Black Cormorant does not disperse inland where the Double-crested Cormorant holds sway. Of British Cormorants, those from the east coast are fairly sedentary whereas some west coast birds move as far as Spain. Dutch Cormorants move into the Mediterranean more than do British Cormorants which tend to move south rather than east.

Dispersal can be extremely limited. Many gulls move no more than a few kilometres from their hatching place. The Kelp Gull, for example, has an average recovery distance even in its first year (which is, in all seabirds, the most nomadic) of only 26.9 kilometres. But some gulls disperse extremely widely, or are nomadic. The Kittiwake crosses the North Atlantic and the Great Black-back disperses thousands of kilometres. In the Pacific, some gulls also disperse widely.

Albatrosses are probably highly nomadic, with a tendency towards continuous migration – strongly directional movement within a broad belt – and perhaps towards true migration. Sightings of flamingo-pink, dyed Wandering Albatrosses feeding off Sydney in July and August and known to have come from Bird Island more than 9600 kilometres away, and recaptures of ringed birds at sea, have shown

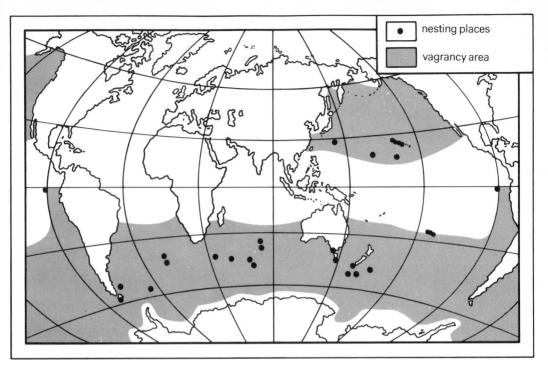

Distribution of the albatrosses, a southern hemisphere family.

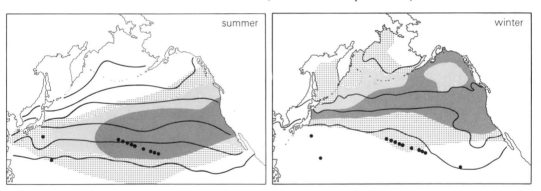

Distribution of the Black-footed Albatross in the Pacific Ocean.

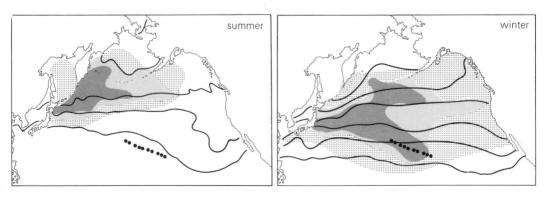

Distribution of the Laysan Albatross in the Pacific Ocean.

175

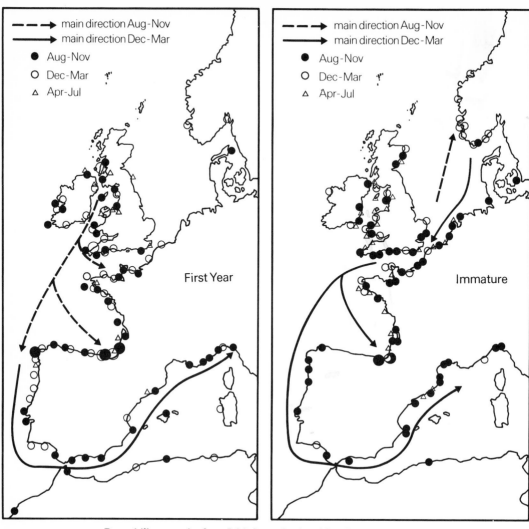

Razorbill recoveries from Irish Sea colonies. After C. J. Mead (1974).

that between breeding seasons some, at least, return precisely to known feeding areas. The navigational ability this requires is common to most seabirds. The Laysan Albatross released away from its colony, returned 6590 kilometres in 32 days and 5120 kilometres in 10 days. Lockley, in a famous pioneer experiment, took Manx Shearwaters to Venice, which lies completely outside their range. One returned within 14 days, over a distance of 5900 kilometres if it travelled by sea. The range restrictions observed by most albatrosses (the 'greats' excepted) are probably imposed by temperature and food and not by the absence of wind. In the southern zone of strong and stable trade winds there are very few albatrosses and even those occur only in winter. However, windless areas such as the Doldrums must act as barriers.

Commonly the movements of seabirds in their first year are more extensive than later—this is so, for example, in Kittiwakes, Shags, Fulmars, Puffins, boobies, frigates and many gulls. Atlantic Gannets show true migration in their first year, followed by more limited and less strongly directional movement thereafter. Juveniles travel south from North Atlantic colonies, to equatorial waters off west Africa (birds from eastern Atlantic colonies) and to the Gulf of Mexico (Canadian birds), a roughly equivalent distance of some 6400 kilometres. Interestingly, the other two Gannets travel much the same distance, again to warmer waters, though the African Gannet goes north and the Australasian west, across the Tasman

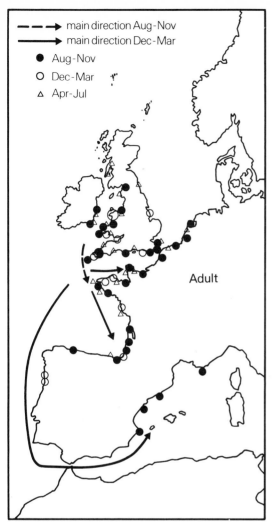

Legend:
- - - → main direction Aug-Nov
——→ main direction Dec-Mar
● Aug-Nov
○ Dec-Mar
△ Apr-Jul

Adult

why they *do* migrate so far. Almost certainly they migrate through areas which demonstrably contain the appropriate food at the required time of year. It may be that, since semi-continuous movement is an effective foraging technique, migration, perhaps initiated long ago by geological change but now no longer necessary, nevertheless continues. Such movement is in any case unlikely to entail more hazards than the birds would meet in one fishing area.

The shearwaters are superb migrants, executing huge and complex movements. The Short-tailed Shearwater flies in a figure of eight from south Australia to the north Pacific and arctic oceans and back again; and it doesn't dawdle. In six weeks, one nestling flew the 16 000 kilometres or so to the Bering Sea (an extremely rich area where many southern hemisphere petrels go to moult and now, incidentally, threatened with oil exploration). It has been suggested, on the basis of birds seen at sea, that the shearwaters zip directly through the tropics without much foraging. Even so, they are still fat when they make their landfall after the southward leg. They are also, incidentally, in an advanced state of readiness to breed, with (in the males) free sperm in the reproductive tract. The decreasing daylength in the north presumably triggers migration but, since the birds are dispersed over 20° of latitude it is not easy to see why some don't set off far ahead of others; yet arrival is well synchronized. Perhaps there is a fixed yearly (circannual) rhythm controlling migration. This would accord with the observation that desertion of the breeding area occurs equally decisively and whilst shearwater food is still abundant. Other shearwaters also migrate far and rapidly. The Manx has been recovered in Brazil 16 days after being ringed in Wales, which means a minimum speed of 740 kilometres per day. It deserts its fat chick, which follows as soon as it can fly. Shearwater migrations are sometimes extremely concentrated, the birds pouring along their flight path at the rate of thousands an hour. This is true of migration visible from the coast and also far out at sea. In fact, one good reason why spot checks at regular intervals, as so often carried out from ships, are no substitute for *continuous* surveillance, is that between checks, major phenomena can be totally missed. The Short-tailed Shearwater's route demonstrates that migrants may follow a complex route which presumably takes advantage of

Sea. Adult Gannets, at least from eastern Atlantic colonies, rarely travel so far south. One may speculate that young birds survive better if they locate warmer areas and those with particular qualities of prey size, density and distribution not available in home waters, but that experienced birds became emancipated from these requirements.

Those seabirds which migrate over the longest distances probably do not show this age-dependent difference. Among the most impressive journeys are the trans-equatorial migrations of the Arctic Tern, Arctic and Long-tailed Skuas, Wilson's Storm-petrel and Leach's Storm-petrel and several of the shearwaters, though this far from exhausts the list. It is sometimes difficult, incidentally, to understand

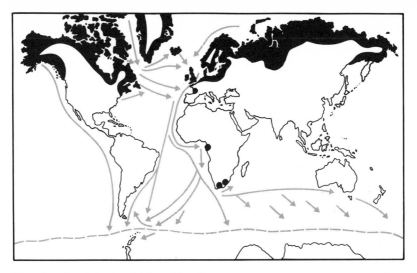

The migration of the Arctic Tern. Breeding area is black; southern boundary of the wintering area is a broken line; direction of autumn migration shown by arrows.

favourable winds and of food. In the Manx Shearwater, the migration of the young bird extends into a period of strongly directional wandering which takes it up the eastern American seaboard, where adult Manx Shear-waters are rarely seen. Several southern shearwaters (Great, Sooty, Cory's, etc.) and sub-tropical petrels, visit north-west European seas, on feeding trips, in late summer. Great Shearwaters leave the Argentine shelf in mid-

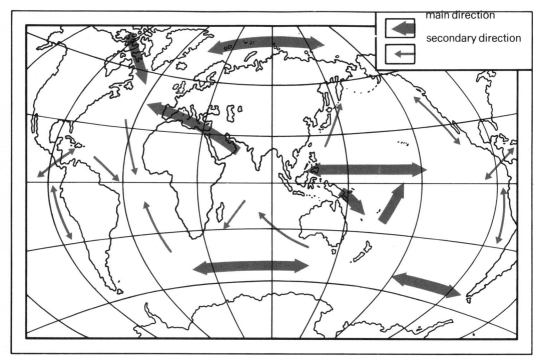

main direction

secondary direction

Probable centres of origin and directions of dissemination of seabirds. Seabird orders and families originated in the Pacific and Indian Oceans and their evolution and dissemination has been proceeding for at least 70 million years. The relationship between the seabird orders is still unclear. After Shuntov (1974).

May when the surface swarms of crustacea sink, and migrate to Nova Scotia, Newfoundland and Labrador in time to catch the spawning capelin, an important prey.

It is difficult to balance the benefits of rapid and direct migration to winter quarters or nursery areas, against extensive feeding *en route*. Feeding conditions can be important determinants of route. In autumn, dense flocks of Sandwich, Common and Arctic Terns migrate through the Gulf of Guinea within 22 kilometres of the shore, which is the zone in which sardines are most abundant. In spring, the fish lie further offshore and, correspondingly, the terns do not migrate along the inshore strip. Comparably, in birds that merely disperse, suitable areas concentrate and retain them. Fulmars congregate over cold water off Newfoundland and Greenland and Kittiwakes over warmer water to the south-east; some auks have their favoured areas in the North Sea and North Atlantic; tropical dispersers concentrate at convergences and so on.

Some tubenoses migrate from one major ocean to another, a much rarer phenomenon than movement within an ocean. Swinhoe's and Matsudaira's Storm-petrels migrate from the north-west Pacific to the Indian Ocean – the former as far as the Arabian Sea. The Streaked Shearwater of the north Pacific visits the Malacca Straits and has reached Ceylon. Several of the gadfly-petrels breed in one ocean and winter in another.

'Eruptions', well known in some landbirds, occur also in seabirds. An eruption is a mass emigration, to areas not normally reached, and depends on conditions at the time, rather than being a regular phenomenon. It is seen most dramatically in the guano birds of Peru, which flood out of their normal area during food shortages caused by warm water incursions, which drive anchovies away. Common Shags show both ordinary dispersal and, in some years, eruptive dispersal. In ordinary dispersal the distance dispersed falls off exponentially, whereas in eruptive dispersal a similar proportion of the total number of Shags involved is found within each 'dispersal distance' (arbitrary blocks, say 6–10, 11–20 kilometres, etc.) from the source of the movement. The implication of this difference is that in eruptive years the Shags, like the Peruvian guano birds, are specifically

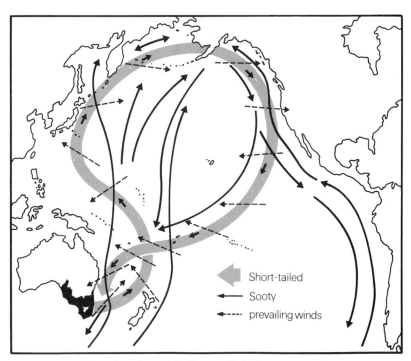

The migrations of the Short-tailed Shearwater and Sooty Shearwater. The breeding area for the Short-tailed Shearwater is shown in black.

179

deserting the unfavourable area, whereas in non-eruptive dispersal they are not moving out of the area of origin at a faster rate than out of any other of the 'areas' within their dispersion limits. The eruption has an external cause whilst dispersion has not.

Most movement of seabirds at sea is concerned with foraging whether it be short or medium to long trips from the breeding colony, or, outside the breeding season, random nomadism, or semi-continuous, global migration. Even the feeding trips of breeding birds can be extensive. It is possible that Short-tailed Shearwaters forage up to 1000 kilometres from the colony and Fulmars may range up to 900 kilometres. Some auks, probably including guillemots and even the diminutive Little Auk, Kittiwakes, petrels and Gannets, among north temperate and arctic species, may fly at least 160 kilometres to feed. Amongst tropical species foraging trips of many days are common in frigates, some boobies, tropicbirds, shearwaters, petrels, tropical albatrosses, etc., and give scope for hundreds of kilometres of travel. These ex-

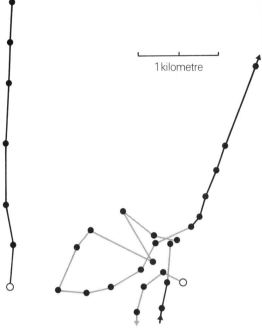

Tracks of an Adelie Penguin (each dot represents a five minute interval). The left-hand bird was released in sunlight (a solid line) and maintained a straight course. The right-hand bird was released under a cloudy sky (tinted line) and headed in the opposite direction until the sky cleared, more clouds left the bird moving at random until the sun returned.
From Emlen and Penney, 'The Navigation of Penguins'.

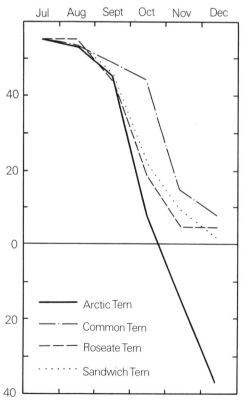

Average latitude of recoveries of four species of tern in their first autumn. After Langham (1971).

tensive foraging movements of seabirds have no precise parallel among landbirds, although they compare in principle with the foraging of some colonial raptors and insectivorous landbirds.

In cool temperate waters the distance and often the direction of foraging movements is species-specific and these feeding flights can give rise to great streams of birds following the sea-paths to favoured areas. When these movements overlap with migration, as in the Gannet, they can obscure the latter.

To deal properly with the movements of seabirds would need a book to itself; the following is merely a digest of the principle points.

Outside the breeding season most seabirds migrate, disperse or wander. These are the most effective ways of using the sea's resources and among immature birds are extended, often, for a lengthy pre-breeding period.

Migrating seabirds may move over a broad

Shy (White-capped) Albatross, the largest of the Albatrosses in New Zealand.

east–west movements, extending between major oceans do occur, and long-distance vagrancy is particularly common among procellariforms.

Foraging movements *within* the breeding season vary in distance and in nature, being either strongly directional or more random. Outside the breeding season they take several forms; e.g. forays from a home-base; local or long-distance nomadism; forays from a temporary-base (a 'nursery' or a wintering area) reached via dispersal or migration; feeding forays carried out whilst on semi-continuous migration; etc.

In strongly seasonal areas, movements outside the breeding season are in some species related to weather, birds moving as conditions dictate (akin to 'hard weather' movements in land birds). The target area of populations (e.g. Norwegian Shags) which migrate over short distances, may change over a period of a few years, in accord with changes in the location of major food concentrations.

Some species spend the winter far at sea, in upwelling areas which may be precisely demarcated. Many seabirds are totally pelagic outside the breeding season. Even species whose breeding habitat is essentially non-marine (Sabine's Gull, Long-tailed Skua, Black Tern) may winter at sea, on the move.

In species with a long and rapid migration, wing moult is usually postponed until winter quarters have been reached. Nomadic seabirds may moult during their wanderings.

Each seabird group shows its specific tendency to migrate, disperse, wander or whatever, although there is much variability between and within species. The most sedentary major group is that containing the cormorants and shags (though many, even of these, are far from sedentary). The auks, penguins, gulls, boobies, frigates, tropicbirds and some terns favour dispersal and/or nomadism. The albatrosses, shearwaters, many petrels and some terns favour rapid, long-distance migration or semi-continuous migration of a variably nomadic nature.

The relative uniformity of the sea allows unimpeded and safe passage over vast distances. Its size and the patchy distribution of food means that only by extensive movement can these local sources be effectively used. The ability to live at sea and to cover enormous distances has, outside the breeding season, enabled seabirds to exploit these features to the full and has contributed largely to their great success.

front, or more narrowly. They avoid land masses and their movements are timed to coincide with appropriate meteorological conditions.

Many use bicoordinate navigation requiring the use of sun or stars and an accurate sense of time, though cruder methods would suffice for coastal and general-direction migrants.

Young birds tend to move further than adults and in some species, true migration occurs in the first year followed in later years by dispersal or nomadism.

The extent of the migration varies hugely, from a few hundred kilometres to trans-equatorial, or even pole-to-pole migration. Even within species there may be regional differences in the scale and direction of the movement. Colonies may have their own wintering areas.

Migration can be extremely concentrated, with birds flowing massively along well-defined routes and for short periods only, or it may be a much looser, broad-front, semi-continuous movement akin to nomadism.

Long-distance migration is often rapid and may entail rather little feeding en route. However, complex routes and semi-continuous movement between breeding seasons are obviously determined largely by the distribution of food. And some species appear to fit their movements precisely to enable them to feed en route.

Latitudinal movements within the same major sea-area are the commonest type but

Seabird populations

Seabirds often nest in large colonies, and, despite the inaccuracy of our counts, (in passing, and to give some indication of the scale of potential errors, it may be noted that an error of between 17 and 46 per cent must be expected on a single count of Razorbills and 13 to 26 per cent on one of Guillemots, whilst rough estimates can be 'out' by several 100 per cent), we are therefore able to make reasonable estimates of local, regional and in some cases world, populations. One of the most basic and stimulating aspects of seabird numbers, or those of any other animal, concerns their control. What determines and maintains the level of the population?

Before discussing this, it is worth taking a few concrete examples. Some seabirds, like some landbirds, are extremely rare. There are, for instance, less than 2000 pairs of Andrew's Frigatebird, all of them on the Indian Ocean Christmas Island, less than 1000 to 1500 pairs of Ascension Frigatebirds, all on Ascension Island, and perhaps 1500 breeding pairs of Abbott's Booby, again all of them on Christmas Island. There are between 6000 and 15000 Galapagos Penguins and 700 to 800 pairs of Galapagos Flightless Cormorants. But there figures are large compared with those of the Cahow or Bermuda Petrel, or the Magenta Petrel of the Chatham Islands, until this year thought to be extinct and of which there are now only one or two pairs known though there are probably more. There are probably only between 75 and 100 Short-tailed Albatrosses in the world. Several seabird species number less than 500000 but more than 100000. For example, the Cape Penguin was estimated to number 295000 adults in 1956 (since when it has decreased); and, in the same year, the Cape Cormorant and the Cape (African) Gannet numbered 122000 and 352000 individuals. The Atlantic Gannet totals around 213000 pairs. Among albatrosses, the tropical Laysan is among the most numerous, with an estimated 1.5 million birds in 1957–58 since when it has probably increased markedly; the Black-footed at that time numbered 300000 birds. Another tropical albatross, the Waved Albatross, is very much rarer, at about 10–12000 pairs, all of them on Hood Island in the Galapagos. Black-browed and Grey-headed Albatrosses each number about 100000 pairs whilst the Wandering Albatross of similar latitudes totals only around 50–60000 birds.

Probably most seabird species number more than a million individuals. Harris has recently made an informed guess that there are of the order of 15 million Puffins, most of them of the race that breeds around Britain (*Fratercula artica grabae*), which coincides remarkably well with Lockley's 1953 estimate. Lloyd's estimate for the world population of Razorbills yields just over 200000 breeding pairs, of which 144000 are in Britain and Ireland, whereas there are at least scores of millions of Common Guillemots. The world population of Guanay Cormorants, all within the small strip of coastal waters of Peru, used to number about 15 million, that of the Peruvian Booby about 3 million and the Chilean Pelican less than half a million. Nobody has estimated the world population of Sooty Terns but it must be scores of millions. Among penguins, Magellanic Penguins number tens of millions, Emperors (some thirty colonies) are to be reckoned in tens of thousands, perhaps short of 50000 birds, and Adelies in millions. The hordes of Little Auks in the Arctic must also qualify for a place in the top few, reaching perhaps hundreds of millions, as also may Wilson's Storm-petrel of the Antarctic.

The range in numbers, among seabirds, is thus enormous. The most populous are small or medium-sized species in the cold, exceptionally productive polar and sub-polar seas, but the vast aggregations of Sooty Terns in the tropics, including some of the most impoverished zones, are a reminder that the right feeding niche (here the ability to forage over vast areas) and breeding strategy can produce almost comparable populations there, too. In tropical seas the more pelagic species are more numerous overall than inshore feeders because the feeding area open to them is much greater. As Diamond has pointed out migratory species are also more populous than sedentary, and for the same reason. However, it is perhaps not the obviously successful species that pose the hardest problems, but the 100 000 pairs of Black-browed Albatrosses, the 200 000 pairs of Razorbills, the 1500 pairs of Andrew's Frigatebirds and so on. What controls numbers?

Some theories on population control

Perhaps the arguments about the regulation of animal populations have largely bypassed the average birdwatcher, so it may not be superfluous to summarize the three main ideas, among whose chief proponents have been David Lack, Andrewartha and Birch, and Wynne-Edwards.

Starting from the observation that bird populations remain more or less stable, rather than fluctuating wildly, it is suggested that they do so via the operation of density-dependent factors. In other words, a high population density soon causes a lowering of the density. It may do so by reducing the rate at which new breeders are added to the population, or by increasing the rate at which members of the population die, the main causes of mortality being starvation, predation and disease, and intra-specific competition for breeding space or sites. There is, it is said, *overt competition* for key resources, whatever their nature, and whenever (in the breeding season or out of it) the competition occurs. Thus, high population density lowers recruitment rate by, for example, reducing the number of young which are reared, and by increasing the age at which birds breed for the first time. In many birds, though not importantly in seabirds, it may reduce clutch size, too. Fewer young are reared because competition for food means that fewer can be fed, and the age of first-breeding is raised because younger,

less experienced birds, find it difficult to rear young in competition with older birds. Similarly, more birds die from starvation and the other causes mentioned above. So, sooner rather than later, the population density comes down to the level which the resources can sustain. For example, in the south of England, the population of Herons decreases markedly after each hard winter and then builds up again, but never to anything like the level which is theoretically possible. So it fluctuates between restricted limits.

This model appears to work well enough for many landbirds, and for some, but not all, seabirds. It is the basic premiss of actual competition that, to me, seems untenable. Competition for food means that the chances of an individual catching an adequate amount, in relation to effort expended, are reduced because of the number of other individuals likewise seeking food. This implies that, as they increase, the birds reduce the amount of available food, either by consuming it or by interfering with each other's success, or both. Whilst this applies convincingly to inshore feeders such as Shags, much as it applies to Herons, it seems quite inapplicable to many offshore feeders. By no feat of imagination can one visualize the numbers of Red-footed Boobies in the Galapagos affecting either the quantity of flying fish and squid in the surrounding Pacific, or the rate at which individual boobies capture them. It is just as difficult to believe that Peruvian Boobies deplete the incalculable squadrons of anchovies and the evidence clearly shows that, prior to disastrous overfishing by man, they did not do so. They had a vast, untapped reserve. And there is, in the Atlantic Gannet, no evidence that inexperienced birds are less able than older ones to gather food for their young. The chicks of first-time breeders grow as quickly as any others. Consider, too, the squid-eating Wandering Albatross, with its total population of 50–60 000 birds and a feeding range covering tens of thousands of productive square kilometres. Is it possible that their numbers could affect the astronomical squid population, or each albatross's hunting efficiency? Possibly the *total population* of squid-eating animals, of which the Wandering Albatross is a miniscule part, could affect the level of this particular food item. If this were so, one might conceivably conclude that the Wandering Albatross population is controlled by the populations of the many squid-eating species, of which huge group it is such an insignificant part. But this is far-removed from the Lackian concept of density-dependent regulation of populations. Indeed, apart from its intrinsic complexity (though complexity is no argument against possibility), it would not accord with the sort of evidence which Lack adduces. Thus, in the Heron case just cited, it is the increase of the *Heron*, and not the increase of any other fish-and-frog eaters, that is held (and I'm sure correctly) to lead to the levelling-off of its population. Conversely, it is the *Heron's* decrease, after a hard winter, that removes the food restrictions and allows Herons to increase again. Nevertheless, competition has been authoritatively defined (by Birch) as occurring when 'a number of animals, of *the same or different species*, utilize common resources the supply of which is short, or if the resources are not in short supply, competition occurs when the animals seeking that resource nevertheless harm one or other in the process'. Of course, food is not necessarily the only limiting common resource, but in the case of the Wandering Albatross, the other candidates are equally improbable.

All this does not imply that food is unimportant. Indeed, as much of the present book tries to show, food is the key influence on breeding strategies and productivity. But, in many cases, it is food *independent* of the birds' numbers, rather than dependent on them. When the seas around the Galapagos suddenly fail to yield easy catches to the Red-footed Boobies, frigates, shearwaters, etc., then the young suffer an abrupt decline and many die. But they would have done so if there had been ten times as many birds or a tenth as many. Again, it is certainly abundant food that allows the Peruvian Booby and Guanay Cormorant to feed four young, and to build up to a population of 30 million in one small strip of sea, but when this food disappears, in an 'El niño' year, the seabirds would fare just as catastrophically whether they were few or many, for the anchovies are affected by oceanographic phenomena and for all practical purposes their numbers are quite independent of the birds. Yet again, the population of Abbott's Booby on Christmas Island was until very recently entirely unaffected by man and yet it is tiny. What keeps it so? Again, in a sense, food, but not density dependent competition for food. Thus, 90 per cent or more of the young starve, before becoming independent, but they do so because the species, has embarked on an evolutionary path that requires it to sustain a dependent youngster throughout the monsoon season, when it is clearly difficult to do so. Maybe the climate has changed, maybe (or in fact almost certainly) Christmas Island has drifted hundreds of kilometres from its original position, which *may* have been nearer to Abbott's Booby's feeding areas. These, or other factors could be the reasons for Abbott's low success, which in turn could explain its low numbers. Maybe it is in very, very slow decline. But whatever it seems self-evident that the number of Abbott's Booby is not controlled by density dependent competition either for food or nest-sites.

This leads me to the second of the three major theories of population-regulation, which holds that density-dependent control is unimportant. Andrewartha and Birch worked largely with insects, which are obviously more susceptible to population control by density-independent climatic factors than are birds. But I believe they were right to reject a *generalized* concept of density-dependent control, with all its many corollaries. I have just tried to show, by selected examples, that for populations of seabirds such a *generalization* is unconvincing, although in *specific cases* it is highly persuasive and, in fact, logically incontestable. Why it should be supposed that there must be a control mechanism which applies to all animals, or even all seabirds, escapes me. Presumably it is thought to be because, like the general theory of evolution, the theory of population-control cannot brook exceptions. If so, this is a false analogy. There *can* be no exceptions to the general theory that animals evolved from pre-existing forms, and ultimately from inorganic materials. But once animals exist, they can evolve so as to counteract environmental influences in many different ways. The evolution of density-dependent control mechanisms is one such way, and the capacity to survive the buffetings of density-independent environmental factors, such as oceanographic ones, is another. And it seems to me that some birds behave in a classically Lackian way, and others, probably including many seabirds, do not. Perhaps this is the sort of thing Andrewartha and Birch meant when they commented that '. . . Generalizations about "density-dependent factors" and competition in so far as they refer to natural populations are neither theory nor hypothesis but dogma'.

The third suggestion is again fundamentally different in approach. Food and, or, other resources, but mainly food, is seen as the ultimate factor controlling population levels, but direct competition for it is emphatically rejected. Instead, the key concept is that of social, or intrinsic regulation of the population. In brief, it is considered that recruitment to the population is adjusted so that it redresses mortality and keeps the population in appropriate balance with resources. Lack, it will be recalled, saw things the other way round – as mortality keeping the balance and recruitment roaring ahead as fast as the breeding pairs could manage. If recruitment is to be adjusted so that the population is kept below the level at which direct, density-dependent competition and mortality ensues, it is clearly necessary for the breeders and potential breeders to adjust their output in accordance with the current state of the food supply. The latter could presumably be monitored physiologically, by the amount of effort expended in feeding; and productivity, in turn, could be adjusted in a number of ways. For example, breeding pairs could refrain from breeding for a year or more; pre-breeders could defer their first breeding attempt, broods could be reduced by the parents, and so on. The net result would be to keep the population, in balance with its resources, that is, below the level at which it over-exploits them, but by 'conventional' means instead of direct competition for the resources. Instead of having its limits imposed on it, the population would impose the limits on itself. This thesis is particularly relevant to seabirds because Wynne-Edwards considers them to be prime examplars of it. Also, it is consistent with one important reality, namely that many seabirds obviously do *not* compete for food. The detailed exposition of this general theme, in Wynne-Edwards' book *Animal Dispersion in Relation to Social Behaviour* created world-wide interest. Perhaps the two major criticisms which have been made are, first that the theory is at odds with what most biologists think they understand about the way natural selection works and second, that the facts don't fit. I won't attempt to go into the first of these objections, except to say that the argument is about the individual versus the group. The individuals that produce the most offspring in their lifetimes, provided that these offspring are fit, will most effectively perpetuate their genes and thus their traits. So natural

selection will favour these 'selfish genes' at the expense of the genes carried within the bodies of individuals who refrain from putting forth their maximum reproductive effort. This view, of course, encompasses kin-selection, for to the extent that one helps another individual (say a brother or sister), who shares ones own genes, to survive, one is helping one's own genes. But many think it does not encompass group-selection on a large scale, that is, altruism (such as non-breeding) which helps others to survive (by conserving resources), when those others do not share an appreciable number of one's own genes. The second objection is that it appears that many seabirds do *not* refrain from breeding in order to reduce the rate at which recruits are added to the population. They refrain from breeding, or they produce few young, because they *can't* do better. Many of the examples I cited when discussing breeding strategies showed that the seabirds in question were maximizing their output. Fratricide in Masked Boobies is not a device for reducing the number of offspring reared, but for *increasing* it. The second chick is there to take over if the first dies early in life. Nor do Atlantic Gannets take rest years; non-breeders are either re-mated birds, or young birds. And the long periods of deferred maturity in many seabirds is probably necessary before birds are capable of breeding effectively. Further, in all the many seabirds which have been given larger-than-normal broods, none except the Atlantic Gannet have proved fully capable of rearing the extra young. In the sulids, which show every gradation from clutches of one to four, the clutch size is clearly related to the number of young that the adults can feed. But it is only fair to add that non-breeding years *do* occur in some species and that the period of deferred maturity seems excessively long in others. Yet non-breeding years may be devices for maximizing output by mitigating stress, and even the longest deferred maturity *may* be necessary.

The subject of competition *between* species has a vast literature of its own, which I have no space to mention. But one example may illustrate the delicacy of the balance between closely-related species. In the east North Atlantic, a proportion of the Guillemots are bridled, with white spectacles and a line behind the eye. This proportion increases as one goes north from Brittany to the Shetlands, but decreases again as one goes north in Iceland. The suggestion is that, in Iceland, the Common Guillemot is in contact with the Brunnich's, and, (though for quite unknown reasons) the bridled form of the Common is less able to withstand the competition.

Where, then, does this take us, when interpreting the population levels of different species? Not, I'm afraid, very far. Why has the population of Wandering Albatrosses levelled out at 50000 instead of 5 million? The answer may be that it has not. It may be very slowly increasing or decreasing. Similarly, the Atlantic Gannet population is not stable at 213000 pairs; it is increasing at about 3 per cent per annum. In other cases, the present population has been grossly affected by man. But why are there n millions of Wilson's Storm-petrels and not $2n$ millions? In some species, nest sites may be limiting, but it is always difficult to be convinced of this.

Species, with small numbers and restricted distribution, fall into several categories. Abbott's Booby, for example, is now restricted to Christmas Island but formerly occurred in the western Indian Ocean on Rodriguez and on one of the Seychelles group (usually said to be Assumption but Glorioso is an alternative) and perhaps in the Chagos of the central Indian Ocean. Its range has shrunk because man has destroyed it and its habitat in the west, but in the east, on Christmas Island, it has not been significantly affected by man, yet its numbers remain small. Conceivably, its numbers fluctuate extremely slowly. Given its absurdly low productivity, certainly less than 0.05 chicks per pair per year, and quite probably only half that, it would take a long time for any favourable environmental change, leading to slightly greater productivity, to show up in numbers. On the other hand, it is difficult to understand why Andrew's Frigatebird numbers less than 2000 pairs whilst the Greater Frigatebird numbers probably well over 100 times as many. Both have similarly low productivity and probably almost identical food spectra. Nor is Andrew's Frigatebird particularly specialized in its nesting-site requirements. By contrast, the low numbers of the Galapagos Penguin (less than 15000) and the flightless cormorant (about 800 pairs) are more easily understood. The former is restricted to the cool waters of the Humboldt, which brush past the southern and western islands in the archipelago. Its breeding and feeding range is thus strictly limited. The

penguin breeds only on Isabela and Fernandina. The cormorant requires a combination of deep water off rocky peninsulas, and gently sloping sandy beaches and is furthermore inhibited from spreading, since this would mean sea-crossings in shark-infested waters. Thus even with their higher productivity, they do not increase and in some years the penguins either do not attempt to breed or are almost completely unsuccessful, even though in others, productivity may be more than 1.3 young per nest. The mortality rate, too, may be unusually high, and in the penguin the main cause of death is failure to gather enough food before moulting, which is an exhausting process and has to leave the penguin in perfect condition if it is to thermo-regulate properly.

Some other rare seabirds, such as the Cahow and the Short-tailed Albatross have simply been victims of straightforward exploitation by man, who has extinguished thriving colonies. As one would expect from the environmental changes that are constantly occurring, seabird populations have to find new points of balance. The rates at which they change are of great interest, even though we rarely know why they do so.

Some examples of changes in population

During the last fifty years the Herring Gull population, has exploded. Since about 1925, in Europe the population has, according to area, doubled, tripled or quadrupled, whilst in New England, this century, it has increased by a factor of between 15 and 30. Now, Herring Gulls are not only a nuisance, but a potential danger. They drive away some other seabirds, notably terns, and foul islands, and because their increasingly urban habits bring their droppings into close contact with people, the danger of disease may become significant. At present, the British population is increasing overall at about 13 per cent per annum, and the figures for most colonies show similar steep rises: The Isle of May population increased from 760 pairs in 1947 to 21000 in 1972, and since 1907 the regular annual increase has been about 13 per cent. On Walney Island off Cumbria, the mixed colony of Herring and Lesser Black-backs increased from 700 pairs in 1950 to 18000 in 1965, which is a yearly increase of 25 per cent—well above the rate at which the colony could have increased

An unattended lorry loaded with barrels of fish provides a free meal for Herring and Lesser Black-backed Gulls, Lerwick Harbour, Shetland.

by its own output. From mortality of first year birds calculated from ringing data, and from adult mortality calculated from direct observations of marked individuals, and assuming 2nd year (and thereafter) mortality to equal adult mortality, and taking first-breeding to occur in the 4th or 5th year and annual productivity to be about one young per pair per year, the calculated rate of population increase is 11–12 per cent per year. This is a good fit with the observed increase. Lesser Black-backs may be capable of somewhat faster increase, perhaps 17–20 per cent. In America, Herring Gulls increased from about 10000 pairs in 17 colonies in 1900 to about 90000 pairs in over 300 colonies in 1967. This increase progressed fairly steadily at 4–5 per cent per year. By 1976, it seems, however, that the breeding population in the eastern United States was about 95000 pairs and that in most parts of America, the population is now stationary or decreasing. Only the southernmost colonies are still increasing rapidly. In Canada the 1976 population of breeding pairs, north to 52°, was estimated to be roughly 125000 and possibly still increasing. Scandinavian populations have also increased.

Besides the Herring and Lesser Black-backed Gulls, the Greater Black-back has also increased markedly. Its present estimated population in Britain and Ireland is more than 22000 pairs, though the largest colony (North Rona) is only some 1800 pairs strong. It has increased its numbers and breeding range markedly this century, especially in Scotland and Ireland, though also in England and Wales. The increase between 1902–1930 in England

and Wales indicated a growth rate of 36 per cent per year, which is extraordinarily high and must have been due to immigration. In America, they first nested in 1926 and increased to about 12000 pairs in 100 colonies by 1965. The increase (estimated 17 per cent per year) was aided by immigration from Canada. In 1976 the United States population was thought to number more than 15000 pairs and to be still increasing.

An intriguing effect of the massive cull of breeding Herring Gulls on the Isle of May (43900 breeding gulls killed between 1972 and 1976) was to alter, drastically, the age-composition of the colony. Before 1972 about 20 per cent of the breeding population consisted of birds breeding for the first time whereas by 1976 this proportion had risen to about 50 per cent. A most interesting facet of this change was that reproductive success was not lowered as a result. The mean annual fledging success of breeding gulls was 0.80 chicks per pair in 1975 and 1976, compared with 0.79 in 1967 and 1968. Yet, as a rule, birds breeding for the first time have a much lower success than older birds.

It is commonly accepted that Herring Gulls, at least, owe much of their increase to an artificially improved food supply, that is augmented by fish-waste, garbage, farm-food, etc. For example, Nisbet relates the Herring Gull's recent decline in certain areas of Canada and America to the decline in total fish landings (Quebec, Maine, Massachusetts, Rhode Island). By contrast, in Newfoundland, New Brunswick, Virginia and North Carolina, where gulls have maintained or increased their numbers, the inshore fishery has been maintained. On the other hand, Harris questions the association between human-provided food and the gull's increase, pointing out that at Milford Haven, in Wales, the amount of fish handled declined dramatically over the period in which gulls in that area were increasing rapidly. However, Herring Gulls will eat almost anything, and it may be that it is not the amount of man-provided food which has increased much – some sources have probably decreased, due to recycling and more efficient disposal of waste – but that Herring Gulls formerly did not take advantage of it, and now do so. Their feeding habits may have changed significantly. In seeming support of this, it is significant that the Herring Gull is *not* now increasing in Iceland,

The annual rate of increase in the number of pairs of Herring Gulls nesting in towns in five regions of Britain. So far all attempts to move colonies of over ten pairs have failed. After Coulson and Monaghan (1977).

even though it was colonized in 1925. There, it subsists largely on natural food and each colony appears to be 'closed' to newcomers. The colonization of Iceland, incidentally, as also of Bear Island (1932) and Spitzbergen (1952), was probably due to amelioration of climate. Correspondingly, the northern Glaucous Gull disappeared from Newfoundland and retreated in Iceland. Among other species of gull, some are increasing and others decreasing. The Kittiwake is increasing around Britain and in Canada; the Black-headed Gull has about doubled in England and Wales since 1958 (now over 100000 breeding pairs, the largest colony, at Needs Oar point in Hampshire containing some 20000 pairs), and increase achievable merely by the survival to breeding age of two or three eggs per 100 pairs per year, extra to those required to keep the population stable; the Silver Gull has started to exploit ploughed fields inland for food in Australia and is increasing; the Ring-billed Gull colonized the Great Lakes, in America, in 1926 and increased to 330000 pairs by 1967; the Southern Black-backed Gull, or Kelp Gull, has increased markedly in sub-Antarctica and New Zealand and is colonizing Australia, and one could add further examples. Not all these increases are susceptible to the explanation suggested above. The main cause of the British Black-headed Gull's increase, for example, is probably increased breeding success due to the creation of more wardened reserves (not intended for the gulls) and in some areas, the provision of new breeding localities such as flooded gravel pits. The Kittiwake's success is certainly not due to scavenging and may reflect a change in the distribution of natural food.

The Herring Gull's new habit of nesting on buildings, usually wedging the nest between chimney pots, seems to have grown most markedly since about 1969, and is increasing fast. Colonies counted in 1969 and again in 1976 had increased by 143 per cent, which, with colonies newly established since 1969, is equal to a *yearly* increase of 17 per cent, and gave a minimum total of some 3000 pairs of roof-top nesting Herring Gulls. New roof-top colonies are being formed at the rate of 9.3 per cent per annum, and it has been estimated that, on present trends, there will be 14000 pairs nesting in 246 towns by 1986. Already, by 1975 and 1976, thirty-one district authorities in Britain had reported complaints from residents; the gulls are noisy, messy and sometimes aggressive in defence of young. Some towns are colonized and then spontaneously deserted, but in most

such cases, only a pair or two had gained a toehold, and in a colonial species, single pairs or very small groups are extremely ill-at-ease. Mostly, the nests are on the tops of tall buildings in the centre of the town. Some Lesser Black-backs and Great Black-backs, also, are now nesting on roof-tops, but Herring Gulls remain the prime exploiters.

Unfortunately, terns are not doing nearly so well as gulls. There is probably no species of tern that is currently increasing rapidly, if at all, and there are many that are seriously on the decline. In northwest Europe the Roseate Tern has declined of late, the 1969 total of 2476 pairs for Britain and Ireland declining to 1414 in 1974 and the Arctic from 35859 pairs to 29569. Others, however, have fared better, the Common up from 9106 to 10613 (though those figures are based on only some of the existing colonies), the Sandwich from 10783 to 29569. Others, however, have fared better, and the Little from 1427 (in 1967) to 1685 in 1974, again based on most of the existing colonies. In America, Common, Arctic, Roseate and Little terns were all greatly reduced by man in the late 19th century, after which they increased to peak numbers between 1920 and 1950 and are now decreasing again, partly due to the occupancy of offshore islands by gulls. Nisbet estimates that at their 'high' and 'low'

The distribution and size of colonies of Herring Gulls nesting on buildings reported in 1969 and 1976. After Coulson and Monaghan (1977).

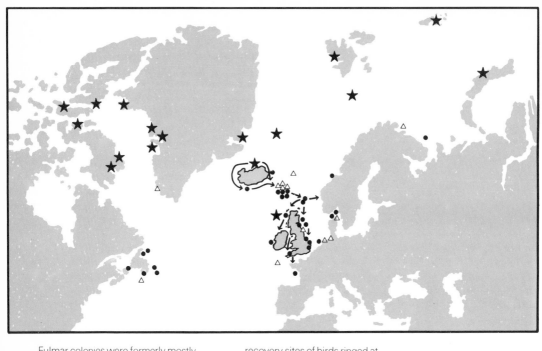

The Fulmar population explosion. After G. M. Dunnet (1977).

points respectively, the numbers of breeding pairs of terns in Massachusetts were: Common Tern, 30 to 40000 and c. 5000; Arctic Tern 300 to 400 and c. 20; Roseate Tern 4500–5000 and c. 2000; and Little Tern 1500 and c. 100. The 1972 figures are even lower. In Holland, Sandwich Terns suffered drastic mortality through poisoning with toxic chemicals and are slowly recovering. For all their huge numbers, Sooty Terns are much reduced, in many areas of the tropics. Gull-billed Terns have declined in recent years due to destruction of breeding and feeding habitat, for these terns feed largely on frogs, lizards and invertebrates in wetlands.

Fulmars have been increasing in the eastern North Atlantic for more than 200 years. Their remains were absent from all of the pre-historic middens found all over Scotland and Ireland, although these contained most other seabirds, from Great Auks to Storm Petrels, and so it seems safe to conclude that they were not at that time breeding in Scotland. However, they were present in numbers, on St Kilda by (at the

latest) the 9th Century, where the population remained more or less stable until 1939, and according to James Fisher, was for long the only colony in the temperate Atlantic–an outpost. After spreading around Iceland, (18th Century) colonizing the Westmann Islands, then the Faroes (early 19th Century) and Foula (Shet-lands) in 1878, the spread continued to the outer Hebrides (by 1889), Orkney and North Highlands (by 1899), Atlantic Ireland (by 1909), Eastern Scotland (by 1914), the inner west (Irish Sea area) and eastern England (by 1919), and the low south-west, including the south coast of England, (by 1934). By 1959 there were 486 breeding colonies, 222 stations being prospected and nearly 100000 occupied sites at the breeding colonies. In 1966, Fisher estimated that by 1969, there would be over 800 stations and 130000 occupied sites, excluding St Kilda (the 'Operation Seafarer' count, 1969–70, gave 306000 pairs, the discrepancy due to more complete coverage). The yearly percentage rates of increase in the number of occupied sites varied, according to region, from 10–27 per cent. Later, with better figures, 'Operation Seafarer' calculated that between 1929 and 1949 the total increase was about 420 per cent and between 1949 and 1969, about 280 per cent, or about 7 per cent per year. In the western North Atlantic the Fulmar has recently extended its range and now breeds in Newfoundland.

Clearly, from the rate at which many areas were colonized, the pioneers were followed by waves of immigrants, who consolidated the territorial gains. Indeed, even assuming adolescent mortality no higher than adult, an increase of only 5 per cent per year would be expected for any colony by its own output. As we now know for several species (Gannets, Kittiwakes, Herring Gulls, Puffins, Manx Shearwaters and others), the immigrant Fulmars are young birds. Fisher attributes this rapid and determined spread to the provision of high-quality food from the offal of, first, the northern whalers and then the trawling industry. Completely different explanations were, however, put forward by Wynne-Edwards and Finn Salmonsen. The former suggested that the Fulmar's spread is a 'natural' phenomenon, perhaps due to the emergence of a new and particularly vigorous genotype, originating in a single individual. The latter suggested that the spread occurred because some pioneer Fulmars moved south into an empty food-niche (the macro-plankton of the offshore waters) and were thus able to thrive. The initial move into this hitherto unexploited area, he ascribes to a change in genotype. He pointed out that only the Fulmars breeding in the warmer boreal waters were involved in the increase, and that the area of warmer water in the eastern North Atlantic had increased during the last 100 years. Later, Dick Brown found that in the western North Atlantic, Fulmar distribution is linked to cool water (and hence plankton density) more than to offal. Fisher emphasized the vast amount of whale offal available in Greenland waters to the Fulmars of Iceland, which spread greatly during the 'right-whaling days', and the geometric build-up of trawling offal which occurred ahead of the Fulmar explosion. He also emphasized the great foraging range of the Fulmar – at least 600 miles – which puts offal within the range of all Fulmars breeding on British and Irish Coasts and obviates the criticism that the details of the Fulmar's spread do not tally well with the location of offal. As he said (in 1966), hardly any of the trawlers operating in waters available to British Fulmars have plants for utilizing fish offal. Almost all of it was thrown into the sea. Before the 1939–45 war, twice the weight, or more, of the entire British and Irish Fulmar population was being dumped *daily* as offal, into some parts of the Fulmar's ocean range. But this statistic is of dubious value since only a fraction could be grabbed by the Fulmars before sinking. Finally, he attributed the decline in the rate of increase in Fulmars, since the 1950's, to a new and much less favourable balance between Fulmar biomass and offal. However, as the 'Seafarer' counts showed, the increase was by no means over by 1960. Several colonies registered huge increases between 1959–1969, especially Orkney, where the increase was some 240 per cent. In the Outer Hebrides, though, it was only 27 per cent. The apparently small increase in the 1950's was probably because many colonies were not counted. Perhaps, the major cause of the Fulmar's increase has been a shift in natural food or in feeding habits, aided at times by offal, even if the latter helped the Fulmar only for a short time each year, when natural food was scarce and young birds vulnerable to starvation.

Two more examples of population changes must suffice. The first concerns the auks, about which there has been much concern in recent years. Around Britain, the Guillemot and the Puffin are the two most numerous auks, with (according to the 1969 'Operation Seafarer' counts) roughly estimated populations of 577000 and 490000 pairs respectively. British Guillemots had not been counted in total before 1969, but a few colonies had, and judging from them, considerable decreases had occurred since 1939, especially in southern England and Wales. But in parts of Scotland, at least, Guillemots increased and are still doing so, and it must be stressed that recent work on the variations in the results of counts carried out at different times means that one-off counts, such as most of those carried out for 'Operation Seafarer', are accurate only to within 26 per cent of the true figure. I believe that a detailed investigation of counting methods, and the factors affecting counts (daily and seasonal, variation in attendance, etc.) and the interpretation of counts, is overdue and will hold some surprises. The British Guillemot population comprises only a fraction of the world's, and the latter has declined markedly in several areas. In the remarks which follow immediately, I do not discriminate between Common and Brunnich's Guillemot, though the figures apply predominantly to the latter, which is an arctic species breeding almost entirely north of 55°. Leslie Tuck in his monograph on the murres (guillemots), cites a figure of 1 645 000 in one of the Russian, Novaya Zemlya seabird 'bazaars' (that in Bezymyannaya Bay) in 1933–34. Eight years later, the population had dwindled to 600 000 and in a further 6 years, to 290 000 birds. Subsequently, however, protection largely restored the population. Again, there were about 750 000 guillemots at Cape Tchernetskin in 1942 (and even this must have been well down on previous numbers, since the 'bazaar' (as these great colonies are termed) had been exploited since 1930), but only 55 000 by 1950. And so it goes on, colonies at Cape Lilye had 200 000 guillemots in 1925 but only 1000 in 1950; exploited and depleted colonies at Kuvshin, the Vily and the Home 'bazaar', etc. When Tuck wrote (1960), there were still nearly fifty bird 'bazaars' in Novaya Zemlya with a total (both species) of about 2 million guillemots.

Then there are the teeming populations, to be numbered in millions, of Bear Island, Spitzbergen (all Brunnich's), and Franz-Josef Land. Tuck, again, hazards a guess at a minimum total of 15 million (almost all Brunnich's) in the Polar Basin, from which he arbitrarily excludes East Greenland. There have been recent massive declines in the West Greenland population, earlier estimated at 2–3 million, mainly in the Upernavik district; the Greenland Brunnich's Guillemots have suffered drastically from salmon-netters and shooters in the last decade. More than 1.25 million birds are killed each year.

In the Canadian Arctic the once populous Common Guillemot has greatly declined and some 90 per cent now breed off east Newfoundland. In New England (New York–New Brunswick) the seabird population reached a low ebb in the early 20th century, due to persecution, and the auks, in particular, have not regained their former abundance. A recent estimate gave some 1.25 million Common Guillemots and over 5 million Brunnich's. On the other hand, the warming up of the Arctic in recent years has had a notable effect on the seabirds of Newfoundland, Labrador, Greenland, Iceland and the Faroes. One effect was an increase in guillemots in the Labrador current area. Comparably, in the Baltic, guillemots are more abundant today than they have been in historical times. On the other hand, in some areas (for instance, the north shore of the Gulf of St Lawrence) there has been a very considerable and very recent decline in auks, especially Razorbills and Puffins. Overall, the picture for auks is at present one of decline. In Norway, too, guillemots are on the decline, although the population is not large in comparison with some of the species' strongholds. The main agents in its decrease have been oil, possibly toxics, in several localities, for the Brunnich's, exploitation by, and fishing activities of, man, and in localized instances, increase in Herring Gulls.

The Razorbill has only a small population (estimated world total 208 000 breeding pairs), and in most areas has not been counted in enough detail to reveal population changes. However, the eastern Canadian population is well-surveyed and David Nettleship cites forty-four colonies in eastern Canada and Maine, totalling some 38 000 birds. Recently, it has declined by probably more than 50 per cent in the Gulf of St Lawrence, perhaps due to oil pollution and toxic chemicals, also in Norway (pollution, hunting and fishing nets), Finland, Sweden, and Denmark. At least 70 per cent of the world population breeds in Britain and Ireland where, it is thought, its numbers are currently fairly stable, after a previous decline. Undoubtedly, it is increasing at some stations, for example the Bass Rock, where in the last five years numbers have at least doubled, and on St Kilda, where it has increased slightly. It is highly vulnerable to oil and toxics in certain key areas such as the Irish Sea, North Sea and English Channel and small increases in the mortality rate of pre-breeders and breeders can soon drastically affect the size of the population.

The British Puffin population has declined markedly since the end of the last century, especially in the southwest of England (e.g. Lundy Island), the Irish Sea (e.g. Grassholm) and southwest Scotland (e.g. Ailsa Craig), where the reductions have been enormous. It has reputedly declined also, at many more northern and western (and ancient) stations such as St Kilda, the Shiants, Clo Mor and North Rona (but see below). Until the 1960s, the spectacle of the St Kildan Puffins was generally described in superlative terms, and estimated, sometimes by experienced observers, at anything up to

Above The Puffin. A favourite auk that has declined drastically in some localities in the last decade or two but may now be recovering.

Below A flock of Little Auks in their breeding grounds in Spitzbergen. Some colonies number more than a million birds.

Below The east coast of Christmas Island, Indian Ocean, one of the world's great seabird stations, with an endemic booby, frigatebird and tropicbird. It is densely covered with rain-forest.

The Noup of Noss in the Shetland Isles (*above*) and the horizontally stratified cliffs of the Orkneys (*right*) provide an ideal nesting habitat for many seabirds such as Guillemots and Kittiwakes.

Opposite A colony of Australasian Gannets (mainland Saddle Colony) at Cape Kidnappers, in New Zealand. Notice the regular spacing in the central part of the colony. The ledges on the rock face in the background are man-made and are to encourage this flat-ground loving bird to nest there.

Left Part of an unusually dense colony of Northern Royal Albatrosses on Sisters Island, off New Zealand.

Below Part of a colony of half a million Royal Penguins at Hard Point, Macquarie Island.

Opposite Following the plough inland has become an important feeding method for Herring, Common and Black-headed Gulls in western Europe. These are Black-headed Gulls in winter and immature plumage.

Left The Short-tailed Albatross, now down to a handful of pairs, suffered massively at the hands of plume-hunters.

Below Fulmars feeding on offal thrown overboard from a fishing vessel. Although huge amounts have been provided it is by no means certain that this offal has been the main or only factor in the Fulmar's dramatic spread in the North Atlantic.

The six auklets showing their
bizarre facial adornments presumably
used in breeding displays: (from left
to right) Cassin's Auklet, Rhinoceros
Auklet, Crested Auklet, Least
Auklet, Parakeet Auklet and
Whiskered Auklet.

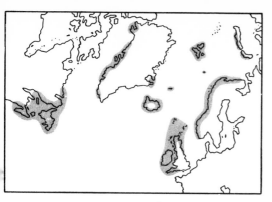

Breeding distribution of the Puffin.

△ increase
■ no change
★ decrease

Recent changes in some British and Irish colonies of Puffins. After M. P. Harris (1976).

3 million pairs, though this figure may well be exaggerated. The causes of the general decline, much of it since 1962, remain somewhat obscure. The poisoning of plankton, upon which Puffins feed extensively in winter, seemed a possibility, especially in view of the indication that levels of PCBs (polychlorinated bi-phenyls)

are higher in plankton from offshore Atlantic waters than from inshore, but is discounted by several authors. Puffins do not figure nearly so prominently as Guillemots among oiled, beached birds, and natural predation is almost certainly negligible. Certain colonies, notably those on Lundy and Ailsa Craig, have been eliminated by rats, but there are no rats on St Kilda. About changes in food availability, nothing is known, though Harris' recent work has shown that St Kildan Puffins certainly find it more difficult to gather enough food than do those from eastern Scotland, on the Isle of May. Since 1972, however, the decline on St Kilda appears to have been arrested. In that year, some recolonization of Hirta, the main group, probably occurred and substantial increases were noted at many of the smaller groups. Moreover, of six other Scottish colonies (Hermaness, Fair Isle, Garbh Eileen, the Shiants, the Isle of May, and Faraid Head) Mike Harris has shown increases at two (Isle of May and the Shiants) and at the others no decline, between 1971 and 1975. He suggests that they are still increasing in the Shetlands, and that on Hermaness and the north coast of Unst there were 'certainly more than the 50 000 pairs (recently) given for the whole of Shetland'. Similarly it *might* have increased on Foula since 1971; is probably increasing on Fair Isle and may not have declined further (since 1968) in the Orkneys. The mainland Clo Mor colony decline mentioned earlier is perhaps dubious. The Flannan colony did not decrease noticeably between 1969 and 1975, whilst on Mingulay there was a marked increase. The spectacular decline of Shiant birds may have been arrested; it had apparently slowed down by 1973. The increase in the east coast has been most spectacular on the Isle of May (5 pairs in 1959 to 2969 occupied burrows in 1975). In England the decline is in many cases still proceeding, although in the north-east of England, as on the Farne Islands, and especially Coquet Island, the population is increasing. In Ireland the decline has been in places spectacular (e.g. Inishtearaght from 20–30 000 pairs in 1968 to 7500 pairs in 1969 and Rathlin 2200 pairs 1967, to 817 pairs 1969) but may not be continuing. In Wales, all colonies have declined but most are now stable, as they apparently are in the Channel Islands. In France, the colony at Les Sept-Iles declined from 10–15 000 pairs to 2500 pairs in 1966 and then, after Torrey

Canyon, to 4–500 pairs in 1969. It is still in slight decline.

North of Britain the picture is not too gloomy: it is holding its own in the Faroes; possibly increasing in Iceland (of the order of 8–10 million birds mainly on the Westman Islands); no obvious signs of change in Norway (estimated 1.25 million pairs). In the U.S.S.R., there has been some regaining of numbers after decline. In Newfoundland and Labrador the population (less than 500000 breeding pairs) has declined considerably this century and again, more than threequarters of the Canadian population breeds in east Newfoundland, mostly at four large colonies in Witless Bay. Harris goes on to tabulate 'calculated guesses' for the sizes of various populations (races) in their various localities and produces a maximum figure of the order of 13 million for the world population, though the figures are not meant to be treated as anything more than orders of magnitude.

Harris' valuable survey puts the Puffin decline in a new and far less pessimistic light. Rightly, I'm sure, he relegates predation, soil erosion, and direct human exploitation, to a secondary role in the overall decline that occurred. Nor does he consider pollution to be important (most birds have low levels of toxics and in any case, many declines pre-dated pollutants). Instead, he supports Lockley's view, expressed twenty-five years ago, that the decline was largely due to oceanographic changes affecting the Puffin's food supply. The seas around southern England warmed up to reach peak temperature in the 1940s and 1950s and since about 1960 have been cooling again. Cooler seas should lead to an increase in the food which pre-eminently northern species such as Puffins and guillemots rely upon.

The Gannet is among those North Atlantic seabirds which are currently increasing. There are now more than 213000 pairs in thirty-four gannetries in the world, of which more than 180000 pairs are in the east. On both sides of the Atlantic the population has been increasing steadily this century, not spectacularly as did the Fulmar and Herring Gull, but climbing at around 3–5 per cent per annum. In its case, there seems no need to postulate an improved food supply or a new genotype. The lifting of the depressing effect of straightforward exploitation by man has been enough to allow the population to increase. Of course, in saying this, one implies that it is climbing back to a

level which it formerly occupied, or perhaps (if things have changed) to a new level. But one cannot say what either of those levels will be. Other members of its family have done less well. The Masked and Brown Boobies have certainly declined steeply over much of their world range, and so, probably, has the Red-footed Booby although its tree-nesting habit may have helped to save it. The major cause is undoubtedly direct exploitation by, or the indirect effects of, man. The Peruvian Booby has declined, probably as a result of man's over-fishing of the anchovy stock; the Blue-footed Booby has probably declined in the Gulf of California and off Peru, and Abbott's Booby's tiny relict population on Christmas Island has lost ground (literally and metaphysically). The Cape Gannet is probably declining but the Australasian is increasing.

Finally, the increase of several antarctic and sub-antarctic seabirds, notably penguins, must be mentioned. Many species (Adelie, Chinstrap, Gentoo, etc.) are increasing rapidly in range and numbers. Nowadays, penguins are the chief consumers of the invertebrate riches of the antarctic seas, and they may, some would say must, have benefited from the demise of the whales, which consumed unimaginably large quantities of euphasids and squids. Furthermore, the penguins suffered heavily at the hands of whalers and others, and the lifting of this pressure must have had an effect.

Lest the picture of the state of health of the world's seabirds appear unwontedly bright from this sketchy survey, it may be added that many relatively common species have suffered heavy losses this century, which have not been made good. I have already instanced seven sulids, and could add most terns, several shearwaters, some albatrosses, some frigatebird populations, some pelicans, the Cape Penguin, the Guanay Cormorant, several more auks, and others. In passing, it may be noted that the seabird populations, even of remote islands, may have been affected by man on a scale which the visitor may not appreciate. On Aldabra, and quite recently, for example, frigatebirds, many of them adult, were killed at the rate of thousands a year. On Christmas Island (Indian Ocean) Andrew's Frigatebird has been killed for food over many years and may owe its present small numbers largely to this. There are at present twenty-eight seabirds on the list of endangered species.

Seabirds and man

Man is a predator. For millions of years he was, a hunter, or possibly in some areas a hunter-gatherer. During all this time, there were seabirds, and seabirds are good to eat. Even our pampered modern palates find them acceptable, and we can be sure that, from Neolithic times onwards, seabirds were taken by man. Identifiable seabird bones have been recovered from many late Pleistocene sites in Scotland and Ireland, and, sometimes in huge quantities, in prehistoric sites elsewhere around the North Atlantic, around the north Pacific, in the southwestern Pacific and in island groups in the southern hemisphere (Chathams, Ascension, Norfolk and others). The Chathams are perhaps the classic example of an island group whose seabirds suffered at the hands of primitive man. These islands were colonized by polynesians, perhaps from the Society Islands, (the Mariories), who multiplied until there were about 2000 of them, all living off seabirds and fish (there were no mammals except the odd seal). Their middens contain vast numbers of seabird bones, especially petrels, of which many belong to the Magenta Petrel hopefully now re-discovered there after fearing it to be extinct. Several petrel species really were brought to extinction by the Mariories, who were themselves eaten in large numbers, at a later date, by the more warlike Maoris. Later still, white men introduced the usual pests and now the Chathams are infested with feral goats, cats, pigs, rats etc. The Magenta Petrels may have survived in the wilder parts of one of the islands.

James Fisher records that of nineteen sites, from Fife to the Orkneys and Shetland, the Hebrides, Ayrshire and Ireland, Great Auks were found in ten, gulls in nine, Gannets and Cormorants in eight, Guillemots in six, Razorbills in four, Puffins in three, and petrels, Shags, Kittiwakes and terns in one each. Later, among the thousands of islands of the western and southwestern Pacific, and the central Pacific, several species, notably the ground-nesting boobies and some albatrosses, must have been highly vulnerable. However, whilst it is possible, or even likely, that pressure might have been locally severe, man's numbers were probably too low to exert a serious effect, though he doubtless helped the wolves and bears (in the northern regions) to encourage seabirds to nest on islands and cliffs rather than the mainland.

Eventually, the skilled and knowledgeable culling of seabirds became a way of life on several northern isles. The St Kildan culture was based entirely on seabirds and astonishing feats of climbing were performed in pursuit of Fulmars and Gannets. The earliest detailed account of the St Kildan's way of life, and perhaps the best, is Martin Martin's account of his voyage to St Kilda, published in 1698. They regulated their harvest according to their own rules, so as not to deplete the stock. This skilful management is seen perhaps even better in the Faroes, where seabirds are still culled. The Westman Islands, Sula Sgeir and Myggenaes in the Faroes, are the only places where Gannets are still regularly taken for human food. Nørrevang, of Denmark, has delved deeply into Faroese lore. Their methods, mainly for catching Puffins, guillemots and Gannets, have been in use for centuries. Puffin colonies were exploited by rotation, once in three years, first by drawing birds from their burrows (only one of the pair), and later by 'fleyging', catching Puffins in mid-air with a net on a pole. (Quite independently the Aleuts of the North Pacific developed a 'fleyg' for catching Tufted Puffins.) The Faroese noted that young, non-breeding pairs did not fly straight into the colony, as breeders did, but approached in a huge circle. Only these birds were caught. A further check on their age was provided by their bill structure, for it takes more than three years for a puffin to acquire a fully adult bill. Similarly with guillemots, the ledges were heavily exploited for several years and then left alone for three years.

At many other places, for example the Bass Rock, Ailsa Craig, Eldey (Iceland) Bird Rocks (Gulf of St Lawrence) and several colonies of the Australasian Gannet, huge numbers of Gannets, adults and young, have, to put it euphemistically, been collected for food or bait. At some of these places, as, for instance, at the Bass and Ailsa, Gannets were 'leased', and they and their eggs were taken regularly for centuries, even though there was never anything like the situation described for St Kilda and the Faroes. At others, as at Bird Rocks, once the largest colony of Atlantic Gannets in the world, wanton destruction continued at a terrific pace for a few years and the colony was virtually wiped out. In this instance, the birds were used largely as bait for the Grand Banks fisheries, as also were the Great Auks of Funk Island. By similar exploitation, the flightless Great Auk was brought to extinction and whalers slaughtered huge numbers of several penguin species. Large amounts of oil were extracted from both auks and penguins. Among the most famous cases of exploitation of seabirds for food is the annual harvesting of fledgling Mutton birds (Short-tailed Shearwaters) of Australasia. They are very fat (over 1000 grams at maximum) and succulent and are eaten fresh or salted, and the oil is used pharmaceutically. Despite the large numbers collected annually (up to 500000) it seems that numbers are apparently not declining and it may still be Australia's most abundant bird. Other shearwaters have also been taken for food, for example 10–20000 Cory's Shearwaters were taken every year on Great Salvage Island.

Exploitation for plumes used to cause immense slaughter. The White-capped or Shy Albatross at Albatross Island (30 kilometres northwest of Tasmania) used to cover acres of ground in a solid mass, but was reduced to 250–300 nests by 1909. Even now, less than 2000 nestlings are produced in a year. One of the most infamously exploited species was the Short-tailed Albatross which between 1887 and 1903 constituted most of the 5 million seabirds killed on Toroshima and other islands south of Japan. In 1922–23 practically the entire breeding population of some 3000 birds was taken, and by 1973 the population was still on 57 pairs, and had been as low as 10 pairs in 1955. Again, plume-hunters practically exterminated the seabirds of New England in the late 19th Century.

Among tropical species, the Sooty, Crested and Bridled Terns, Brown Noddies and others, the three boobies, especially the two ground-nesters (Masked and Brown), have endured centuries of egg-collecting on a heroic scale. In the Caribbean, on an isolated coral island (Bird Island) to the west of the Antillean Arc, eight men reputedly killed 5000 birds in six weeks and reckoned to obtain 1000 eggs per day. On Walrus Island in the North Pacific, six men loaded a badarrah (boat) with guillemot eggs until it could hold no more without sinking. The boat was capable of carrying 4 tonnes, excluding crew, and they filled it in less than three working hours (July 5 1872). Again, just short of 2 million Sooty Tern eggs were taken per year, in good years, from the Seychelles. Examples of this sort of thing could be multiplied many times throughout the world. Nor is it surprising, for seabird eggs are extremely nourishing and palatable. Guillemot eggs give 1988 calories per kilogram compared with an average 1358 for beef and both eggs and seabirds can be an important element in a people's diet. An estimated 2 million guillemot eggs are eaten each year. So, over the centuries, one can guess that not a few colonies have been decimated. Even today, large seabird colonies are sometimes virtually wiped out in a few years, as fishermen acquire boats in which they range further and stay out longer. The Brown Booby colony on Pulau Perak, in Malaysia, has dwindled from more than 6000 pairs to a handful, in a few years; fishermen leave evidence of mass killings on islands in the Seychelles, Coral Sea, Caribbean, southwest Pacific and so on.

An unusual case of direct exploitation by man – or more accurately, in this case, children – concerns the taking of British and European terns, Common, Roseate, Arctic and Sandwich, in West Africa. In the last ten years, many thousands have been snared with fine nooses, fish-baited, on the tideline. So far, nearly 1400

St Kildans catching a Fulmar. The St Kildan culture was based entirely on seabirds and astonishing feats of climbing were performed in pursuit of Fulmars and Gannets.

ringed Sandwich Terns have been recovered, and since only a proportion of the birds are ringed, and not all ringed birds are reported, it is no wonder that the scale of the killing is causing concern to conservationists in Europe. The drastic effects of the introduction of rats, cats, dogs, pigs, goats and donkeys to many seabird islands has already received mention. Polynesian rats are known to kill adult albatrosses on some Pacific islands, literally eating them alive as they incubate, the birds being apparently unequipped to react to this novel form of predation. Rats, which reached Lord Howe Island from a wrecked steamer, in two years nearly exterminated the native birds. Cats are thought to have destroyed ground-nesting seabirds on Ascension, donkeys are a pest in the Chagos archipelago, pigs root out shearwater burrows and have extirpated whole colonies of Muttonbirds. They got onto Clipperton, in the eastern Pacific, around 1897, probably from the wreck of the British ship 'Kinkora', and reduced the vast population of frigates, Sooty Terns and Masked and Brown Boobies from, in the case of the Masked, perhaps the largest colony in the world, to a handful of non-breeding pairs in 1958. Ten years later, after the pigs had been destroyed by Kenneth Stager, who deserves a medal, over 4000 boobies were nesting. The destruction of vegetation on the South Atlantic Island of South Trinidad, once covered with beautiful brazil-wood trees (*Caesalpina*) but now barren, is attributable to goats and has exterminated a great colony of Red-footed Boobies. In New Zealand, where so many petrels have suffered at the hands of man and his animals, there has been a great decline in the breeding area of the Mottled Petrel, among others, due to the introduction of wild and domestic animals. Man-caused fires have had disastrous effects on some oceanic islands, such as Rodriquez (Mascarenes), Madeira and Muttonbird islands off Tasmania.

Disturbance by man can cause a colony of seabirds to desert their breeding area completely, as sometimes in Sandwich Terns, or it can spoil their breeding success to varying degrees. In many cases, bereaved birds begin to interfere with other nesters, thus compounding the damage and, incidentally, supporting the idea that one function of synchrony is to minimize interference by conspecifics. It would be tedious and unnecessary to document specific cases, but it is worth emphasizing that in these days, when more people have the time, money and inclination to visit islands and other seabird haunts, as indeed to visit wildlife reserves of all kinds, their effect can be substantial. A single brash intrusion into a seabird colony can cause the loss of hundreds of eggs or small young, and repeated several times a season can reduce productivity practically to zero. Usually, this is because there are Herring or Black-backed Gulls in attendance, waiting to snap up exposed eggs or chicks. Or in other parts of the world, perhaps frigates or skuas. Disturbance is something which the researcher too has to bear in mind, for he may get a false picture, not only of breeding success but also of the timing of laying and of fidelity to site and mate. The year *after* a disturbance, the pattern of return and laying may be materially affected, as happened with certain groups of Gannets on Ailsa Craig. Thus, even mild disturbance can have effects on breeding biology which the worker may never suspect. In the case of rare and vulnerable species such as the Galapagos Penguin or the Flightless Cormorant, disturbance could be highly dangerous, but the remedy is obvious. Indiscriminate intrusion simply has to be prevented, and disturbance kept down by the use of suitably placed trails and hides. Even careful research work can, and usually does, cause appreciable loss. It was estimated that the task of checking ringed Eynhallow Fulmars on their nest sites caused up to 25 per cent egg-loss and there are many cases of bird-ringing causing substantial chick mortality, though in this case it results from over-keenness and lack of care, which the British Trust for Ornithology does everything within its power to correct. Perhaps more significant than the instrusions of visitors, because less easily controlled, is the intrusion of fishermen. There are countless regions in which fishing boats plunder seabird colonies. Among more recent phenomena, sonic booms have caused large scale desertion of breeding colonies by Sooty Terns in the Dry Tortugas.

Nevertheless, seabirds are lucky in that the kind of breeding places they favour are often not much sought after by man. Still, it is desirable to have as many islands and mainland seabird areas as possible, safe from untoward disturbance. In Britain, several of the finest ones are now safe in the care of one body or another. Some of the finest seabird stations in Britain, like the Bass Rock, Ailsa Craig and

Skokholm and Eynhallow (Orkneys) are privately owned. Seabird stations are rarely 'managed' by man, except by removal of pest species, largely gulls, by one means or another. Although it is a value-judgement to kill gulls for the benefit of other seabirds, there is obvious sense in preventing one species from increasing too far and damaging others, such as terns, Gannets, guillemots, Puffins or shearwaters. Also, Herring Gulls foul islands, and cause the fine-leaved, turf-like grasses to be replaced by lush, nitrogen-loving species such as *Holcus mollis* and by nettles, docks etc. The trouble is that in a long lived species it is ineffective to kill young gulls, and even if adults are destroyed, the cull has to go on year after year. Otherwise the colony is simply repopulated from outside. In Massachusetts, foxes and racoons were introduced into Herring Gull colonies where they wiped out the young, took a few adults and caused major reductions in the colonies and the abandonment of one. But at this stage, the predators starved and the islands were re-colonized by gulls. From the point of controlling numbers, sterilizing adults, which then continue to occupy breeding space but without producing young, is more effective than killing them. But although 'Sudan black' has been used to sterilize Herring Gulls, for example, it is not permanently effective. Control methods used have included netting, shooting, trapping, poisoning, narcotizing, and neutralizing eggs by spraying, pricking etc. But there is no single, effective means of controlling them, and the gaps will always be filled by gulls from elsewhere, so long as they are increasing at their present, rapid rate. The guano has been harvested on a continuing basis, at around 100 000–200 000 tonnes a year – and the birds carefully conserved. Indeed, mainland colonies have been established on headlands. The Gulf of California also had extensive deposits and the guano islands off the South African cape are still worked. These three major areas are all in the region of productive upwellings, which is why they support exceptionally large numbers of seabirds. The phosphate islands of Nauru and Ocean Island have also yielded vast quantities and at present Christmas Island in the Indian Ocean is producing more than 2 million tonnes each year, though it has not yet been established that the phosphate stems from bird guano rather than fossilised marine deposits. From the seabird point of view, man's guano gathering activities disturb them, often kill them, completely destroy vegetation and top-soil and may thus destroy the bird's habitat. I say 'may', because where islands are utterly barren anyway, seabirds and guano gathering can co-exist, as in Peru.

Destruction of breeding habitat, fortunately, is not as serious a threat to seabirds as it is to some landbirds, where drainage of wetlands, destruction of rain forest, and burning and overgrazing sparse savanna with subsequent desertification, affects vast areas. Mostly, seabird islands are too remote, small and barren to suffer in this way. But destruction, or at least pollution, of the marine habitat is a much more potent threat. There are two major types of pollution. The main ones are oil and toxic chemicals, which themselves are of several kinds, and minor ones include waste netting and general rubbish such as plastic, rubber and metal items, some of which is picked up by seabirds.

It is estimated that 2–5 million tonnes of oil are lost in the world's oceans each year. This problem and the effects of oil pollution on seabirds are too well known to merit elaboration. Large numbers of seabirds of many species become oiled although so far, apart from the serious sufferings of the seabirds off the Cape of South Africa, especially Cape Penguins, the principal victims are in the North Sea, English Channel, Irish Sea and North Atlantic and come ashore around Britain and on the western seaboard of Europe. The following figures convey some idea of the scale of mortality involved: 6124 kilometres of the Netherlands coast yielded 23 067 oiled birds between 1962 and 1968, whilst between 1968–70, 4128 were picked up along 1597 kilometres of east Scottish coast. More than 17 000 auks are known to have been involved in an Irish Sea/Clyde oiling incident in September/October 1969. In the winter of 1970, an estimated 50 000 seabirds were killed by oil off the east coast of Britain; 7757 auks were actually picked up. Up to 10 000, mainly Guillemots, were killed in the spring of 1971 off north-western Scotland. The Torrey Canyon disaster, on the Seven Stones Reef between Cornwall and Scilly Isles, in 1967 and the Santa Barbara oil-drilling accident off California in 1969 are now landmarks, since these, the names Amoco Cadiz, Eleni V, Christos Bitas, Betelgeuse, and Esso Bernicia have become notorious in pollution history.

It is difficult to calculate an accurate figure for the number of deaths caused by oil, but scores of thousands perish annually around Britain and Europe. Expressed as seabird corpses per kilometre of coast, the highest figure appears to be that for Poland, with an average of 5.2, of which 73 per cent were oiled (1970–71). Working through the information on the location of oiled birds, Bill Bourne concludes that perhaps the worst area in the world is in the approaches to the Baltic. The southern shores of the North Sea hold the record for the bird mortality caused by one pollution incident; 500 000 (though the figure is disputed and may have been much lower) said to have been killed by 9000 tonnes of crude oil from a grounded tanker at the mouth of the Elbe in January 1955. Severe oil pollution incidents have occurred in the English Channel, Irish Sea, North Sea and the Atlantic approaches. As mentioned, oil pollution off South Africa has increased greatly since the Suez Canal was closed, as it has, also, off Argentina and the offshore southern South American oilfields. There is little evidence of serious loss of life amongst tropical seabirds due to oiling, but a lot of reports of oil patches and tar balls, and there can be no doubt that a great deal of illegal dumping of oil, from ships clearing their tanks, occurs all over the tropical oceans.

Apart from clogging the plumage, destroying insulation and killing through chilling and stress, it is thought that oil ingested by preening can kill the bird through internal damage, by adversely affecting the transport of nutrients from the gut to the blood. Auks are particularly vulnerable to oil because they swim far underwater and may surface in a slick.

Oiled seabirds can be rehabilitated, but to do so requires skill, facilities and time. As soon as possible after discovery they should be rehydrated by passing a warm, weak solution of glucose and salt into their stomachs, using a tube passed down the throat. Rehydration is then needed every day, perhaps more than once a day and certainly after the stressful business of cleaning off the oil, which is done when the bird is in the best possible physical condition, and not *necessarily* immediately unless the oil is one of the more toxic ones. The bird should be cleaned with a mild detergent in warm water, followed by thorough rinsing with warm, clean water. It should then be swabbed off and dried with warm air, and kept in a warm, dry, shady

An oiled Guillemot. Auks are particularly vulnerable to oil because they swim far underwater and may surface in a slick.

place free from straw or other particulate matter. If necessary it should be force fed, with multi-vitamins included in the fish every other day. Before release it should be capable of picking up fish for itself and of swimming and preening without becoming waterlogged. Details of treatment are to be found in a free (single copies only) booklet 'Saving Oiled Seabirds' available from:

Distribution Services,
American Petroleum Institute,
2101 L St., N.W.
Washington, D.C. 20037.

There is considerable anxiety about, among others, the recent oil developments near to Shetland and Orkneys. The prospect of giant tankers plying these waters, among Britain's finest seabird colonies, is not a tranquil one. Good intentions are expressed all round, but the truth is that communication procedures are still inconsistent and slow, when accidents threaten or have happened, and that the emergency procedures for dealing with oil spillages have proved at best disappointing, at worst hopeless. Whilst moulting, soon after leaving the breeding colonies in July/August, guillemots are flightless and could be extremely vulnerable. So, for that matter, could young Gannets, flightless for a few days after leaving the colony. The only solution is prevention, which presumably depends upon tight control of navigation channels and a strictly observed procedure in the event of problems arising. Of course, oil pollution affects all marine life, not merely seabirds, and fishery interests are vitally important and have to be considered in any procedures evolved to deal with oil pollution. The detergents used to disperse oil may be more toxic than the oil itself and their use is often, understandably, opposed by fishery and other interests even if bird conservationists want to use them. Given the will, the pollution caused by merchant ships clearing out tanks, and depositing used engine oil and bilge oil, could be largely eliminated by the provision of facilities at port and compulsion to use them. At the moment, there are many countries that are not constrained by their own laws, from dumping on the high seas, and controls within territorial waters are no substitute for this.

The principal toxic chemical pollutants are the organochlorines, the PCBs (polychlorinated bi-phenyls) and the heavy metals, principally mercury and cadmium. Of the latter, cadmium, at least, occurs naturally in seawater and is present in high concentrations in many pelagic seabirds, which may well be adapted to deal with it. But a wide variety of highly toxic wastes are dumped at sea, including chlorinated dioxins, dibenzofurans and napthalenes. The discovery that pollution of seabird tissues had become world-wide, with DDT derivatives in antarctic penguins, and the well-documented cases of mass mortality or de-rangement of reproductive processes, which were incontestably due to poisoning by toxic chemicals, such as the virtual destruction of the Dutch population of Sandwich Terns by organochlorines and the decimation of Florida Brown Pelicans due to egg-shell thinning, caused widespread concern. The pelicans, incidentally, are now increasingly productive and egg shells are thickening as the DDE concentration in their food decreases. There have also been less clear-cut cases, in which large numbers of seabirds which died after exposure to natural stress (bad weather, food shortage) were found to have high levels of toxics. Because toxics may fail to kill a bird until it mobilizes its fat, in which they commonly concentrate, and may even then be an important contributory factor rather than the sole cause of death, it has been suggested that toxics may not be as detrimental as some people suppose. But this attitude seems singularly negative. We know that they are highly poisonous, we know they occur in seabirds in damaging concentrations and that they sometimes kill, and that means that it is highly undesirable to spread them throughout the world's ecosystems. The effects of the well-nigh limitless number of possible combinations of exotic chemicals, now brought together in the world's seas, is further cause for concern. If we know so little of their effects singly, how can we be complacent about the potentially new forms that could arise by combination.

Even more influential, on seabird populations, could be changes in their food due to man's activities. The Fulmar's explosive increase may have been, initially at least, partly due to man-provided offal, and the increase in large gulls certainly owes a lot to man's provision of food. The increase in some penguins has been attributed to the removal of the competition for krill, represented by whales. On the other hand, the meteoric rise of the Peruvian anchovy fishing industry, which put Peru at the head of the world's fishing catches by 1969, (more than 14 million metric tonnes), has had serious effects on the huge population of seabirds (up to 27 million in total). Until about 1965, they speedily recovered from the periodic catastrophes which befell them in the bad Niño years. But, by then, the fishery was taking more than the stocks could withstand without crashing. The combination of a bad Niño and an overfished stock of anchovies apparently proved too much, and the birds failed to recover at their usual speed. Latterly, the fish stocks are beginning to recover, but the seabirds, especially the Guanay Cormorant, remain low. Formerly, the Guanays were by far the most numerous of the 'big three' (Peruvian Booby, Guanay Cormorant and Brown Pelican). Predictably, as fish yields began to fall, the fishing interests cast disapproving eyes on the seabirds and suggested that they be eliminated. The craziness of the situation is almost beyond belief. The populace of a protein-starved nation (Peru), pay high prices for fish, whilst turning most of their catch into fish-meal to feed chickens upon which an obese America, spending millions on anti-fattening drugs, can batten, or use as fertilizer. At the same time, Peru suggests that its important guano fertilizer industry be eliminated. But no doubt economists would justify it.

Laysan Albatross colony by the runway on Midway Island, Hawaii. Between 1959 and 1963 there were 300 to 400 strikes a year.

Large numbers of Peruvian seabirds were in fact killed. Similarly in South Africa, the fishing lobby has in the past, pressed for the elimination of *its* guano-producing seabirds.

In the eastern North Atlantic there has been a four-fold increase in fish landings since 1910, though the pattern varies according to species, and industrial fishing is only a recent threat. Around the British Isles, the herring stock has been badly overfished. In the North Sea, catches peaked in 1965 (1.3 million tonnes) and have since declined. Attention is inevitably turning to other species. Now, mackerel are being heavily fished. Present technology, enables entire shoals to be netted in one fell swoop. Factory ships standing by to receive as much as an endless stream of suppliers can provide, means that stocks are facing a new level of exploitation. Since catches peaked in 1967, this may mean that we are already partway down the hump of the over-exploitation curve. Sand-eels, sprats, Norway pout, blue fish,

and others are now being taken in greater quantities in the North, Norwegian Sea and Barents Sea than ever before, although industrial fishing, for fish-meal, is still light, west of Britain. And all the time, the pressures grow. Membership of the European Economic Community endangers any realistic conservation policy, and beyond that lies the threat of eventual world shortage of protein. However, it would be quite wrong to see seabirds as direct competitors. In fact, it is the considered conclusion of a recent and detailed investigation of North Sea fisheries, that bird competition is of marginal importance. The total biomass of small (non-commercial) fish, potentially available to seabirds, is probably in excess of 2 million tonnes in the North Sea alone, and there are not more than some 2 million seabirds, requiring perhaps 75 000 tonnes per year. These figures compare with an annual catch of about 2.5 million tonnes by the fishing industry. When one considers that the roughly estimated stock of 1 million tonnes of North Sea sprats may themselves produce another million tonnes in a year, at present levels of exploitation, and roughly the same figures apply to sand-eels, too, it can be seen that seabirds are unlikely to be taking more than an insignificant percentage of the yearly production. But the birds may not see it this way. For them, the competition provided by man may prove to be highly significant. The removal of a major component of the ecosystem, does not simply leave a hole. It alters the proportions of other species. Also, the removal of certain year-classes alters the proportions of the year-classes and thus of the sizes of fish. Both these factors may be extremely important to seabirds, and some students of seabird biology believe that eventually the result will be a great reduction in seabird numbers. Indeed, one researcher's computer simulation of the relation between fish production, human fishing and fishing carried out by Shetland seabirds indicates that the birds require between 20 and 35 per cent of the annual food fish production from within a 45 kilometre radius of each colony, and that seabirds, predatory fish and industrial fishing are in direct competition. But the issue is enormously complicated and predictions in fishery matters are notoriously unreliable. Usually, the experts are wise after the event.

For some people, these considerations raise the matter of priorities. In a world short of protein, have those interested in seabirds any right to raise their voice? Of course they have, on at least two counts. First, fish stocks which are so overexploited that they cannot even support seabirds are indeed in a bad way and no sensible long term policy would even contemplate reducing them this far. Second, there may be quite a few generations of man still to come. They *may* be less destructively self-centred than we are, and may even value wildlife. Seabirds were here long before us and fortunately, try as we might, it is unlikely that they will become extinct before we do.

Study techniques

There is not space to detail the common marking and study techniques used on seabirds but the former include numbered metal rings (all of which, except for stainless steel, wear and corrode far too quickly) rings made of coloured synthetics such as 'Darrie', wing tags, flipper tags for penguins, feather dyeing, leg streamers and bill tags. Among study techniques, the next step forward in marking seabirds will probably be with radio transmitters whose signals can be picked up by satellite. This could give at least four fixes per day, and would be an ideal method, accurate to within about 5 kilometres, of tracking the paths of individual seabirds. The trouble seems to be devising a flat package and a suitable method of fixing it to the bird. A harness, such as those used for game birds, would be totally inappropriate on a seabird, though the total weight, mainly of batteries, could probably be reduced to 200 grams and could be borne by the larger species. Emperor Penguins have carried 700 gram depth-recorders and other apparatus for short periods, but it is a different matter living with them. Tiny transmitters, weighing only 18 grams have been superficially implanted into the abdominal cavities of penguins, but the range over which the pulses can be picked up is small.

Continuous recording of behaviour reveals many fascinating and otherwise inaccessible facets of the relationships of the pair. Time lapse photography has been successfully used on Kittiwakes, though in the special circumstances of the warehouse colony at North Shields, in which cameras can be installed behind the nests. Radio-active rings have also been used, to give individually recognizable signals, so enabling the attendance patterns of the pair to be continuously recorded. In this way, incompatible pairs could be recognized, and their breeding success and subsequent fidelity monitored. It would be interesting to let cameras look continuously at selected parts of several different colonies, for a whole breeding season. In this way, the levels of all the social behaviour patterns could be chekced against the features of the colonies, which should be chosen to differ widely in location, and to have different topographies, different size and so on. However, it would probably take a lifetime to analyse one season's recording!

Apart from Tinbergen's attempt to devise a realistic model of a Black-headed Gull which could be operated electronically so as to respond to the signals of a real gull in whose territory it had been planted, nobody has tried to 'talk back' to a behaving bird in natural surroundings. And this pioneering attempt was not wholly successful. Kortlandt first used the demanding method of long-term watches of behaviour from a hide, in his case in a cormorant colony. One lives in the hide, rather than merely spending a few hours there, and many fascinating and otherwise unobtainable observations can be made.

The rare Bonin Petrel near its nest burrow, on Midway Island, Hawaii. The drastic decline of some gadfly-petrels has been due to their vulnerability to introduced mammalian predators.

Not all the interaction between man and seabirds is one way – detrimental to the latter. Amongst the ways in which seabirds – although in fact almost always, gulls – damage man's interests are: endangering aircraft, polluting drinking water and possibly transmitting disease, and being a general nuisance. Informed opinion does not construe their feeding activities as competition with man.

Probably the most general offenders at airports are gulls, which, often, are attracted to nearby sewage works, refuse tips and reservoirs. The Danish Airport at Saltholm is nested on by 30000 gulls, which feed in Copenhagen. In the United States commercial carriers reported 476 strikes in 1966 and 2196 between 1961 and 1967. Although 73 species of bird were involved, gulls and waterfowl were the chief victims or culprits, according to viewpoint. Much work has been carried out on the subject of birds and airports, but its general import is simple enough to grasp without citing details. It is that the siting of the airport is the most important factor. If it *must* be in a silly place, in terms of bird strikes, then an adequate advance-warning system, by radar, for signalling the presence of birds must be used, together with a battery of techniques for scaring them off, and keeping them away (these include distress calls; presence of raptors; ultra-sonic sound, flashing lights, etc.). The situation on Midway Island in the Pacific, where Laysan and Black-footed Albatrosses collided with the Pentagon and reeled back, bruised and bloodied, was quite exceptional. Then, when Midway became a staging post for Pan-Am jets, there were 300 to 400 strikes each year between 1959 and 1963. Preventive measures cost the species many thousands of lives, as the United States shovelled the albatrosses aside, but the species is now recovering.

In Britain salmonellae were isolated in 52 out

of 111 samples of reservoir water, though never from incoming water; gulls were almost certainly responsible. Tubercle bacilli have been found in gulls, also in Britain and could infect cattle with avian tuberculosis. Gulls have been implicated, also, in the spread of bovine cysticerosis and can be the intermediate hosts for stages in the life cycles of tapeworms and flukes.

Under 'general nuisance' comes eating food intended for domestic stock (in the Ythan valley, Aberdeenshire, pig-farmers estimate that the 40–80000 Herring Gulls eat up to 33 per cent of the food put down for outdoor pigs), destroying other species, (terns, especially) nesting on buildings and transporting dangerous objects (tins, etc.) to pastures and runways and ruining grouse-moor shoots (if that is a nuisance). It is not without its humorous side that the gull whose numbers now engage man's fairly strenuous control measures, was given the impetus to increase by man himself. Control measures have included netting, shooting, trapping, narcotizing, neutralizing eggs, and importing predators.

In sum, the main threats to seabirds from man either have been, or are: direct taking of adults, young and eggs, pollution by oil and chemicals, fishing procedures and their effects on stocks, disturbance and tourism, alteration of species composition *via* gull increases.

The most valuable contributions man could now make, from the seabirds' viewpoint, are: produce effective inter-government legislation on offshore pollution; make national pollution control more stringent and effective; control disturbance (very difficult, but effective in selected cases); wherever possible set aside seabird breeding habitats as reserves (under the control of existing bodies); implement all I.C.B.P. resolutions; continue the sort of research which leads to better census techniques (since changes in numbers are basic indicators of the species' status) and to better understanding of the relationship between seabirds and their food (a very tall order).

Before listing currently endangered species it is worth mentioning that, in the recent past, several seabirds have been thought to be extinct, and have then been rediscovered, even, sometimes, in reasonable numbers. The gadfly-petrels have figured prominently in this way. The drastic decline of several once-numerous gadfly-petrels has been due to their vulnerability to introduced mammalian predators, which have been particularly troublesome because the petrels live in habitats in which the predators can readily survive the lean season, and so can multiply to pest proportions. Also, some of the gadfly-petrels (the 'muttonbirds' of some islands) have been sought by man, as food. Among species which have been heavily reduced by man and pests are the Kermadec Petrel, Cook's Petrel (nearly wiped out by cats and dogs on Little Barrier Island, New Zealand), the Mottled Petrel, and Solander's Petrel (wiped out on Norfolk Island). The Dark-rumped or Hawaiian Petrel, endemic to Hawaii and the Galapagos is rare in Hawaii and endangered by land clearance and introduced mammals in the latter. The Guadalupe Storm-Petrel, known to have nested off Mexico, is probably extinct as a result of introduced cats. The Black-capped Petrel of the West Indies suffered from man and the mongoose and is now restricted to the highlands of Haiti. The Cahow or Bermuda Petrel similarly taken by man and harassed by pigs, rats and cats was 'lost' for some 300 years before its rediscovery in 1951. It is still in great peril and rears very few young. Tropicbirds compete with it for holes (originally the Cahow was found well inland), though this problem has been partly met by providing artificial holes inaccessible to tropicbirds; also DDT has been implicated in the Cahows reduced breeding success. Though not known to do so, the Jamaica Petrel may still survive on Jamaica. The cliffs of Réunion harbour several petrel species. As well as the Cahow, the Mascarene and Magenta Petrels may have been rediscovered after presumed extinction. The Magenta Petrel is a particularly fascinating story. Known from only one specimen collected in the South Pacific in 1866 and rather dirty and undistinguished by the time Bill Bourne made his pilgrimage to Turin to contemplate the skin, it seemed to him to resemble another petrel, the Taiko, which used to occur on the Chathams along with several others now extinct. Not al' authorities agreed with him, but the apparent rediscovery of the Magenta Petrel on the Chathams in 1978, by David Crockett, appears to confirm his identification. Perhaps even more surprisingly, new petrels have been discovered (Jouanin's Petrel, and Barau's Petrel, a new species which is actually numerous on Réunion).

Appendices

SPECIES OF SEABIRDS OF THE WORLD

(Mainly after E. P. Edwards, 1974, *A Coded List of Birds of the World*.)

The symbols for distribution of the species indicate that the bird occurs in some part of a certain region or sub-region, as follows:

H	Holarctic
HP	Palearctic only
HN	Nearctic only
N	Neotropical mainland and nearby islands all around
NI	West Indies, except Trinidad and Tobago
N + I	Neotropical mainland, nearby islands, and West Indies
E	African mainland, north to Sahara, and western islands
EI	Islands off east coast of Africa
E + I	Africa, and all islands
O	Oriental mainland, Hainan, Taiwan, Ceylon, small islands near India

OI	Malay Archipelago to Borneo and Bali; Andamans, Phillipines, Ryukyus
O + I	Oriental mainland and islands to Borneo and Bali
AI	Australasian islands from Celebes, Lombok, the Marianas, to New Guinea, Midway, Hawaii, the Tuamotu Archipelago
AU	Australia (incl. Tasmania)
AZ	New Zealand
AIU	Australasian islands and Australia
AIZ	Australasian islands and New Zealand
AUZ	Australia and New Zealand
A	entire Australasian region
Ant.	occurs on the Antarctic continent

(Symbols for penguin distribution enclosed in parentheses indicate that the species occurs on sub-antarctic islands south of the region indicated.)
w. refers to where the bird spends the non-breeding season. Regions or parts of regions where the species is only a transient between wintering and breeding grounds are not listed.
example: HP;w.HP,O breeds in Palearctic; some individuals spend the winter in the Palearctic and some in the Oriental mainland as defined above.

SPHENISCIFORMES–PENGUINS

Spheniscidae–Penguins

Aptenodytes patagonicus	King Penguin	(N, E, AZ)
Aptenodytes forsteri	Emperor Penguin	Ant., (N)
Pygoscelis papua	Gentoo Penguin	Ant., (N, E, AZ)
Pygoscelis adeliae	Adelie Penguin	Ant., (N)
Pygoscelis antarctica	Chinstrap Penguin	Ant., (N, E)
Eudyptes pachyrhynchus	Fiordland Penguin	AUZ
Eudyptes crestatus	Rockhopper Penguin	(N, E, AUZ)
Eudyptes scalateri	Erect-crested Penguin	(AZ)
Eudyptes schlegeli	Royal Penguin	(AZ)
Eudyptes robustus	Snares Island Penguin	(AZ)
Eudyptes chrysolophus	Macaroni Penguin	(N, E)
Megadyptes antipodes	Yellow-eyed Penguin	AZ
Eudyptula minor	Little (Blue) Penguin	AUZ
Eudyptula albosignata	White-flippered Penguin	AZ
Spheniscus demersus	Cape Penguin	E
Spheniscus humboldti	Humboldt Penguin	N
Spheniscus magellanicus	Magellanic Penguin	N
Spheniscus mendiculus	Galapagos Penguin	N

PROCELLARIIFORMES–ALBATROSSES, PETRELS

Diomedeidae–Albatrosses

Diomedea exulans	Wandering Albatross	N, E, A
Diomedea epomophora	Royal Albatross	N, AUZ
Diomedea irrorata	Waved (Galapagos) Albatross	N
Diomedea albatrus	Short-tailed Albatross	H, OI, AI
Diomedea nigripes	Black-footed Albatross	H, OI, AI
Diomedea immutabilis	Laysan Albatross	HN, AI
Diomedea melanophris	Black-browed Albatross	N, E, A
Diomedea bulleri	Buller's Albatross	N, AIZ
Diomedea cauta	Shy Albatross	N, E, A
Diomedea chlororhynchos	Yellow-nosed Albatross	N, E, A
Diomedea chrysostoma	Grey-headed Albatross	Ant., N, E, A
Phoebetria fusca	Sooty Albatross	Ant., N, E, A
Phoebetria palpebrata	Light-mantled Albatross	Ant., N, E, A

Procellariidae–Petrels, Shearwaters

Macronectes halli	Northern Giant Petrel	E, AZ
Macronectes giganteus	Southern Giant Petrel	Ant., N, E, AUZ
Fulmarus glacialoides	Antarctic Fulmar	Ant., N, E, AUZ
Fulmarus glacialis	Northern Fulmar	H
Thalassoica antarctica	Antarctic Petrel	Ant., N
Daption capense	Cape Petrel	Ant., N, E, A
Pagodroma nivea	Snow Petrel	Ant., N
Pterodroma macroptera	Great-winged (Grey-faced) Petrel	N, E, A
Pterodroma aterrima	Mascarene Petrel	EI
Pterodroma rostrata	Tahiti Petrel	AI
Pterodroma lessonii	White-headed Petrel	Ant., N, E, A
Pterodroma hasitata	Jamaica (Black-capped) Petrel	N + I
Pterodroma cahow	Cahow (Bermuda) Petrel	HN
Pterodroma baraui	Barau's (Réunion) Petrel	EI
Pterodroma phaeopygia	Hawaiian Petrel	N, AI
Pterodroma externa	Juan Fernandez Petrel	N, AI
Pterodroma incerta	Atlantic Petrel	N, E
Pterodroma alba	Phoenix Petrel	AI
Pterodroma inexpectata	Mottled Petrel	HN, AIZ
Pterodroma solandri	Solander's Petrel	HP, AIU
Pterodroma ultima	Murphy's Petrel	AI
Pterodroma brevirostris	Kerguelen Petrel	E, A
Pterodroma arminjoniana	Herald Petrel	N, EI, AI
Pterodroma neglecta	Kermadec Petrel	N, AI
Pterodroma magentae	Magenta Petrel	AI
Pterodroma mollis	Soft-plumaged Petrel	N, E
Pterodroma cooki	Cook's Petrel	HN, N, AIZ
Pterodroma leucoptera	Gould's Petrel	N, AIU
Pterodroma pycrofti	Pycroft's Petrel	AI
Pterodroma hypoleuca	Bonin Petrel	AI
Pterodroma axillaris	Chatham Island Petrel	AI
Pterodroma nigripennis	Black-winged Petrel	AI
Halobaena caerulea	Blue Petrel	N, E, A
Pachyptila vittata	Broad-billed Prion	N, E, A
Pachyptila salvini	Medium-billed Prion	E, AUZ
Pachyptila desolata	Antarctic (Dove) Prion	Ant., N, E, AUZ
Pachyptila belcheri	Thin-billed Prion	N, E, AUZ
Pachyptila turtur	Fairy Prion	N, E, AUZ
Pachyptila crassirostris	Fulmar Prion	E, A
Bulweria bulweri	Bulwer's Petrel	HP, AI
Bulweria fallax	Jouanin's Petrel	OI
Bulweria macgillivrayi	Macgillivray's Petrel	AI
Procellaria cinerea	Grey Petrel (Pediunker)	N, E, AZ
Procellaria aequinoctialis	White-chinned Petrel (Shoemaker)	N, E, A
Procellaria westlandica	Westland Petrel	AZ
Procellaria parkinsoni	Black Petrel	N, AZ
Calonectris leucomelas	Streaked Shearwater	HP, OI, AI

Calonectris diomedea	Cory's Shearwater	H, E
Puffinus creatopus	Pink-footed Shearwater	HN, N
Puffinus carneipes	Flesh-footed Shearwater	H, N, A
Puffinus gravis	Great Shearwater	H, N, E
Puffinus pacificus	Wedge-tailed Shearwater	H, N, EI, AI
Puffinus bulleri	Buller's Shearwater	H, N, AZ
Puffinus griseus	Sooty Shearwater	H, N, O+I
Puffinus tenuirostris	Short-tailed Shearwater	H, O+I, A
Puffinus heinrothi	Heinroth's Shearwater	AI
Puffinus nativitatis	Christmas Island Shearwater	AI
Puffinus puffinus	Manx Shearwater	H, N+I, AI
Puffinus gavia	Fluttering Shearwater	A
Puffinus assimilis	Little Shearwater	HP, N, E, A
Puffinus lherminieri	Audubon's Shearwater	HN, N+I, EI, O, AI

Hydrobatidae–Storm-petrels

Oceanites oceanicus	Wilson's Storm-petrel	Ant., H, N+I, E+I, OI, A
Oceanites gracilis	Graceful Storm-petrel	N
Garrodia nereis	Grey-backed Storm-petrel	N, E, A
Pelagodroma marina	White-faced Storm-petrel	HP, N, E, A
Fregetta grallaria	White-bellied Storm-petrel	N, E, AIZ
Fregetta tropica	Black-bellied Storm-petrel	N, E, AIZ
Nesofregetta albigularis	White-throated Storm-petrel	AI
Hydrobates pelagicus	(British) Storm Petrel	HP, E+I
Halocyptena microsoma	Least Storm-petrel	HN, N
Oceanodroma tethys	Galapagos Storm-petrel	N
Oceanodroma castro	Harcourt's (Maderian) Storm-petrel	HP, N, E+I, OI, AI
Oceanodroma monorhis	Swinhoe's Storm-petrel	O
Oceanodroma leucorhoa	Leach's Storm-petrel	H, N, OI, AI
Oceanodroma markhami	Sooty Storm-petrel	HP, N
Oceanodroma melania	Black Storm-petrel	HN, N
Oceanodroma matsudairae	Matsudaira's Storm-petrel	OI, AI
Oceanodroma homochroa	Ashy Storm-petrel	HN
Oceanodroma hornbyi	Ringed Storm-petrel	N
Oceanodroma furcata	Grey Storm-petrel	HN

Pelecanoididae–Diving-petrels

Pelecanoides garnotii	Peruvian Diving-petrel	N
Pelecanoides magellani	Magellanic Diving-petrel	N
Pelecanoides georgicus	Georgian Diving-petrel	N, E, AZ
Pelecanoides urinatrix	Common Diving-petrel	N, E, A

PELECANIFORMES–PELICANS, BOOBIES, CORMORANTS

Phaethontidae–Tropicbirds

Phaethon aethereus	Red-billed Tropicbird	N, EI, O+I, AI
Phaethon rubricauda	Red-tailed Tropicbird	N, EI, AIU
Phaethon lepturus	White-tailed (Yellow-billed) Tropicbird	HN, N+I, EI, AI

Pelecanidae–Pelicans

Pelecanus onocrotalus	Eastern White Pelican	HP, E, O+I
Pelecanus rufescens	Pink-backed Pelican	E+I
Pelecanus philippensis	Spotted-billed Pelican	O
Pelecanus crispus	Dalmatian Pelican	HP, O
Pelecanus conspicillatus	Australian Pelican	AU
Pelecanus erythrorhynchos	American White Pelican	HN; w.HN, N
Pelecanus occidentalis	Brown Pelican	HN, N+I

Sulidae–Gannets and Boobies

Sula bassana	Atlantic Gannet	H
Sula capensis	African Gannet	E
Sula serrator	Australasian Gannet	AUZ
Sula nebouxii	Blue-footed Booby	N

Sula variegata	Peruvian Booby	N
Sula abbotti	Abbott's Booby	OI
Sula dactylatra	Masked Booby	N, E + I, OI, A
Sula sula	Red-footed Booby	N + I, EI, OI, AIU
Sula leucogaster	Brown Booby	HN, N, E + I, OI, A

Phalacrocoracidae–Cormorants

Phalacrocorax auritus	Double-crested Cormorant	HN
Phalacrocorax olivaceus	Olivaceous Cormorant	HN, N + I
Phalacrocorax sulcirostris	Little Black Cormorant	OI, A
Phalacrocorax carbo	Common Cormorant	H, E + I, O + I, A
Phalacrocorax fuscicollis	Indian Shag	O
Phalacrocorax capensis	Cape Cormorant	E
Phalacrocorax nigrogularis	Socotra Cormorant	E + I
Phalacrocorax neglectus	Bank Cormorant	E
Phalacrocorax capillatus	Japanese Cormorant	HP
Phalacrocorax penicillatus	Brandt's Cormorant	HN
Phalacrocorax aristotelis	Common Shag	HP
Phalacrocorax pelagicus	Pelagic Cormorant	H
Phalacrocorax urile	Red-faced Cormorant	H
Phalacrocorax magellanicus	Rock Cormorant	N
Phalacrocorax bougainvillii	Guanay Cormorant	N
Phalacrocorax varius	Greater Pied Cormorant	AUZ
Phalacrocorax fuscescens	Black-faced Cormorant	AU
Phalacrocorax lucidus	White-breasted Cormorant	E
Phalacrocorax carunculatus	New Zealand King Cormorant	AZ
Phalacrocorax verrucosus	Kerguelen Cormorant	E
Phalacrocorax gaimardi	Red-legged Cormorant	N
Phalacrocorax punctatus	Spotted Shag	AIZ
Phalacrocorax atriceps	Blue-eyed Shag	Ant., N, E, A
Phalacrocorax albiventer	King Cormorant	N, E, AU
Phalacrocorax melanoleucos	Little Pied Cormorant	OI, A
Phalacrocorax africanus	Reed Cormorant	E + I
Phalacrocorax niger	Little Cormorant	O + I
Phalacrocorax pygmeus	Pygmy Cormorant	HP, O
Phalacrocorax harrisi	Galapagos Cormorant	N

Anhingidae–Darter, Anhinga

Anhinga rufa	Darter	HP, E + I, O + I, AIU
Anhinga anhinga	Anhinga	HN, N + I

Fregatidae–Frigatebirds

Fregata aquila	Ascension Frigatebird	EI
Fregata andrewsi	Christmas Island Frigatebird	OI
Fregata magnificens	Magnificent Frigatebird	HN, N + I, E
Fregata minor	Greater Frigatebird	NI, EI, OI, AIU
Fregata ariel	Lesser Frigatebird	NI, EI, O + I, AIU

LARIFORMES-GULLS, TERNS, AUKS

Stercorariidae–Skuas, Jaegers

Catharacta skua	Great Skua	H
Catharacta lonnbergi	Southern Skua	N, E, AUZ
Catharacta maccormicki	Antarctic Skua	Ant., N
Stercorarius pomarinus	Pomarine Skua (Jaeger)	H; w.H, N, E + I, O + I, AIU
Stercorarius parasiticus	Arctic Skua (Parasitic Jaeger)	H; w.H, N + I, E + I, O + I, A
Stercorarius longicaudus	Long-tailed Skua (Jaeger)	H; w.H, E

Laridae–Gulls, Terns

Leucophaeus scoresbii	Dolphin Gull	N
Pagophila eburnea	Ivory Gull	H
Larus pacificus	Pacific Gull	AU
Larus fuliginosus	Lava (Dusky) Gull	N
Larus modestus	Grey Gull	N

Larus heermanni	Heermann's Gull	HN, N
Larus leucophthalmus	White-eyed Gull	E
Larus hemprichii	Sooty Gull	E, O
Larus belcheri	Band-tailed Gull	N
Larus crassirostris	Black-tailed Gull	HP, O
Larus audouinii	Audouin's Gull	HP
Larus delawarensis	Ring-billed Gull	HN; w.N+I
Larus canus	Common Gull	H; w.H, O+I
Larus argentatus	Herring Gull	H, E; w.H, N+I, E+I, O
Larus thayeri	Thayer's Gull	HN
Larus schistisagus	Slaty-backed Gull	H
Larus fuscus	Lesser Black-backed Gull	HP; w.HP, E
Larus californicus	California Gull	HN; w.HN, N
Larus occidentalis	Western Gull	HN, N
Larus dominicanus	Kelp (Dominican) Gull	N, E, AZ
Larus marinus	Great Black-backed Gull	H
Larus glaucescens	Glaucous-winged Gull	H
Larus hyperboreus	Glaucous Gull	H
Larus glaucoides	Iceland Gull	H
Larus ichthyaetus	Great Black-headed Gull	HP; w.E, O
Larus atricilla	Laughing Gull	HN, N+I
Larus brunnicephalus	Brown-headed Gull	HP; w.O
Larus relictus	Relict Gull	HP
Larus cirrocephalus	Grey-headed Gull	N, E+I
Larus serranus	Andean Gull	N
Larus pipixcan	Franklin's Gull	HN; w.N
Larus novaehollandiae	Silver Gull	E, A
Larus melanocephalus	Mediterranean Gull	HP
Larus bulleri	Black-billed Gull	AZ
Larus maculipennis	Brown-hooded Gull	N
Larus ridibundus	Black-headed Gull	HP; w.HP, E, O+I
Larus genei	Slender-billed Gull	HP, E, O
Larus philadelphia	Bonaparte's Gull	HN; w.N
Larus minutus	Little Gull	HP
Larus saundersi	Saunders's Gull	HP; w.O+I
Rhodostethia rosea	Ross's Gull	HP; w.H
Rissa tridactyla	Kittiwake	H; w.H, E
Rissa brevirostris	Red-legged Kittiwake	HN
Xema sabini	Sabine's Gull	H; w.N
Creagrus furcatus	Swallow-tailed Gull	N
Chlidonias hybrida	Whiskered Tern	HP, E+I, O+I, A
Chlidonias leucopterus	White-winged Black Tern	HP; w.E+I, O+I, AIU
Chlidonias niger	Black Tern	H; w.N, E
Phaetusa simplex	Large-billed Tern	N
Gelochelidon nilotica	Gull-billed Tern	H, N+I, E, O+I, AIU
Hydroprogne caspia	Caspian Tern	H, E, O+I, A
Sterna aurantia	River Tern	O
Sterna hirundinacea	South American Tern	N
Sterna vittata	Antarctic Tern	Ant., N, E, AZ
Sterna virgata	Kerguelen Tern	E
Sterna hirundo	Common Tern	H, N+I, E+I, O+I, AIU
Sterna paradisaea	Arctic Tern	H; w.Ant., N, E, AU
Sterna dougallii	Roseate Tern	H, N+I, O+I, AIU; w.E, N+I, O+I, AIU
Sterna forsteri	Forster's Tern	HN; w.N
Sterna trudeaui	Trudeau's Tern	N
Sterna striata	White-fronted Tern	AZ; w.AUZ
Sterna repressa	White-cheeked Tern	E, O+I
Sterna albistriata	Black-fronted Tern	AZ
Sterna sumatrana	Black-naped Tern	EI, O+I, AIU
Sterna acuticauda	Black-bellied Tern	O
Sterna aleutica	Aleutian Tern	H
Sterna lunata	Spectacled Tern	AI
Sterna anaetheta	Bridled Tern	N+I, E, O+I, AIU
Sterna fuscata	Sooty Tern	HN, N+I, E+I, OI, AIU
Sterna nereis	Nereis Tern	A

Sterna superciliaris	Yellow-billed Tern	N
Sterna balaenarum	Damara Tern	E
Sterna lorata	Peruvian Tern	N
Sterna albifrons	Little (Least) Tern	H, N + I, E + I, O + I, A; w.N, E + I, O + I, A
Sterna saundersi	Saunders's Little Tern	HP; w.E + I, O
Sterna bergii	Great Crested Tern	HP, E + I, O + I, AIU
Sterna maxima	Royal Tern	HN, N + I, E; w.N + I, E
Sterna bengalensis	Lesser Crested Tern	HP, E + I, O + I, AIU
Sterna zimmermanni	Chinese Crested Tern	O
Sterna elegans	Elegant Tern	HN; w.N
Sterna sandvicensis	Sandwich Tern	HP, N + I; w.HP, N + I, E,O
Sterna eurygnatha	Cayenne Tern	N
Larosterna inca	Inca Tern	N
Procelsterna albivitta	Grey Ternlet	N, AI
Anous stolidus	Brown Noddy	N + I, E + I, OI, AIU
Anous tenuirostris	Black (Lesser) Noddy	N, E + I, O + I, AIU
Gygis alba	Fairy Tern	N, E + I, OI, AI

Rynchopidae–Skimmers

Rynchops niger	Black Skimmer	HN, N
Rynchops flavirostris	African Skimmer	E
Rynchops albicollis	Indian Skimmer	O

Alcidae–Auks, Guillemots, Puffins

Alle alle	Little Auk (Dovekie)	H
Alca torda	Razorbill	H
Uria lomvia	Brunnich's Guillemot (Murre)	H
Uria aalge	Common Guillemot (Murre)	H
Cepphus grylle	Black Guillemot	H
Cepphus columba	Pigeon Guillemot	H
Cepphus carbo	Spectacled Guillemot	HP
Brachyramphus marmoratum	Marbled Murrelet	H
Brachyramphus brevirostre	Kittlitz's Murrelet	H
Endomychura hypoleuca	Xantus's Murrelet	HN
Synthliboramphus antiquum	Ancient Murrelet	H
Synthliboramphus wumizusume	Japanese Murrelet	HP
Ptychoramphus aleuticus	Cassin's Auklet	HN
Cyclorrhynchus psittacula	Parakeet Auklet	H
Aethia cristatella	Crested Auklet	H
Aethia pusilla	Least Auklet	H
Aethia pygmaea	Whiskered Auklet	H
Cerorhinca monocerata	Rhinoceros Auklet	H
Fratercula arctica	Common Puffin	H
Fratercula corniculata	Horned Puffin	H
Lunda cirrhata	Tufted Puffin	H

ENDANGERED SPECIES

The 'red list' of endangered species (after the IUCN) contains the following:

V Cape (Jackass) Penguin	E Bonin Petrel	R Galapagos Flightless Cormorant
E Short-tailed Albatross	R Gould's Petrel	
V Westland Petrel	E Magenta Petrel	V Andrew's Frigatebird
E Black Petrel	R Madeiran Soft-plumaged Petrel	R Ascension Frigatebird
E Mascarene Petrel	E Hawaiian Petrel	R Relict Gull
I Tahiti Petrel	I Heinroth's Shearwater	R Audouin's Gull
E Bermuda Petrel	V Newell's Shearwater	E Lesser Tern
E Cook's Petrel	E Abbott's Booby	R Damara Tern
V Jamaica Petrel	R New Zealand King Cormorant	I Chinese Crested Tern

Key to symbols: E in danger of extinction; V likely to move into the endangered category; R rare; small world populations that are at risk; I suspected as belonging to one of the above but insufficient data available.

Acknowledgements

Photographs
Aquila–187, H. Kinloch 47; Ardea–199, T. Beamish 135 top, M. D. England 142 top, P. Germain 42 bottom, 207 bottom, C. R. Knights 195 bottom, E. Mickleburgh 26, V. Taylor 143; N. P. Ashmole 162; Bruce Coleman Ltd–J. and D. Bartlett 38–39; Cross Sections–K. Westerskov 48, 181; D. F. Dorward 17; B. Hawkes 210; E. Hosking 15, 71, 85, 106, 121, N. Rankin 90, 120, 201; Jacana–Benoit 43, Eliott 130, Ermie 40, B. Hawkes title page, 207 top, Suinot 34 top, 34 bottom, Varin-Visage 111 top, Ziesler 35, back jacket; Natural History Photographic Agency–S. Dalton 195 top, B. Hawkes 206, P. Johnson 33 top, 138–139, 155, K. B. Newman 46–47, J. Tallon 44, 138 bottom; J. B. Nelson front jacket, 103, 111 bottom, 114, 131 top, 131 bottom, 135 bottom, 138 top, 144, 146, 149, 198 bottom, 202, back flap; C. J. R. Robertson 203 top; Royal Society for the Protection of Birds–M. Richards 208; B. Sage 198 top, 212; N. Tinbergen 70; J. Warham 91, 92, 109, 122, 159, 203 bottom; Wildlife Service, New Zealand 38, 39, 42 top, 142 bottom, 148; G. Ziesler 29, 33 bottom, 46, 134–135, 171. Painting on page 194 by K. Lilly.

References cited in diagrams
Where appropriate, the source material for line drawings has been acknowledged. However, in some of the composite drawings, derived from several widely disparate sources, acknowledgement has not been practical.

Ashmole, N. P. 1971. *Avian Biology* Vol. 1. Academic Press, London.
Carrick, R. 1972. *Population ecology of the Australian Black-backed Magpie, Royal Penguin and Silver Gull.* The Mawson Institute for Antarctic Research, University of Adelaide.
Dunnet, G. M. 1977. Dramatic spread of the Fulmar. *Wildlife*, London.
Emlen, J. T. & Penney, R. L. 1966. The Navigation of Penguins *Scientific American*. W. H. Freeman.

Feare, C. J. 1976. The breeding of the Sooty Tern (*Sterna fuscata*) in the Seychelles and the effects of experimental removal of its eggs. *J. Zool. London.* 179.
Harris, M. P. 1976. The present status of the Puffin in Britain and Ireland. *British Birds 69.*
Lack, D. Interrelationships in breeding adaptations as shown by marine birds. *Proceedings XIV Int. Orn. Congr.*
Lamb, H. H. Our understanding of the global wind circulation and climatic variations. *Bird Study 22.*
Langham, N. P. E. 1971. Seasonal movements of the British terns in the Atlantic Ocean. *Bird Study 18.*
Mead, C. J. 1977. The results of ringing auks in Britain and Ireland. *Bird Study 21.*
Monaghan, P. & Coulson, J. C. 1977. Status of large gulls nesting on buildings. *Bird Study 24.*
Nash, A. 1975. A speculation on Puffin fishing. *Bird Study 22.*
Olson, S. 1977. *A lower Eocene Frigatebird from the Green River Formation of Wyoming.* Smithsonian contributions to Paleobiology No. 35.
Pearson, T. H. 1968. The feeding biology of seabird species breeding on the Farne Islands, Northumberland. *J. Animal Ecology 37.*
Potts, G. R. 1969. The influence of eruptive movements, age, population, size and other factors on the survival of the Shag (*Phalacrocorax aristotelis*). *J. Animal Ecology 38.*
Shuntov, V. P. 1974. *Seabirds and the biological structure of the ocean.* (from: Dalnevostochnoe Knizhnoe Izdatelstvo, Vladivostok, 1972) Translation of Bureau of Sports, Fisheries and Wildlife. U.S. Dept. Interior. Washington D.C.
Storer, R. W. 1952. A comparison of variation, behaviour and evolution in seabird genera, *Uria* and *Cepphus*. Univ. Calif, Publ. Zool. Vol. 52. No. 2.
——1958. Evolution in Diving Birds. *Proceeding XII Int. Orn. Congr.*
Tuck, L. M. 1960. *The Murres.* Canadian Wildlife Series No. 1.

✳   ✳   ✳

Selected bibliography
The literature is so vast that all I can do is to select a few examples which give the 'feel' of seabird research and which illustrate both the range of enquiries and publications.

Ashmole, N. P., & Ashmole, M. J. 1967. Comparative feeding ecology of seabirds of a tropical oceanic island. *Yale Peabody Museum Nat. Hist. Bull. 24.*
Bourne, W. R. P. 1963. A review of oceanic studies of the biology of seabirds. *Proc. XIII Int. Orn. Congr. 831–854.*
—— 1976. Seabirds and pollution. *Marine Pollution.* Academic Press.
Coulson, J. C. 1966. The influence of the pair-bond and age on the breeding biology of the Kittiwake Gull *Rissa tridactyla. J. Animal Ecology 35.*
Cramp, S., Bourne, W. R. P. & Saunders, D. 1974. *The Seabirds of Britain and Ireland.* Collins.
Drent, R. 1973. The natural history of incubation. From *Breeding Biology of Birds.* Nat. Acad. Sciences. Washington D.C.
Fisher, H. I. 1976. Some dynamics of a breeding colony of Laysan Albatrosses. *Wilson Bull. 88.*
Fisher, J. & Lockley, R. M. 1954. *Seabirds.* Collins.
—— & Vevers, H. G. 1943–44. The breeding distribution, history and population of the North Atlantic Gannet *Sula bassana. J. Animal Ecology 12*

Harris, M. P. 1969. Breeding seasons of seabirds in the Galapagos Islands. *Journal Zoology 159*, London.
Kadlec, J. A. & Drury, W. H. 1968. Structure of the New England Herring Gull population. *Ecology 49.*
Mills, J. A. 1973. The influence of age and pair-bond on the breeding biology of the Red-billed Gull *Larus novaehollandiae sopulinus. J. Animal Ecology 42.*
Nelson, J. B. 1970. The relationship between behaviour and ecology in the Sulidae with reference to other seabirds. *Oceanogr. Mar. Biol. Rev. 8.*
—— 1978. *The Gannet.* T. & A. D. Poyser, Berkhamsted.
Nettleship, D. N. 1972. Breeding success of the Common Puffin (*Fratercula arctica* L.) on different habitats at Great Island, Newfoundland. *Ecol. Monogr. 42.*
—— 1976. Census techniques for seabirds of arctic and eastern Canada. *Canadian Wildlife Service. Occasional Paper No. 2*
Stonehouse, B. (ed.) 1975. *The Biology of Penguins.* Macmillan Press.
Tinbergen, N. 1953. *The Herring Gull's World.* Collins.
—— 1959. Comparative studies of the behaviour of gulls (Laridae), a progress report. *Behaviour, 15*
Tuck, L. 1960. *The Murres.* Canadian Wildlife Series No. 1.
Udvardy, M. D. F., Zoogeographical study of the Pacific Alcidae *Pacific Basin Biogeography.*

ndex

adaptive radiation, 7-8
air-strikes, 210, 212
albatrosses,
Black-browed, 38
   breeding season, 144
   breeding success, 164
   colony, 132, 136
   incubation, 145
   mortality, 169
Black-footed, 27
   chick, 116
   colony, 134, 212
   courtship, 87, 88, 90-91
   distribution, 175
   incubation, 145
   territoriality, 75
breeding habitats, 11-12
Buller's,
   courtship, 39, 90
   fidelity, 165
clutch, 12
courtship, 85, 87
distribution, 11, 175
feeding, 43, 44-45
feeding young, 108, 109
fighting, 70
fledging, 114, 148,
   161-162
flight, 13
fossil, 6
Grey-headed, 38
   breeding season, 144
   breeding success, 164
   colony, 132, 136
   incubation, 145
   mortality, 169
Laysan, 27
   air-strikes, 210, 212
   breeding, 24
   colony, 134, 210
   courtship, 87, 88, 90-91
   distribution, 175
   fledging, 114
   incubation, 145
   movements, 176
   'rest-years', 152
   site-fidelity, 164
   territoriality, 74
maturity, 150, 151
mortality, 165, 166, 167
nomadism, 174, 176
plumage, 58
population, 182
Royal,
   colony, 203
   courtship, 87, 90
   fledging, 114
   incubation, 145
   pre-laying period, 145
   size, 45, 61
Short-tailed, 182, 186, 200,
   207

Shy, 181, 200
structure, 4
territorial behaviour, 74
Wandering, 9, 26, 38
   age, 11
   aggression, 76
   breeding attendance, 145
   colony, 136
   courtship, 87, 90-91
   fledging, 114, 147
   incubation, 145
   movements, 174, 176
   plumage, 11
   population, 182, 183, 186
   size, 11
Waved,
   breeding season, 139
   care of young, 110
   courtship, 88-89, 90-91
   fighting, 69, 75-76
   incubation, 105, 106, 145
   site-establishment, 65
   site-fidelity, 164
   'sway-walk', 67
Yellow-nosed, 9, 27
auklets,
breeding habitats, 23
Cassin's, 200
   breeding cycles, 23, 139
   colony, 134
   courtship, 100
   diet, 63
   feeding young, 108
   fighting, 69
   fledging, 148
   moult, 153
   predation, 163
   'rest-years', 152
Crested, 129, 200
   feeding, 23
Least, 129, 200
Parakeet, 63, 129, 200
Rhinocerous, 54, 139, 162,200
species, 22
Whiskered, 57, 200
auks,
adaptive radiation, 61, 63
breeding habitats, 23
courtship, 100, 101-102
distribution, 22, 173
feeding young, 109, 146
fledging, 148, 162
fossils, 22
Great, 7, 9, 48, 63, 200
Little, 9, 14, 22, 28, 195
   bill, 62
   courtship, 100, 102
   diet, 54, 63
   feeding, 32, 146
   nest-sites, 129
   population, 182
   predation, 51
   'wrecks', 168
Lucas, 7
   plumage, 22, 58
   population, 182
   predation, 163
   post-hatching
      development, 23
   species, 22
   territorial display, 79

behaviour,
   definition, 64

of young, 110-115
ritualized, origin, 66-67
territorial, 65-79
sexual, 79-103
body care, 115
boobies,
Abbot's, 16, 128, 146
   appeasement, 70, 73
   bill, 62
   breeding cycles, 140
   breeding success, 160
   clutch, 155
   courtship, 92
   development, 158
   egg weight, 145
   fledging, 147
   greeting, 80, 106
   nest-building, 104
   nest-sites, 130
   population, 182, 184,
      186, 196
Blue-footed,
   courtship, 67, 92, 93, 97
   diving, 43, 46
   nest-building, 104
   population, 196
Brown, 27, 144
   appeasement, 60, 73
   breeding cycle, 63, 133,
      144, 149
   clutch, 155
   exploitation, 200
   feeding, 46
   fidelity, 164
   fledging success, 161
   nest-building, 66
   plumage, 59
   population, 202
   predation, 206
   sibling murder, 110
Masked, 9, 15, 27, 60
   breeding strategy, 139
   clutch, 155
   courtship, 92, 93
   feeding, 46
   fidelity, 164, 165
   greeting, 80
   nest-building, 104
   plumage, 47
   population, 202
   predation, 206
   sibling murder, 110, 111
   sunning, 117
Peruvian, 16
   clutch, 63, 104, 155
   colony, 128, 133
   courtship, 93
   nest-building, 104
   nest-sites, 118
   population, 182, 184, 202,
      209
   predation, 161
   starvation, 168
Red-footed, 9, 15, 26, 60
   clutch, 155
   colony size, 131
   copulation, 103
   courtship, 92, 93
   dispersal, 171
   feeding, 46
   incubation, 145
   nest-building, 104
   nest-site, 70, 130, 131
   piracy, 51, 53
   plumage, 59

population, 183, 184, 202
predation, 206
size, 46
temperature regulation,
   110, 116
sunning, 117
species, 14
bosunbirds, see tropicbirds
breeding cycles,
   length, 144-150
breeding strategies,
   timing, 137-144
brood patches, 104

Cahow, 13, 186
   population, 182
   predation, 51, 213
Cape Pigeon, 12, 27
   feeding, 41, 44, 54
   nest-sites, 131
care of young, 107-110
chick, 157-160
   starvation, 157-159
   temperature control, 159
clutch,
   size, 155-156
colony,
   definition, 132
   density, 133
   disadvantages, 136
   size, 133
   synchrony, 135
colonial habit, 131-137
copulation, 102-103
cormorants,
Black, 174
Cape, 182
   clutch, 17
Common, 15
   colony, 47, 49, 132
   courtship, 96, 97
   dispersal, 174
   feeding, 48, 49, 56
   fledging, 147
   incubation, 104
   nest-building, 104
   territoriality, 78
courtship, 95-96
Double-crested, 48, 157
edibility, 17
feeding, 48-49
Flightless, 7, 15
   breeding, 16
   colony, 132, 137
   population, 182
fossil, 6, 7
Guanay, 16
   colony, 46, 132, 133
   feeding, 48
   nest-building, 104
   plumage, 58
   population, 49, 182, 184, 209
   starvation, 168
Little Black, 48
Little Pied, 49
Pied, 17, 58, 96
Red-faced, 49
Red-legged, 118
site-fidelity, 164
species, 14
currents, 28-30

darters, 14, 49
diet, 53-55

disease, 168-169, 212-213
dispersal, 170, 171, 172
displays, 71-79
diving-petrels,
  colonies, 14
  diet, 54
  distribution, 14
  plumage, 58
  species, 14
Dovekie *see* Auk, Little
dreads, 65

eggs, 154-157
eruptions, 179
evolution, 6, 7, 178

feeding,
  postfledging, 149
feeding methods, 31-63
fidelity, 104-105
fighting, 66, 68-69, 70-71
fishing industry, 27, 169,
  210-211
fledging, 111-112, 147-148
  success, 161-162
flightlessness, 7
foraging, 180, 181
frigatebirds,
  Andrew's, 127
    population, 182, 186, 196
    weight, 41
  Ascension Island,
    nest, 17, 130
    plumage, 42
    population, 182
    predation, 162
  bill, 62
  breeding strategies, 18, 42
    136-137
  clutch, 18
  courtship, 95
  dispersal, 171
  distribution, 18, 173
  egg weight, 145
  Eocene, 23
  feeding, 41, 42, 115
  fidelity, 164
  fighting, 70
  fledging, 114, 147
  fossil, 6
  Greater, 27, 149
    bill, 60
    breeding cycles, 140
    display, 127
    feeding, 42, 115
    fighting, 77
    incubation, 106
    nest-site, 131
    piracy, 53
    population, 186
  Lesser, 9
    bill, 60
    feeding, 42
    plumage, 59
  Magnificent, 9
    feeding, 41
    fidelity, 165
    predation, 53
  maturity, 151
  piracy, 51, 52-53
  plumage, 17-18, 42, 58
  predation, 53, 161
  species, 14
  structure, 17

sunning, 116, 117
territoriality, 76
wing-loading, 17
Fulmar, 42
  bill, 60
  breeding attendance, 145
  courtship, 80, 91
  distribution, 12, 28
  feeding, 45, 52, 54, 207
  fidelity, 165
  fledging, 113
  nest-sites, 120
  population, 190, 191, 209
  site-establishment, 65
  species, 12
  territorial displays, 76
fulmar-petrels, 12

gadfly-petrels,
  breeding strategies, 141, 142
  distribution, 13
  feeding, 45
  species, 12, 13
Gannets,
  accidents, 168
  African, 47
    greeting, 121
    migration, 176
    nest-building, 104
    population, 202
    temperature regulation,
      110, 121
  Atlantic,
    appeasement, 73
    bill, 60
    breeding success, 160
    care of young, 109, 110
    colony, 132-137
    copulation, 103
    cull, 204
    development, 158
    distribution, 28
    diving, 47
    egg, 154
    feeding, 46, 52
    fidelity, 164, 165
    fighting, 68, 70
    fledging, 111, 112, 147
    greeting, 81, 106
    incubation, 104, 106,
      107, 145
    landing, 120
    maturity, 176
    migration, 176
    piracy, 52
    population, 182, 186, 202
    preening, 116
    weight, 16, 46
  Australasian, 26
    aggression, 76
    colony, 202
    migration, 176
    population, 196
    breeding success, 163
    clutch, 104, 155
    courtship, 92
    fledging success, 161
    moult, 153
    nest-building, 104
    nest-sites, 118, 120
    plumage, 47, 58
    population, 182
    site-establishment, 65
    territorial displays, 77

guano, 207, 209-210
guillemots,
  Black, 28
    colony, 133, 137
    courtship, 100, 101, 102
    distribution, 20
    feeding, 32
    incubation, 146
    nest-sites, 129
    'rest-years', 152
  Brunnich's,
    aggression, 79
    colony, 118
    courtship, 100
    distribution, 21, 174
    egg, 154
    fighting, 70
    incubation, 146
    mortality, 169
    nest-sites, 120
    population, 192
  clutch, 156
  colony, 134
  Common,
    aggression, 79
    appeasement, 73, 79
    bill, 60, 62
    bill-touching, 80
    breeding season, 144
    chick, 114
    colony, 118, 132, 196-197
    courtship, 101, 102
    dispersal, 172
    distribution, 21, 174
    fighting, 70
    fledging, 112, 148
    incubation, 146
    nest-sites, 120
    plumage, 59
    population, 191, 192
    predation, 51
    races, 185-186
  courtship, 101-102
  egg-collecting, 204
  egg loss, 161
  feeding, 43, 48, 63
  fledging, 113
  mortality, 168, 169
  moult, 153
  Pigeon,
    breeding season, 139
    courtship, 100
    fighting, 69
    incubation, 104
    nest-sites, 129
    predation, 161, 163
    site-fidelity, 164
gulls,
  Audouin's, 19 ♂
    bill colour, 108
  Black-billed, 105, 129
  Black-headed,
    care of young, 107
    displays, 82, 83
    distribution, 19
    piracy, 53
    population, 188
    predation, 53, 136, 161
    site-establishment, 66
  Black-tailed, 19
  brown-gulls, 131
  clutch, 19, 156
  Common, 19, 56
  dispersal, 174
  displays, 82, 83

Dominican, 18, 124
  clutch, 157
  dispersal, 174
  population, 188
  feeding young, 108, 109,
    150
  fledging, 148, 162
  following plough, 206
  Franklin's, 74
  Glaucous, 51, 188
  Great Black-backed, 9, 19
    disposal, 174
    population, 186
    predation, 136, 169
  Grey, 19
    body temperature, 160
    care of chick, 116
    clutch, 156
    nest-sites, 129
  Heermann's, 124
  Herring,
    bill, 60
    care of young, 107, 108,
      115
    clutch, 156
    colony, 133
    control, 137, 213
    copulation, 103
    courtship, 82, 83
    development, 158
    disease, 169
    distribution, 18
    fighting, 66, 68, 72
    fledging, 112, 114
    hybridization, 18
    incubation, 104, 105, 106
    maturity, 151
    population, 186-189
    predation, 53, 136, 161,
      163, 206-207
    rest-years', 152
    scavenging, 52, 187, 213
    site-establishment, 66
    stimulation, 135
    territorial displays, 72,
      74, 82
    wing-pulling, 70
  Ivory, 28
  Kelp *see* Dominican
  Laughing, 53, 74, 157
  Lava, 71, 74
  Lesser Black-backed,
    appeasement, 73
    bill, 60
    colony, 133, 189
    diet, 56
    hybridization, 18
    population, 187
    predation, 51, 53
    wing-pulling, 70
  Little, 9
  Pacific, 19
  plumage, 18, 58
  Red-billed, 83, 156
  Ring-billed, 19, 188
  Ross's, 18, 28, 117
  Sabine's, *title page*, 19, 28
  Silver, 74, 188
  species, 18-19
  success, 19
  Southern Black-backed *see*
    Dominican
  Swallow-tailed, 124
    breeding cycle, 140

courtship, 86
  nest-building, 104
Thayers, 28
Western, 156
wing, 7

habitats,
  breeding, 118-131, 119,
    193
  cliff, 118, 119, 198-199

incubation, 104-107,
  144-146

Kittiwake,
  bill, 60
  breeding success, 161, 163
  clutch, 157
  colony, 136, 194-195
  development, 159
  diet, 56
  dispersal, 174, 179
  displays, 82
  distribution, 19
  egg weight, 139
  feeding young, 108
  fidelity, 165
  fighting, 66
  fledging, 114
  incubation, 105
  nest-sites, 118, 120, 123
  piracy, 52
  population, 188
  scavenging, 52

maturity, 150-152
migration, 170-180
mollymawks see albatrosses
mortality rates, 165-169
moult, 153
murrelets,
  Ancient, 63, 139
  clutch, 156
  Craveri's, 115, 148
  diet, 54, 63
  Kittlitz's, 23, 63, 113
  Marbled,
    adaptation, 63
    breeding season, 139
    nest-site, 23, 113, 131
  species, 22
  Xantus's, 63, 148
murres see guillemots
muttonbird see Shearwater,
  Short-tailed, Sooty

nest-building, 103-104
noddies,
  Brown, 27, 130
  Black, 83, 120, 130
  Common, 59, 60
  feeding, 42, 44
  Grey, 60
  Lesser, 60, 66, 169
  White-capped, 123
nomadism, 170, 171, 172

oceans, endpapers, 24-30
oil pollution, 169, 192, 207,
  208-209

pelecaniforms, 14-18
pelicans,
  Australian, 46
  breeding habitats, 16
  breeding strategies, 16
  Brown, 171
    courtship, 92, 95
    diving, 29, 43, 46, 56
    fighting, 68
    population, 209
  Chilean,
    nest-building, 104
    population, 209
    starvation, 168
  courtship, 92, 94
  distribution, 16
  feeding young, 109, 150
  species, 14, 16
  structure, 14-15
  territorial displays, 77
  White,
    aggression, 76
    care of young, 107, 110
    copulation, 103
    crèche, 109, 110, 111, 135
    display, 80
    feeding, 32
    fledging, 147
    group feeding, 43, 46
    temperature regulation,
      116
penguins, 8-11
  Adelie,
    appeasement, 73
    breeding cycle, 142-143
    breeding season, 144
    clutch, 156
    colony, 132
    copulation, 103
    courtship, 96, 99, 101
    diet, 49
    fighting, 66, 69, 70
    fledging, 114, 147
    incubation, 145
    movements, 180
    plumage, 58
    population, 182
    predation, 163
    'rest-years', 152
    territorial display, 78
  Black-footed see Jackass
  breeding habitat, 10, 129
  breeding strategies, 11, 140
  Cape see Jackass
  Chinstrap
    colony, 132
    nest-sites, 129
  clutch, 11
  colony, 10-11, 132
  courtship, 96-102
  Crested, 66, 70
  development, 157
  distribution, 10
  egg weight, 145
  Emperor, 9, 33, 43
    aggression, 71
    breeding cycle, 142
    clutch, 155
    crèche, 110, 111
    diet, 49
    display, 98
    diving, 48, 50
    incubation, 104, 106, 145
    population, 182
    territoriality, 78

feeding, 49-50
fledging success, 162
Fiordland,
  breeding cycle, 143
  colony, 132
fossil, 6
Galapagos,
  population, 182, 186
  temperature regulation,
    117
Gentoo,
  appeasement, 73
  .clutch, 155
  seal reaction, 169
  territorial display, 78
incubation, 104
Jackass, 33
  diet, 49
  population, 182
King,
  breeding cycles, 141, 142
  clutch, 155
  copulation, 103
  courtship, 96, 97, 98, 101
  diet, 49
  feeding young, 109, 110
  fidelity, 165
  fighting, 68, 70
  fledging, 147
  incubation, 104, 106
    107, 145
  porpoising, 49, 50
  seal reaction, 169
Little Blue, 9
  breeding season, 144
  fledging, 147
  territoriality, 78
Macaroni, 155
Magellanic,
  colony, 40, 132
  diet, 49
  incubation, 145
  nest-sites, 131
  population, 182
moult, 153
Peruvian,
  diet, 49
plumage, 58
population, 196
Rockhopper,
  breeding cycle, 141, 143
  clutch, 155
  colony, 132
  fledging, 147
  plumage, 57
Royal,
  breeding cycle, 141, 143
  breeding state, 65, 163, 164
  colony, 132, 203
  maturity, 151
  predation, 163
Snares Crested,
  bill, 62
  development, 157
  nest-sites, 130
  species, 8
  territory, 78
  wing, 7
Yellow-eyed,
  breeding age, 65
  clutch, 154
  incubation, 104
petrels,
  Antarctic, 12, 45
  Barau's, 213

Black, 13, 32
Black-capped, 213
Blue, 14, 54
Bonin, 27, 212
Cook's, 213
feeding methods, 32
fighting, 76
fledging success, 162
Giant, 12, 26
  aggression, 76
  bill, 62
  feeding, 43, 45, 52
  predation, 43, 163, 169
Grey-faced, 141, 142
Hawaiian, 162, 213
incubation, 161
Jamaica, 213
Jouanin's, 213
Kermadec, 213
Least, 32
Madeiran, 105
Magenta, 13, 182, 203, 213
Mottled, 206, 213
Phoenix, 60
Snow, 54, 130
Solander's, 213
species, 12
Westland Black, 13, 42
plumage, 57-58, 59, 61
populations, 182-202
predation, 51, 53, 163, 169, 206
preening, 115
prions, 12, 26
  Antarctic,
    breeding attendance, 145
    feeding, 41
    nest-sites, 130
    predation, 136
  Broad-billed, 12, 62
  Dove see Antarctic
    feeding, 41, 54
  Medium-billed, 12
  Thin-billed, 12, 41
procellarids, 58, 148
productivity, 160-165
Puffins, 193
  bill, 22, 60
  colony, 124, 125
  courtship, 67, 101-102
  dispersal, 172
  distribution, 22, 28
  feeding, 32, 56, 108
  fledging, 148
  greeting, 80
  Horned,
    bill, 62
    plumage, 57
  moult, 153
  piracy, 52
  population, 191, 193-200
  Tufted,
    breeding season, 139
    distribution, 174

Razorbill,
  bill, 60
  colony, 133
  courtship, 94, 100, 101-102
  diet, 63
  fledging, 113
  greeting, 80
  mortality, 168, 169

moult, 153
movements, 176
nest-sites, 120
population, 182, 192
wing, 7
rest-years', 152

shags,
Black, 49
Blue-eyed, 26
Common,
bill, 60
clutch, 157
colony, 137
courtship, 96, 97
diet, 49, 56
disease, 168
dispersal, 179
diving, 48
fidelity, 164, 165
fighting, 66
fledging, 147
mortality, 166, 167, 169
nesting, 47, 49
plumage, 59
site-establishment, 65
territoriality, 78
King, 46
Pied, 49
Spotted, 48, 49
White-breasted, 49
shearwaters,
Audubon's, 13
bill, 60
feeding, 45
moult, 153
billing, 80
Christmas, 27, 45, 60
Cory's, 27
cull, 204
feeding, 45
nest-sites, 129
courtship, 91
distribution, 12
feeding, 44-45
fighting, 70
Flesh-footed, 45
Great, 42
colony, 133, 137
feeding, 45
fledging, 113
migration, 178-179
nest-sites, 130
plumage, 59
Little,
courtship, 86, 91
feeding, 41, 159
fighting, 76
nest-sites, 130
Manx, 12, 28
breeding season, 138, 145
development, 157
egg weight, 139, 145
feeding, 45
fighting, 76
fledging, 112, 113
migration, 170, 176, 177, 178
predation, 136
site-establishment, 66
migration, 177
Pink-footed, 13
Short-tailed,12
breeding season, 138

courtship, 92
cull, 204
migration, 177, 179
Slender-billed, 76
Sooty, 12, 42
disease, 168
migration, 178, 179
nest-sites, 131
piracy, 51
species, 12
Streaked, 179
terratoriality, 76
Wedge-tailed, 27, 60, 76, 168
Shoemaker, 13, 131
site-establishment, 65-66
size-range, 9, 61
skimmers, 106
skuas,
Arctic,
display, 75
migration, 177
piracy, 52-53
plumage, 19
Great,
clutch, 155
displays, 74, 75, 94
distribution, 19
fighting, 70
piracy, 51, 52
predation, 53, 136
Long-tailed, 156, 177
piracy, 52-53
plumage, 58
Pomarine, 42, 75
predation, 163
species, 19
territorial displays, 74, 75
species, 6
starvation, 163, 167-168
Storm Petrel,
feeding, 31, 32
incubation, 146
size, 61
territoriality, 76
storm-petrels,
Ashy, 153
Black-bellied, 145
clutch, 14
diet, 32, 54
distribution, 14, 28
feeding, 43
feeding methods, 31-32
Galapagos, 14, 130, 141, 148
Grey-backed, 131
Guadalupe, 213
Leach's,
diet, 32
fighting, 76
migration, 177
moult, 153
nest-sites, 130
longevity, 14
Madeiran,
breeding attendance, 145
breeding cycle, 141
fighting, 76
nest-sites, 130
mass fights, 76-77
Matsudaira's, 179
plumage, 58
species, 14
Swinhoe's, 179
White-faced, 76, 130

White-throated, 60
Wilson's,
breeding cycle, 143
breeding success, 161
feeding, 31, 41
migration, 177
population, 182
territoriality, 76
study techniques, 211
sulids see boobies and
Gannets

temperature regulation, 116, 117
Ternlet,
Grey, 54, 56
terns,
Arctic,
breeding success, 163
care of young, 107
diet, 56
displays, 74, 83, 84
distribution, 19-20
migration, 177, 178, 179, 180
population, 189, 190
Black, 53, 74
Black-naped, 32
breeding strategies, 21-22
Bridled,
breeding cycle, 140
feeding young, 115
moult, 153
nest-sites, 129
Caspian, 9
mortality, 169
clutch, 22, 156
Common,
breeding success, 163
care of young, 107
diet, 56
displays, 74
egg laying, 135
feeding, 42, 44,
migration, 179, 180
piracy, 53
courtship, 83, 84, 94
Crested, 60
display, 84
distribution, 19
egg-collecting, 204
Elegant, 115
Fairy, 27, 123
bill, 60
feeding, 44
fighting, 66
moult, 153
nest-site, 71, 104, 130
plumage, 44, 59
feeding, 43
feeding young, 108, 150
fledging, 114, 148, 162
Grey-backed, 27, 60
Gull-billed, 53, 190
Inca, 21, 57, 129
Little,
care of young, 107
colony, 133
courtship, 85, 86
feeding, 36, 115
population, 189, 190
nesting habitats, 21, 120

plumage, 20-21, 44, 58, 7[
Roseate,
courtship, 84
feeding, 115
migration, 180
piracy, 53
population, 189, 190
Royal, 114, 115
Sandwich,
care of young, 107, 114[
115
colony, 106, 107
courtship, 84, 85
diet, 56
disturbance, 206
feeding, 42
migration, 170, 179, 18[
piracy, 53
population, 189, 190
site-establishment, 65
territoriality, 74
Sooty, 27
bill, 60
breeding cycles, 140
care of young, 110, 115
colony, 123, 132, 13 4
courtship, 83, 84, 85
development, 158, 163
feeding, 42, 44
feeding young, 109
fighting, 66
incubation, 104, 106
mass flights, 65
migration, 170
mortality, 168
moult, 153
plumage, 59
population, 182, 190
predation, 53, 161, 162,
163, 206
site-establishment, 65
species, 19
structure, 20
territorial displays, 74
toxic chemicals, 209
tropicbirds,
breeding strategies, 18
distribution, 18
feeding, 46
feeding young, 108, 150
fighting, 70, 77
fossil, 6
Red-tailed, 27
bill, 60
competition, 70
courtship, 94, 95
development, 158
nest-sites, 131
species, 14, 18
territorial display, 77
White-tailed, 135
courtship, 95
feeding, 46
fledging, 113
intraspecific killing, 51
nest-sites, 70, 130, 131
Yellow-billed see White-
tailed
tubenoses, 11-14
species, 11
structure, 11
Tysty see Guillemot, Black

Wideawake see Tern, Sooty